CONTINUING CARE

The Process and Practice of Discharge Planning

Nancy C. Zarle, RN, MS
Beth Israel Hospital

AN ASPEN PUBLICATION©
Aspen Publishers, Inc.

1987

Rockville, Maryland
Royal Tunbridge Wells

Library of Congress Cataloging in Publication Data

Zarle, Nancy C.
Continuing care.

"An Aspen publication."
Bibliography: p.
Includes index.
1. Hospitals—Admission and discharge—Planning. 2. Hospitals—After-care—Planning.
I. Title. [DNLM: 1. After Care. 2. Home Care Services. 3. Nursing Process. 4. Patient
Care Planning. 5. Patient Care Team. 6. Patient Discharge. WY 100 Z37c]
RA971.8.Z37   1987   362.1′4   87-17408
ISBN: 0-87189-382-7

Editorial Services: Lisa J. McCullough

Library of Congress Catalog Card Number: 87-17408
ISBN: 0-87189-382-7

Printed in the United States of America

1 2 3 4 5

To the Primary Nurses at Beth Israel Hospital

Table of Contents

Contributors

NANCY BROWN, RN, BSN
  Clinical Nurse II, Research
  Beth Israel Hospital
  Boston, Massachusetts

PATRICIA CASACCIO, RN, BSN
  Clinical Nurse II, Neurology
  Beth Israel Hospital
  Boston, Massachusetts

AURELIE C. CORMIER, RN, BSN
  Clinical Nurse II, Oncology
  Beth Israel Hospital
  Boston, Massachusetts

SUSAN C. KINNELL, RN, BSN
  Unit Teacher, Orthopedics
  Beth Israel Hospital
  Boston, Massachusetts

ELLEN CREGAN KITCHEN, RN, BSN
  Clinical Nurse III, Medicine
  Beth Israel Hospital
  Boston, Massachusetts

NANCY P. O'ROURKE, RN, BSN
  Clinical Nurse III, Medicine
  Beth Israel Hospital
  Boston, Massachusetts

HEIDI PICARD, RN, MS
  Head Nurse, Surgical
  Beth Israel Hospital
  Boston, Massachusetts

KATHLEEN A. SMITH, RN, BSN
  Clinical Nurse III, Medicine
  Beth Israel Hospital
  Boston, Massachusetts

EVELYN STELMACK, RN, BSN
  Clinical Nurse III, Medicine
  Beth Israel Hospital
  Boston, Massachusetts

DEBORA J. TOBOJKA, RN, BSN
  Unit Teacher, Surgical
  Beth Israel Hospital
  Boston, Massachusetts

Preface

Patients and their families have many questions and concerns when they are told about the impending discharge. They feel immediately that the patient is not ready to go home, that the discharge is premature.

Today, however, patients do not have the option to remain in the acute care setting until they are completely well. New government and insurance directives require discharge as early as possible. Nevertheless, this change can be viewed positively because recovery occurs faster at home for some persons; for others, discharge to an alternative care facility is the best plan.

Because these "quicker-and-sicker" discharges make continuing care planning imperative and because the continuing care literature is still meager, I have felt the need of a theoretical and practical textbook to assist the professional in the many facets of a continuing care program. This book, then, has been written for all professional disciplines involved in the continuing care planning process. It can be especially useful to nurses, physicians, social workers, and administrators in a variety of health care settings.

The book provides the health care professional involved in the continuing care planning process with a framework for a continuing care program and also the steps that lead to` an effective discharge planning process. Moreover, because the prospective payment system based on the diagnosis-related groups (DRGs) has caused many chang-

es in our health care delivery system, this book can assist the health care provider to identify new sources of home health care, ambulatory care, and other relevant services offered by agencies and organizations. Systematizing the continuing care planning process deserves special attention in these days of economic cutbacks. This book emphasizes the importance of a process and the tools and strategies for an appropriate and timely continuing care plan.

As a continuing care nurse specialist, I feel privileged to be a member of Boston's Beth Israel Hospital family. Here I have been given the opportunity to grow and to be creative in my specialty area. Here I have been surrounded by the support of the nursing and hospital administrations, nursing leaders, and primary nurses.

To Bentley College and to all my friends, thank you—especially Beth who unselfishly gave me hours of typing time and much encouragement. The interest shown and the encouragement given to me daily by these communities of professionals and friends are greatly appreciated.

Finally, my family (Tom, Gretchen, and Stig) deserves my very special thanks and loving appreciation—especially Tom, who has been a wonderfully supportive husband during the time spent in research and writing. He patiently endured a seemingly endless number of evenings and weekends without me while I was writing. To my father, Nils, for his constant support, thank you.

1. Continuing Care: The Process and Practice of Discharge Planning

Continuing care planning, one of the most important and critical components of the health care delivery system today, is one of the most rapidly developing areas of concentration in the health care field. Moreover, this development demands a specialized knowledge base for the continuing care professional. As the emphasis on continuity of patient care increases and as the rigorous monitoring of discharge-planning activities by the regulatory agencies and third party reimbursers continues, the professional must be ready to accept the challenge. Many health care providers may be victimized by the new pressures of the present health care economic scene; others, however, perceive this pressure as an opportunity to become more effective and efficient in the daily practice of continuing care and discharge planning.

This chapter presents a basic philosophy of continuing care, a purpose for continuing care planning, a definition of continuing care, a definition of discharge planning, discharge-planning standards, the American Nurses' Association Resolution on Admission and Discharge Planning, and the goals and objectives of a continuing care program.

BASIC PHILOSOPHY

Within the basic philosophy of any continuing care program developed by an acute care institution, the following considerations should be included:

- All persons admitted to the hospital must be considered for continuing care planning.
- An interdisciplinary approach to the problems and issues of continuing care is needed.
- Because nurses are in a favorable position to assess the needs of the patient, they are valuable members of the interdisciplinary team.
- Physicians are important to the continuing care planning process because they communicate the ongoing, complex medical needs of the patient—a key component in planning the discharge.
- Social Service, a significant member of the interdisciplinary team, plays an important role in evaluating the emotional and environmental needs, the strengths, the limitations, the coping capacity, and the resource networks of the patient and the family.
- Continuing care involves helping patients to plan for their psychosocial and physical needs.
- Successful continuing care plans must involve the patients and the people close to them in the decision making.

PURPOSE

The purpose of continuing care planning is to assure individuals and their families that, beginning on the day of the patient's admission into the hospital, every effort is directed toward helping them to develop an adequate continuing care plan in preparation for discharge from the hospital to home or to an alternative care facility (ie, a hospital for the chronically ill, a rehabilitation hospital, a visiting nurse program, a home health care program, an adult day-care center, a skilled-nursing-care facility, or a hospice program.) In addition to reinforcing the gains made in the acute care setting, this continuing care plan must be tailored, as much as possible, to the patient's needs and wishes. The plan should also include assisting the patient to deal with the limitations imposed at the time of discharge by the health care system and the stresses and losses experienced as a result of the illness and diagnosis.

CONTINUING CARE

Continuing care is defined as the coordination of services rendered to patients throughout three phases of their illness: (1) prehospitalization, (2) hospitalization, and (3) posthospitalization. Figure 1-1 depicts this illness-wellness continuum.

Prehospitalization

The prehospital phase of the care continuum is concerned with health maintenance and health prevention. This care is accomplished in a variety of ways. The term *self-care* (the terminology frequently used to describe the process by which individuals or groups take control of their lives) is appropriate because the focus of health and environmental issues has a personal impact on their individual well-being or upon the population at large.

The principle of responsible action in self-care issues brings people to participate actively in exercise groups for health and fitness (walking, running, bicycling) and in support groups for sharing concerns about proper nutritional intake and production of our food. In addition, community health education programs built around issues of alcohol and drug abuse, elder and child abuse, and support groups assist in making persons informed consumers in the health care marketplace. Industrial and school health education and hypertension screening programs (to name a few) also contribute to a knowledge base for the consumer's self-care and health-option focus. These programs are examples of a community of people involved in many activities, working toward preventing a hospital admission.

Hospitalization

During a person's lifetime, a hospital admission may be necessary. This event moves continuing care into the second phase of the planning continuum—hospitalization. Hospitalization becomes necessary because an acute care intervention must take place. This intervention may be the result of an injury by mechanical, physical, or self-induced means or by the acute onset of a sudden illness that cannot be managed in the community. While in the acute care setting, the patient is diagnosed and treated appropriately in preparation for the next phase of the planning continuum.

Posthospitalization

The last phase of the continuum is the posthospital phase. Everyone who enters the acute care setting is discharged, and the discharge occurs in one of four ways:

1. The patient returns home.
2. The patient returns home, receiving assistance from family or community services.
3. The patient goes to an alternative care facility.
4. The patient dies.

Home

To go home is the goal that most patients, their families, and health care professionals must work toward. Patients returning home without family or community supports are assumed to be able to return to their community and occupation in the physical and emotional condition they enjoyed before entering the health care system for medical intervention. In these cases, it is assumed that the normal life style of the individual and the family will resume after a recuperative period.

Home-with-Assistance: Family Members

Assessment of the patient on admission may determine that home-with-assistance is the discharge goal. At this point, several considerations need to be made. To return home with the assistance of family members may be the only support the patient needs. For example, an elderly patient may be capable of assuming all the activities of daily living but may need minimal supervision (eg, medication compliance and nutritional support). In such cases, the family often agrees to assume the responsibility without additional community support. Of course, they must be instructed by the nurse in how to administer care (eg, a dressing-change technique). Health care providers must be open to this option for all patients.

Because the family has been defined in many ways (depending on the theoretical orientation of the "definer"), it is important as the plans for continuing care are developed to have a clear understanding of its meaning for each patient. This definition can have an impact on the continuing care plan for the patient and can often make the difference in a consideration of the option of home placement versus placement in an alternative care facility. The definitions of family differ.

For the purposes of this text, family is defined in the broadest sense to allow sufficient flexibility when assessing this social unit for continuing care planning: A family is a group of two or more persons related by marriage, blood, adoption, or emotional involvement with each other, who

Figure 1-1 Continuing Care Planning Continuum

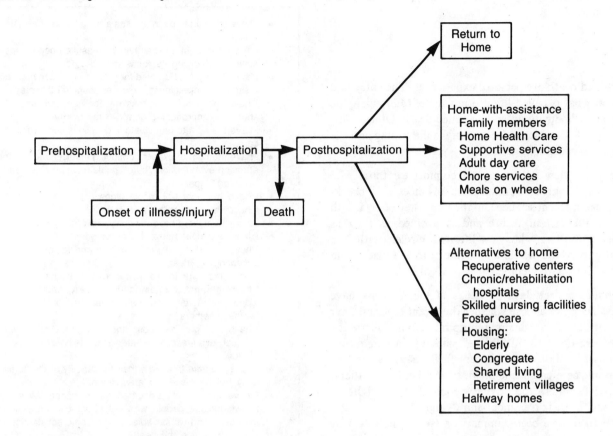

Source: Adapted from "Illness-Wellness Continuum through Discharge Planning" in *Discharge Planning Handbook* by B.M. Steffl and I. Eide with permission of Charles B. Slack, Inc., © 1978.

live and interact together intimately in a common residence or live in close geographic proximity.

Home-with-Assistance: Community Assistance

A hospital stay is a dramatic interruption in a person's life. For many, a stay in the hospital is for only a few days, followed by a return to the normal, healthy life style. But for some who are seriously ill or injured, the stay is longer, and special care is still needed after their hospitalization. For this patient home health services provide a broad range of assistance.

Home care services include skilled nursing, social services, speech therapy, occupational therapy, physical therapy, community services, home health aide, and homemaker services. These services are available to such persons as patients recently released from hospitals, the elderly and others with chronic illness, persons who are terminally ill, persons requiring instruction about and monitoring of their medications and treatments, and new mothers and their babies. Health counseling and support are also available. (See Chapter 8 for a detailed array of

services that can enable a patient to return home with assistance.)

Alternative Care Facility

Some choices of alternative care are easier to make than are others. When planning with the patient and family, two important factors must be considered. First, patients must be given an opportunity to express their desires; secondly, families must express their needs and evaluate what they can realistically provide in the given situation. Families must evaluate their strengths and weaknesses, their financial assets and health care benefits, their emotional attitudes about the presenting illness, and their spiritual strengths.

The alternatives to home care are several. The patient may have a short-term impairment and so may need a facility for only a short period of recuperation. Those faced with a more difficult and involved prognosis may need a chronic or rehabilitation facility before returning home. For others, long-term care is the only option, and so placement in a nursing home must be considered. Foster care, elderly and congregate housing, retirement villages, and halfway houses are also alternative options to home (see Chapter 8).

Death

Birth and death are personal experiences. The entry and exit from what is called life is done alone. Many view life as a straight line with an ending called death. Others view life as a circle in which the beginning is the ending and the ending is the beginning.

The linear view provides great comfort for those who hold onto the great technological advances and breakthroughs in medical science and the hope they offer. Death is off in the distant future and is avoided as long as possible. For those who view life as a circle, death is a natural part of the whole and a return to the place from which a person has come.

Even in the last days or weeks of life, patients have choices. They can choose whether they want to spend their final time at home or in a hospital. Home offers the greatest freedom to fulfill the patient's last requests. Hospitals and skilled-nursing-care facilities are an option when home care cannot be provided for the dying patient. In these facilities, too, dying people have a right to participate in their treatment and dying. These rights of a dying person have been summarized (see Exhibit 1-1) by an unknown author.

Families are not to be blamed when circumstances limit choices and they have made each decision in the best interest of the patient, considering each circumstance. No one option fits every person or situation. In continuing care planning, remember the individuality of each patient and family and then address the options appropriately.

DISCHARGE PLANNING: DEFINITION

Discharge planning is best defined as the vehicle used to move a patient from one level of care to another. For example, discharge planning occurs when a patient is moved from the recovery-room level of care to an intensive-care-unit (ICU) level of care. Communication between health care professionals must be both verbal and written, so that the discharge from unit to unit can be timely, efficient, safe, and comfortable for the patient.

Both a concept and a function, discharge planning is necessary for high quality patient care and sound patient-management practices. Discharge planning is also an organizational management tool that coordinates individual units and disciplines to mobilize the resources necessary to assure a timely discharge from one level of care to another.

Exhibit 1-1 The Dying Person's "Bill of Rights"

- I have the right to be treated as a living human being until I die.
- I have the right to maintain a sense of hopefulness, however changing its focus may be.
- I have the right to be cared for by those who can maintain a sense of hopefulness, however changing this may be.
- I have the right to express my feelings and emotions about my approaching death in my own way.
- I have the right to participate in decisions concerning my care.
- I have the right to expect continuing medical and nursing attention even though "cure" goals must be changed to "comfort" goals.
- I have the right not to die alone.
- I have the right to be free of pain.
- I have the right to have my questions answered honestly.
- I have the right not to be deceived.
- I have the right to have help from and for my family in accepting my death.
- I have the right to die in peace and dignity.
- I have the right to retain my individuality and not to be judged for my decisions, which may be contrary to the beliefs of others.
- I have the right to discuss and enlarge my religious or spiritual experiences, whatever these may mean to others.
- I have the right to expect that the sanctity of the human body will be respected after death.
- I have the right to be cared for by caring, sensitive, knowledgeable people who will attempt to understand my needs and will be able to gain some satisfaction in helping me face my death.

DISCHARGE PLANNING: STANDARDS

JCAH Standards

The Joint Commission on Accreditation of Hospitals (JCAH) has published standards for services and functions within the hospital. For each standard there are interpretations, some of which address continuing care planning. JCAH standards do not consider continuing care and discharge planning as separate entities; rather, they view them as the responsibility of several disciplines and services. Utilization review is also closely tied to the continuing care planning process in these standards.

The following are examples of a few of the JCAH standards and interpretations that are concerned with continuing care planning.

Nursing Services

Standard No. IV. Individualized, goal-directed nursing care shall be provided to patients through the use of the nursing process.

Interpretation: As appropriate, such measures should include physiological, psychosocial, and environmental factors; patient/family education; and patient discharge planning.[1]

Standard No. VI. Written policies and procedures that reflect optimal standards of nursing practice shall guide the provision of nursing care.

Interpretation: The role of the nursing staff in discharge planning.[2]

Social Work Services

Standard No. II. Social work service personnel shall be prepared for their responsibilities in the provision of social work services through appropriate training and education programs.

Interpretation: Assisting the medical, nursing, and other health care personnel in arranging for prescribed medical (including psychiatric) alternative treatment; and participating in discharge planning functions. To facilitate continuity of care, assistance should be provided to the patient and the patient's family in adapting to the patient care plan, whether the service provided is to be continued in a home care or out-of-home care setting.[3]

Standard No. III. Social work services shall be guided by written policies and procedures.

Interpretation: The role of the social work service in discharge planning.[4]

Standard No. V. The quality and appropriateness of social work services provided to patients shall be regularly reviewed, evaluated, and assured through the establishment of quality control mechanisms.

Interpretation: Particular attention shall be given to the appropriateness and effectiveness of the transfer of patients to the long-term care facilities and to home placement with supportive services.[5]

Utilization Review

Standard No. I. The hospital shall demonstrate appropriate allocation of its resources through an effective utilization review program.

Interpretation: To facilitate discharge as soon as an acute level of care is no longer required, discharge planning shall be initiated as early as a determination of the need for such activity can be made. Criteria for initiating discharge planning may be developed to identify patients whose diagnoses, problems, or psychosocial circumstances usually require discharge planning. The utilization review plan may specify the situations in which nonphysician health care professionals may initiate preparations for discharge planning. Discharge planning shall not be limited to placement in long-term care facilities, but shall include provision for, or referral to, services that may be required to improve or maintain the patient's health status.[6]

AHA Guidelines

The American Hospital Association also has set forth guidelines for discharge planning. These approved guidelines were developed by the society for hospital social work directors of the AHA to assist hospitals in evaluating and improving their discharge-planning functions. These guidelines recognize that each institution has a set of different resources and organizes its services to meet the specific needs of its patient population and the community it serves.

The AHA believes that coordinated continuing care planning is essential for hospitals in order to maintain high quality patient care. The belief is that continuing care planning facilitates appropriate decision making by the patient and the family. Decreasing hospital length of stay—thereby, decreasing health care costs—is also an important outcome of efficient and timely discharge planning.

To ensure a high quality continuing care planning program, the AHA states that the hospital will[7]

- Assign responsibility for the coordination of discharge planning.
- Identify as early as possible, sometimes before hospital admission, the expected posthospital care needs of patients, utilizing admissions and preadmission screening and review programs when available.
- Develop with patients and families appropriate discharge care plans.
- Assist patients and their families in planning for the supportive environment necessary to provide the patient's posthospital care.
- Develop a plan that considers the medical, social, and financial needs of patients.

The AHA also lists the following elements essential to accomplishing the hospital's goals for high quality, cost-effective patient care:[8]

- Early identification of patients who are likely to need complex posthospital care.
- Patient and family education.
- Patient/family assessment and counseling.
- Plan development.
- Plan coordination and implementation.
- Postdischarge follow-up.

These guidelines recognize the rapid changes that are experienced in an acute care setting and the effects these changes have on planning activities. Nevertheless, continuing care planning is recognized as an important activity for the hospital and the health care professional.

BRCCN Standards

In addition to the JCAH and AHA guidelines, a set of discharge-planning standards has been written by the Boston Regional Continuing Care Nurses (BRCCN). A group of hospital-based registered nurses in the greater Boston community, they are involved in the field of continuing care. This group was organized in 1974 and completed writing a set of nursing standards for discharge planning in 1984. Exhibit 1-2 depicts the efforts of this group.

These standards, which clearly address the assessment, legislative, communication, networking, documentation, and evaluative process of a continuing care planning program, represent the cornerstone of a knowledge-building process for the continuing care professional today.

Exhibit 1-2 BRCCN Discharge-Planning Standards

Discharge-planning standards have been established by the Boston Regional Continuing Care Nurses to identify the essential components of the discharge-planning process. These standards must include, but are not restricted to, the following:[9]

1. All patients have the right to discharge planning, which begins with the initial patient care assessment at the time of admission.
2. All patients have the right to discharge planning, which includes legal/civil rights and the principles of the least restrictive alternatives to care.
3. Discharge planning should be initiated by the primary health care providers. Assessments should be based on skilled nursing care needs in addition to psychosocial, economic, legal, and environmental factors.
4. Discharge planning must be multidisciplinary.
5. A mechanism for consultation and/or coordination by a continuing care nurse should be established among the multidisciplinary planning team. The continuing care nurse is vital to the assessment process in determining patient's medical and nursing needs after discharge. Based on his/her nursing knowledge and community health expertise, the nurse appropriately identifies specific levels of nursing care required, while recognizing and utilizing appropriate resources.
6. Documentation of the discharge must be consistently recorded on a permanent multidisciplinary sheet in the medical record. Written documentation must be provided to facilities at the time of discharge. The Patient Care Referral Form is the vehicle for transfer of patient care information between agencies.
7. Evaluation is a necessary component of the discharge-planning process, as it serves as a mechanism for identifying gaps and inadequacies in the health care services provided by both the hospital and the community. This information must be used to generate action in health planning and regulatory activities.

ANA Standards

One more example of discharge-planning standards can be cited from the resolution formulated at the 1974 meeting of the American Nurses' Association (Exhibit 1-3).[10] The statement supports the role of the professional nurse in this process.

GOALS AND OBJECTIVES OF A CONTINUING CARE PROGRAM

Continuing care is a decision-making process that focuses on the patient and significant others as the principal decision makers. The role of the professional provider in continuing care is that of facilitator in the decision-making process.

To carry out this process effectively, continuing care planning must be a multidisciplinary program. Moreover, the goal of the program must be to ensure that patients who enter the acute care institution have a planned program for their continuing care needs and a follow-up plan when they leave the hospital. The program must be structured so that it prepares patients and their families for the next level of care—an alternative care facility or the patient's family home. Such effective discharge planning can assure the patient of high quality health care.

A comprehensive continuing care planning program provides the patient with—

Exhibit 1-3 ANA Resolution on Admission and Discharge Planning

- Whereas, there has been a tremendous increase in hospital costs during the last five years and costs continue to rise, and
- Whereas, often there is not an effective, efficient, and appropriate utilization of institutional facilities and community resources, and
- Whereas, hospital care is often followed by care in the nursing homes, rehabilitation facilities, or in other institutions and by home health agencies, and/or various community resources, and
- Whereas, there is a need to assist individuals and their families to cope when there are disruptions due to illness, disability, or other services requiring admission to a health care institution or service from a community agency;

Therefore, be it

- Resolved, that nurses in every health care institution and community agency assume responsibility for planning for the patient's/client's admission and discharge, and be it
- Resolved, that continuing care planning be an integral part of every patient/client care program, and be it further
- Resolved, that nurses in every health care institution and community agency develop well-defined programs and procedures for referral and discharge, demonstrating there has been an effort to provide continually and that there has been patient and family involvement in the planning.

- access into the health care system,
- assessment of post hospital needs,
- a collaborative plan designed to meet identified continuing care needs,
- an implementation plan,
- an evaluation process of the plan in order to identify met or unmet needs.

A comprehensive program should also be able to do the following:

- Identify patients who may require continuing care needs.
- Identify patients who may require long hospitalization.
- Identify patients with unique social circumstances that can complicate a timely and efficient discharge.
- Educate the professional staff about available resources.
- Educate the professional staff about continuing care planning trends and their implications.
- Coordinate patient planning conferences.
- Provide a milieu for policymaking.
- Monitor ongoing continuing care planning activities.
- Maintain accurate records and statistics, and report activities to the administration and the professional staff.

PREADMISSION PLANNING

Under the prospective pricing system, hospitals are being challenged to reduce unnecessary hospitalizations and to reduce the length of stay. Hospitals are finding that increased emphasis is being placed on early discharge, which will require early discharge planning. Discharge planning must begin before a patient's admission so that those patients whose posthospital needs are expected to be complex can be identified early. Plans can then be made to move the patient through the health care system at the lowest appropriate level of care in the shortest amount of time while maintaining a high level of quality.

Although preadmission review programs are mentioned frequently in the literature, these programs are generally established by insurance companies (eg, Blue Cross and Blue Shield) or the federal government (for Medicaid and Medicare beneficiaries). Many of these programs differ structurally; however, they all share the same goal—to reduce unnecessary hospitalization. There is evidence that preadmission review programs are reducing hospital inpatient use.[11] Although these programs operate at the state level, the concept can be applied to a particular hospital in the form of a preadmission planning program.

A preadmission planning program differs from a preadmission review program in that a planning program is hospital based and is therefore geared toward the resources of one hospital. Several programs using preadmission discharge planning are already in existence and more are being developed. However, most of these programs are experimental and are limited to a specific group of patients.[12]

In a typical hospital's patient-admission department, about 40 percent of the patients are admitted electively for planned hospital stays, as elective surgeries or as diagnostic workups. Approximately 30 percent are unplanned admissions but are not admitted as emergencies. The remainder are true emergencies, admitted through the hospital's emergency unit.

A preadmission planning program can directly affect the elective admissions and can have an impact on a portion of the other admissions. Such a program ensures that patients are moved through the hospital system at the most appropriate level of care, within the shortest length of time possible, and at the highest level of quality of care. In addition, a program of this nature could prevent unnecessary hospitalization, particularly for the elderly. The elderly are often admitted with a minor diagnosis because they can no longer be managed at home and are in need of home health care or nursing-home placement. A preadmission program would prevent unnecessary hospital stays for this group in particular and would provide for the arrangement of the necessary social supports to be made on an outpatient basis.

Preadmission planning can assist in the continuing care planning process and in the use of outpatient preadmission testing programs. Preadmission planning is intended to be a resource for the physician, the physician's office personnel, the primary nurse, and the social worker as they help to plan for the patient's hospital stay and discharge. A program such as this can assist the patient—and the family—in making an easier transition from home and community into the hospital. The medical staff should view this program, however, as a resource they can use to get the patient through the system in the most cost-effective way, not as an intrusion on their right to practice medicine.

The advantages of a preadmission planning program are as follows:

- To identify before admission the expected posthospital-care needs of patients using admission and preadmission screening programs.
- To identify early those patients whose posthospital needs are expected to be complex, so that the necessary posthospital resources can be secured in a timely fashion.
- To familiarize patients and their families with the available community resources.

- To coordinate all bookings with physicians and to screen them for appropriateness of admissions, using preestablished admission review criteria.
- To increase efficiency in the scheduling of diagnostic procedures on an outpatient basis.
- To support quality assurance, utilization review, and risk management efforts by involving patients and families in long-term planning.
- To initiate patient education and pre-op teaching before admission for elective surgical patients with a selected diagnosis.
- To help the continuing care primary team to begin the discharge-planning process sooner and to alert them to those patients with complex discharge needs.
- To help decrease the length of stay and to prevent unnecessary admissions.

CONCLUSION

Continuing care has become a vital component of the health care delivery system today. Furthermore, it encompasses a specialized body of knowledge, which is the result of the increased emphasis on the continuity of patient care and the intense monitoring of the health care system by regulatory agencies and third party payers. Continuing care professionals, privileged to be in a rapidly growing specialty of health care, face enormous responsibility in helping patients and their families to meet their ever-changing needs. These persons are important to the hospital because of their role in reducing patient length of stay and decreasing health care costs.

REFERENCES

1. *Accreditation Manual for Hospitals* (Chicago: Joint Commission on Accreditation of Hospitals, 1983), p. 118; p. 119, 11.6–8.
2. *Ibid.* p. 120, 1.30.
3. *Ibid.* p. 178, 11.9–15.
4. *Ibid.* p. 179; p. 180, 11.1–3.
5. *Ibid.* p. 180, 11.39–42.
6. *Ibid.* p. 193; p. 194, 11.25–32.
7. *Discharge Planning Guidelines* (Chicago: American Hospital Association, April 11-12, 1984), Catalog No. 004170. 15 M-6/84-4. 0899.
8. *Ibid.*
9. *Discharge Planning Standards* (Boston: Boston Regional Continuing Care Nurses, 1982).
10. American Nurses' Association Resolution on Admission and Discharge Planning, *Summary of Proceedings of ANA House of Delegates 49th Convention* (American Nurses' Association Publication Code No. G-117-1500, 1975).
11. T. Shahoda, "Preadmission Review Cuts Hospital Use," *Hospitals* **58**, 54 (August 1984).
12. G. Willihnganz, "The Next Step: Preadmission Planning for Discharge Needs," *Coordinator* **3**, 20 (April 1984).

2. A Theory and Model for Continuing Care Planning

The health care delivery system of today is becoming so complex that a model is needed to offer some direction toward goal unification and clarification. Nurses are seeking more effective and efficient ways to provide quality care. Of equal concern is the manner in which that care is planned. Moreover, the growing influence of patient-centered approaches to nursing care creates the necessity of having a theoretical basis for nursing practice.

A systems model can provide such direction and the theoretical basis for nursing care. It is composed of interrelated interacting components and has a purpose, a process, and a content. The *purpose* is a goal to be accomplished that gives direction to the system; the *content* is the components that make up the system; the *process* is the function of the parts in fulfilling the purpose for which the systems model was developed.

A *model* can be defined as a "symbolic depiction in logical terms of an idealized relatively simple situation showing the structure of the original system."[1] A model, then, is a conceptual representation of reality. A *theory* may be defined as a scientifically acceptable general principle that governs practice or is proposed to explain observed facts. Theory, then, becomes a deeper level of reality representation than a model and provides the working insides of a model. Viewed in this way, a model represents structure; theory depicts function.

The continuing care planning model (Figure 2-1) in this book has been developed from the Roy Adaptation Model for nursing practice. It provides the theoretical base for a framework to practice within the continuing care planning process. The nursing process is also used in this model as a series of actions intended to encompass all the steps taken to ensure high quality care for the patient.

In this chapter, the discussion of the continuing care planning model focuses in particular on the Roy Adaptation Model; the nursing process; general systems theory (open and closed system); the definition and role of the primary team, the resource team, and the community team; the role description and the responsibility of an interactive, interdisciplinary continuing care planning team; and an introductory description—with definitions—of the nursing process in continuing care practice (assessment, planning, implementation, and evaluation).

ROY ADAPTATION MODEL

The Roy Adaptation Model had its beginning in 1964 when Sister Callista Roy was challenged to develop a conceptual model for a seminar in Los Angeles. The model is primarily a systems model. In the model, humans are seen to have four subsystems by which they adapt: (1) physiological, (2) self-concept, (3) role function, and (4) role interdependence.

The human adaptation level is determined by the force of the confronting or focal stimuli and other nonspecific or residual stimuli. Nursing seeks to assess the patient's behavior and the factors influencing the human adaptation level. Intervention involves the manipulation of the influencing factors or stimuli in order to change the person's response potential by bringing the stimuli within the zone in which a positive response is possible. The Roy Adapta-

Figure 2-1 A Model for Continuing Care Planning

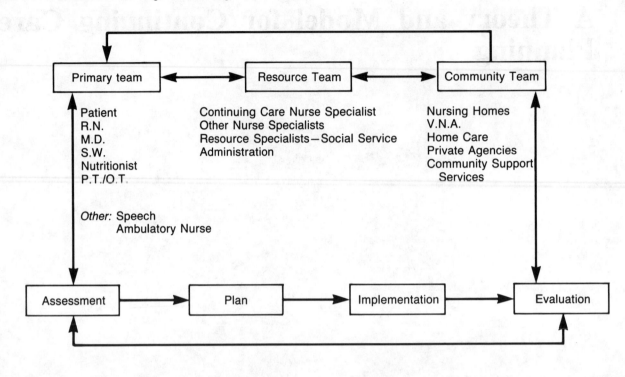

tion Model, consequently, describes the goal of nursing as that of assisting humans to adapt in the four adaptive modes—physical, self-concept, role function, and role interdependence.

In defense of the model, Roy states, "This model of nursing can show us what factors to assess in our patients, what behaviors require nursing intervention, and what factors are relevant to our solution of the problem. It enables us to establish a clear goal for care and provides us the data to be used in selecting nursing approaches."[2]

The Roy Adaptation Model begins with the patient, the recipient of the nursing care. Humans as biopsychosocial beings are constantly interacting with their environment. Daily, humans confront physical, social, and psychological changes in their environment. To respond to the demands placed on them, persons attempt to cope by responding with innate and acquired mechanisms that are biological, psychological, and social.

Health and illness are inescapable facets of human existence. They form a continuum along which at any point persons receive a variety of stimuli to which they must respond. In order to respond positively to the environmental changes around them, humans must adapt.

Human adaptation is a function of the stimulus the person is exposed to and of the person's adaptation level. Adaptation decreases the number of responses necessary to cope with the predominant stimulation and increases human sensitivity to the complementary stimuli. The adaptation level is determined by the pooled effect of the three classes of stimuli:

1. *focal stimuli*—stimuli immediately confronting the person
2. *contextual stimuli*—all other stimuli present
3. *residual stimuli*—beliefs, attitudes, traits, and other factors from past experiences that are relevant to the present situation

Adaptation begins with a stimulus that demands an adaptive response. Any impulsion to act or to respond comes from the disparity between the stimulation level and the adaptation level. The disparity sets up a gradient that determines the strength of the response: the steeper the gradient the greater the impact of the stimulus on the person and the greater the person's response to it. With a decline on the gradient between the stimulus and the adaptation level, the magnitude of the person's response is lessened. The human adaptation level is such that it comprises a zone that indicates the range of stimulation that leads to a positive response. If the stimulus is within the zone, the person responds positively. If the stimulus is outside the zone, the person cannot make a positive response. For example, if a person puts his hand into a basin of very hot water, he will remove it quickly; if the water is cooler, the magnitude of the response is less.

In Roy's model, humans are conceptualized as having various modes of adaptation (a mode of adaptation is a way of adapting).[3] "First, man adapts to his physiologic needs," states Roy, and secondly, man's self-concept is determined by his interactions with others. Thirdly, role function is the performance of duties based on given positions within society. The way one performs these duties is constantly responsive with others; man adapts according to a system of interdependence. This system involves his way of seeking help, attention, and affection.

Mode of adaptation, however, is not the only element in a systems model. The elements of a practice-oriented model include also values, goals, the recipient, and the intervention. In the Roy Adaptation Model, four basic values are implied.[4]

1. Nursing's concern with man as a total being in the areas of health and illness is a socially significant activity.

2. The nursing goal of supporting and promoting patient adaptation is important for patient welfare.

3. Promoting the process of adaptation is assumed to conserve patient energy; thus, nursing makes an important contribution to the overall goal of the health care team by making energy available for the healing process.

4. Nursing is unique because it focuses on the patient as a person adapting to those stimuli present as a result of his position on the health-illness continuum.

Because nursing is concerned with a person as a total being located at some point along the health-illness continuum, the function of nursing is to support and to promote patient adaptation. Nursing focuses on the patient as responding to the stimuli that are present because of the person's particular position on the continuum. The goal is to bring about an adaptive state in which the patient is forced to respond to other stimuli. This process can be assumed to conserve the patient's energy, thus contributing to the overall goal of the health team by making energy available for the healing process.

The nurse's role in promoting adaptation involves two factors: (1) assessment and (2) intervention. *Assessment* includes the recognition of a person's position on the health-illness continuum, the evaluation of the forces acting on the person, and the effectiveness of the person's coping mechanism within the given situation. The question is, How well is the person able to adapt? The nurse intervenes to promote adaptation. *Intervention* involves changing the person's response potential by bringing the stimuli within the zone in which a positive response is possible. The nurse does this by changing the contextual stimuli or the residual stimuli.

USE OF THE NURSING PROCESS WITHIN THE ADAPTATION MODEL

The human being responds to environmental forces in a singular yet integrated fashion. The specific symptoms of a disease process may emphasize some bodily functions more than others, but the person involved responds in a distinctive way. Decisions for nursing intervention must be based, then, on the unique behavior of the individual. When nursing intervention influences adaptation favorably, the nurse is acting in a therapeutic sense; when nursing intervention cannot alter the course of adaptation, the nurse is acting in a supportive sense. It is impossible to measure the degree to which each of many factors affects the individual behavior that characterizes the adaptation taking place. However, it is possible to understand the adaptation more clearly if the variety of factors that might influence it are known.

The adaptation model of nursing implies a process similar to that which has been developed over the years of nursing history. There are two major reasons why nursing uses a problem-solving-based nursing process. The first reason is the patient-centered goal of nursing; the second is the accountability of the profession as a scientific discipline that is service oriented.

According to the adaptation concept of nursing, nursing aims to promote adaptation in health and illness. It is a basic assumption of the model that this service is valued by society. The model shows that nursing activities can change a situation of maladaptation into a solution of adaptation. To do this the nurse must assess adaptation, plan the care, implement the plan, and evaluate the effectiveness of the process. To this end, the data are collected, the problem is defined, and the approach is selected.

GENERAL SYSTEMS THEORY: OPEN VERSUS CLOSED

General systems theory is an analytical framework that guides observations (regardless of the the system) and avoids observations based on only one thing. The system takes into account the growing realization that whatever is studied or observed is not a single entity behaving or acting alone; rather, there are a number of interacting components (in operation at the same time) that have to be planned, arranged, maintained, or managed—whether they are living organisms or machines. Therefore, a broad understanding and many techniques are needed to see the interrelationships that exist between all elements of society, institutions, or organisms. It is important to recognize that nothing is determined by a single phenomenon, but rather by the conglomeration of parts interacting with each other openly and in a broad context to produce an end-goal or an effect. Thus general systems theory provides an interdisciplinary framework for the study of a process, such as nursing, in a continuing care planning model.

The 1980s is a decade in which health care practices in the United States have been challenged; change has been demanded. The critics have called for an evaluation of the existing health care system and for the development of imaginative new ideas that can provide the best possible health services to meet the diverse health needs for the diverse cultural groups that make up the United States. In this context, it is important to support an open system of health care delivery rather than a closed system.

Closed System

A closed system is one in which there is limited or no interchange in components, such as materials and energy, within the total environmental context. Closed systems tend to be insulated and to level out differences in their structure in the interest of maintaining an equilibrium. The closed system, therefore, seriously limits the full rendering of health services to clients by professional groups and according to each professional's particular expertise. As a result, authority and accountability for professional services to patients tend to be seriously hampered, weakened, and confused.

Open System

An open system, on the contrary, encourages and accommodates a continuous interchange and flow of input from the total environment. (This continuing care planning model is built on the open-system concept.) The open system offers the patient a choice of services and supports from several health care disciplines. It also offers earlier, prompter, and easier access to health care services according to the patient's health problem. For example, the patient may not need to see a physician if the problem can be handled effectively and appropriately by a nurse or by a social worker. The system also permits professional contributions from many different health groups, all of them expected to assume responsibility and accountability for their services to the patient, whether they be provided independently or in collaboration with the other disciplines. In other words, an open system uses and effectively integrates the skills and contributions of all health care professionals. Moreover, an open system is always responsive to change. An open exchange of ideas and input is encouraged; so is feedback. Feedback, which may be both positive and negative, is sought from the individual within the primary team, the resource team, and the community team (or the teams as a whole) in order to improve and to develop a process or plan that is sensitive to inputs from within or from outside of the systems model. Modifications

and changes can then be made to meet the needs of the patient, the community, the professional, or the identified health care team more appropriately. Finally, an open system fosters the development of multiple kinds of patient-professional relationships and permits comparisons of different kinds of health services.

In summary, the open, patient-centered continuing care model is presented in this text as a model to stimulate new ideas and directions in conceptualizing the total health care area of continuing care planning.

DEFINITION OF THE INTERDISCIPLINARY TEAMS

The purpose of continuing care planning is to assure persons and their families that every effort—from the time of admission to the hospital—is directed toward planning and providing adequate and continued care for the patient in preparation for discharge. To carry out that purpose, the interdisciplinary team approach is vital—especially in a restrictive political and economic environment. Moreover, it is extremely easy to develop "turf" issues if the discharge planning responsibility is divided. When this fragmented approach occurs, patients are denied not only a basic right but a comprehensive assessment, coordination, and plan for their continuing care needs.

Crossing disciplines requires collaboration and flexibility. Members of the interdisciplinary team must be bound together by a common philosophy of care and must have mutually established goals. What is more, each team member must understand his or her own role and must communicate it to fellow members of the team. There are specific expectations of each team member. If these expectations are not communicated, role ambiguity and role conflict can occur. The concept of continuing care planning, therefore, must be viewed and practiced within this philosophy in order to provide continuity of care that spans from hospital admission back to the home and community or to alternative care placements.

Primary Team

In the continuing care planning model presented in this book, the *primary team* is the interdisciplinary, interactive group of health care providers charged with the following responsibilities:

- to assess the patient for continuing care needs
- to develop a plan of care with goals and objectives that can enable the patient to move along the continuing care planning continuum toward an optimal level of functioning
- to implement the plan of care, each health care discipline offering the patient expert quality care for the identified health problem.

The plan must be evaluated frequently while the patient is in the acute care setting because of the rapidly changing nature of the patient's situation. Initial conclusions from assessments provide the basis for anticipating outcomes and then projecting a course of action. Evaluations assist the primary team not only in determining problems that have been resolved and those that need to be reassessed and replanned but in diagnosing new health problems and identifying issues and needs of the patient and family members. Evaluating the effect of actions during and after the implementation phase also determines the patient response and the extent to which immediate, intermediate, and long-range goals are achieved.

The primary team consists of the patient, the nurse, the physician, the social worker, the nutritionist, the physical therapist, and the occupational therapist. When the patient's plan of care determines that it is necessary, the ambulatory nurse and the speech therapist also may be included as active members of the primary team.

Resource Team

The *resource team* is a group of persons within the acute care setting who are available to the primary team as consultants for the patient's health care needs. These persons, trained in specialty health care fields, are used as resources and educators to the primary team. They assist in the implementation process as their expertise dictates.

Community Team

The *community team* consists of persons from various community agencies and programs—chronic and rehabilitation hospitals, nursing homes, visiting nurses associations, private home care agencies, and community support services. They are the nurses, social workers, physicians, physical and occupational therapists, and the like who are able to assist in the discharge-planning process. Many times the patient has already been followed in the community by these persons, and so they can offer invaluable information and assistance to the primary team as it plans for the patient's discharge. The importance of communicating with the community cannot be stressed enough. The community team professionals continue in the community the plan of care that has been developed and carried out in the acute care setting. The essence of continuing care is established here when open communication is ongoing with the community team and when planning is an interdisciplinary team effort.

CONTINUING CARE PLANNING TEAM MEMBERS: ROLE DESCRIPTIONS AND RESPONSIBILITIES

If personal health is primarily the responsibility of the patient, where do other persons from various disciplines fit into a continuing care model? Each professional discipline has a specific body of knowledge, and so the various disciplines have the responsibility of integrating continuing care into their delivery of health care. Continuing care is a decision-making process focusing on the patient, the family, and the significant others as the principal decision makers. The role of the health care professional is decision facilitation.

Primary Team

Patient

The most important member of the team is the *patient*. Illness or injury is a personal experience; therefore, all efforts, decisions, and the support of the team are directed toward the benefit of the patient. Patients must actively participate in the planning process if they are able. If not, family members or significant others should become active team participants. Patients not only have the right to receive the benefit of quality continuing care planning, but they should play the main role in coordinating the plan of care with their primary provider.

Registered Nurse

In a primary nursing care practice system such as this model is built upon, the primary nurse has the professional responsibility to evaluate patients for continuing care needs and to work with other members of the continuing care planning team to see that these needs are met. Nursing is the only discipline on the team that is a stable entity—routinely and immediately available to every patient and family on a 24-hour basis. Nursing is in a unique position, then, to provide the critical coordinating link between the patient and all other team members. This position maximizes the nurse's ability to facilitate communication and cooperative planning among the health care team members about acute inpatient activities and continuing care planning. Frequently, the primary nurse recognizes less obvious problems that require intervention by another team member. The primary nurse establishes a trusting relationship with patients, their families, and the significant others as a result of ongoing and consistent interpersonal exchanges.

The professional primary nurse spends the most time with the patient and, as a result, is in an advantageous position to evaluate the kinds of services the patient may require at the time of discharge. If this evaluation is neglected, patients may be discharged without any knowledge of their health needs and problems or the health services they desperately need and have a right to expect. Clearly, the primary nurse plays an important role as the coordinator of the continuing care planning team.

Physician

The physician as a member of the primary team in the acute care setting is involved in spending time efficiently caring for patients who have acute or ongoing medically complex problems. Because physicians determine who is hospitalized and the plan for the diagnostic workup and treatment of the hospitalized person, they must begin at the time of admission to discuss with the patient, the family, and the significant others plans for discharge. Failing to look beyond the time of admission and focusing only on the presenting acute illness of the patient only promotes discontinuity in the discharge planning process. Some basic questions the physician should ask and consider at the time of admission are, Where did the patient come from, and is a return to the same place possible? If so, what additional supports will be required? If not, what are the alternatives? These basic questions start the basic discharge planning process and assist the patient, the family, and the other team members to look at these issues early, before compromises are required by the pressures to expedite discharge.

The physician clearly has an important role to play on the primary team. With effective communication and documentation by the physician, the continuing care needs of the patient can be addressed through the interdisciplinary team model process.

Social Worker

Continuing care implies that a social worker also has an important place on the primary team. As a health care professional skilled in interviewing, the social worker's sole responsibility is to assess the patient in the psychosocial and behavioral environment. Through an assessment process, the social worker must obtain the following important information from the patient:

- primary concerns
- living situation and life-style
- understanding of the illness, the proposed treatment, and the continuing care needs
- emotional and environmental needs
- coping capacity
- family relationships
- strengths and limitations (patient and family)
- finances
- resource networks
- desires, beliefs, and plans

Empathy is the social worker's ability to perceive and to encourage expression of the patient's and the family's anxieties, fears, hopes, and struggles so that the patient, with the assistance of others (ie, the family, significant others, and the primary continuing care team), can ultimately make the best decision about continuing care needs.

The social worker is responsible also for conducting weekly primary team rounds for the purpose of addressing the continuing care needs of patients. In these rounds, all new admissions to the unit are reviewed and assessments are discussed; initial plans for discharge from the acute care setting are identified; goals and objectives are stated; and the continuing care process continues. Frequently, patients are admitted and discharged before they are presented at primary team rounds. In these cases, the primary nurse—the coordinator of patient care needs—would communicate continuing care concerns to the primary team or to individual primary team members as dictated by individual patient needs. Planning, at this point, must be addressed and promptly initiated.

In summary, the social worker's role in the continuing care planning process is to assist the patient, the family, the significant others, and the primary health care team to understand the effects of the presenting health problem on the patient and family members. Often, the social worker as the balance wheel of the team enables involved members to set realistic goals for meeting the continuing care needs of the patient. With patient participation and primary team collaboration and cooperation, timely and effective discharge planning can take place.

Physical Therapist

Physical therapy as an involved discipline on the primary team is focused chiefly on the improvement of the patient's mobility or a return to normal function. In the context of this book, *mobility* is defined as the extent to which persons can perform those tasks necessary to carry out the activities of daily living (ADL) and to function within their environment.

One important factor that influences both the length of the hospital stay and the extent of further continuing care is mobility. The physical therapist as a primary member on the continuing care planning team in an acute care setting is qualified to provide quality care for a timely and effective discharge from the acute care setting back to the community or to an alternative care setting. The therapist plans and administers treatment programs for patients of all ages in order to restore function; to relieve pain; and to prevent disability after disease, injury, or loss of body parts. The therapist also contributes valuable insights about a patient's functional independence and level of mobility.

In the acute care setting, the physical therapist makes a thorough evaluation of the patient, noting such factors as age, the level of mobility before admission, the social and living environment, the physical performance capabilities (eg, strength, endurance, range of motion, balance, transfers, mobility, joint functions, gait analysis, and pain status) and the goals and expectations of the patient, the family and the other members of the primary team. Goal setting and the attainment of these goals is a dynamic process that involves constant and continual monitoring of the patient's progress and adaptive processes by the therapist and the total primary team. Realistic changes must be made when they are necessary in order to provide the maximum benefit to the patient. As early as possible in the acute care hospitalization phase, physical therapy intervention must begin. Early intervention in this phase can only enhance the effectiveness of attempts to attain the immediate goals of increasing mobility and thereby possibly to reduce the number of days required for the hospital stay.

The priorities and the recommendations for the physical therapy health care needs of the patient must be communicated to the members of the primary team. Medical record documentation is an effective method of communicating the functional and rehabilitation status and the needs of the patient to the primary team, the resource team, and the community team. Because the pace is very fast in an acute care facility, the patient cannot receive the high quality care that is deserved if these particular continuing care needs are not documented or communicated.

Peteet states that there are five general characteristics needed by the physical therapist for participation in the continuing care planning process. The characteristics are as follows:[5]

- Commitment to, and ability to plan for, patient and family involvement.
- Ability to provide clear and objective chart documentation, including short and long-term goals from admission to discharge.
- Understanding of regulatory requirements as they relate to reimbursement for patient services.
- Knowledge of the availability of community services and general insurance coverage (eg, for patient equipment).
- Clear understanding of the roles of licensed physical therapists, physical therapist assistants, aides, and other health team members, to facilitate appropriate delegation of responsibility.

The physical therapist is, therefore, an important member of the continuing care primary team. Without the objective assessment and evaluation of the functioning and mobility status of a patient, an important factor in creating an atmosphere of constructive effort toward the goal of wellness will be missing.

Occupational Therapist

The occupational therapist brings to the continuing care primary team the professional ability to view patients as holistic human beings who can return to their community or to an alternative care facility placement able to meet the demands of their prospective environments as independently and as capable of self-care as possible. Occupational therapists work in a variety of settings. In the acute care setting, the therapist primarily consults, provides, or supervises the direct care of the patient for occupational therapy needs.

To determine continuing care needs, the therapist completes an assessment of the patient in the following areas:

- psychological adjustment and transitional support with a physical disability
- role of the family
- social and recreational needs and activities
- need for assistive devices: prescription and utilization
- activities of daily living, mobility, self-care skills
- perceptual skills, concentration, and decision making
- therapeutic exercises
- patient concept of self and ego functions

The patient's ability to participate in the program is extremely important to the outcomes of occupational therapy goals. These goals are to retrain the patient to accomplish specific activities of daily living. ADL is a broad term used to include such tasks as the use of public transportation, driver training, body functional restraining activities as they relate to social and recreational needs, and communication skills. Homemaking skills are also included in the occupational therapy program. Every effort is made to use assistive devices, strengthening exercises, safety training, work simplification, stress reduction, and any other technique training in order to enable the patient to return to independent living.

Occupational therapists have the professional knowledge and the skill training to retrain patients in perceptual skills, concentration, decision making, and reality orientation function programs. In addition, spatial relations, depth perception, and other perceptual cognitive skills are assessed by using theories of learning and development.

In preparation for the patient's timely and efficient discharge to home or community, the occupational therapist, with the assistance of the patient and the family members, assesses the following:

- architectural barriers and environmental adaptations
- family education and support
- prevocational training and adjustment to job placement
- homemaking skills

When a patient is transferred or discharged to an alternative care facility, the occupational therapist has the professional responsibility to assist in making a smooth transition for the patient. The therapist can assure the patient, the family, and the continuing care primary team that the placement of choice is specifically able to meet the continuing care needs of the patient. Often therapists make site visits before the discharge of a patient.

Documentation of occupational therapy activities is a crucial component of the effective communication process for the continuing care planning primary team. When documenting action in the medical record, the therapist addresses the following:

• range of motion and muscle status
• sensation
• perceptual and cognitive fields
• ADL, functional status, self-care skills
• community mobility
• course and response to treatment: psychosocial attitudes
• contraindications to therapy
• discharge plans
• recommended equipment
• occupational therapy goals

The occupational therapist is a valued member of the continuing care primary team. Through early referrals, the process of assessing appropriate discharge considerations can begin in order that the optimal treatment plan can be fully operational for the patient so that the patient can return to home and community living at the optimal level of functioning ability. The occupational therapist contributes to the continuing care planning process by incorporating a total picture of the patient's functional progress as it relates to total functional abilities.

Nutritionist

Because food and nutrition are integral parts of the life cycle, getting patients to eat well is important but often difficult. Illness has a way of destroying appetites; yet the body must have the proper nourishment. Life cannot be sustained without food.

The clinical nutritionist's role on the continuing care primary team is to assess the nutritional status, to identify problems, and to plan and administer nutritional care to patients in various illness-wellness life situations. The nutritionist also acts as a resource person to other members of the primary team.

It is the responsibility of the nutritionist to educate and to instruct the patient and family members in special diet needs that are identified by the primary team. The nutritionist also assists patients in carrying out their religious and cultural beliefs about their dietary patterns so

that their specific life-style and commitment can be maintained. Similarly, the nutritionist can help patients to interpret how they can substitute cultural foods for items in a special clinical diet.

The nutritionist is responsible for delivering optimal nutritional care to the patient. Two areas of concern for the patient are (1) the short-term restorative care and (2) the long-term continuing care nutritional needs. In planning for the patient's nutritional needs, the nutritionist must address the following areas with the primary team and must isolate the areas that are significant:

• past and present medical history as it relates to the patient's nutritional status: laboratory data and medication history
• physical milieu: living situation, available resources (ie, transportation, food, finances, family members, friends)
• psychosocial milieu: ethnic background, cultural habits, religion, education level, motivation, goals, recreation, exercise patterns

As a primary team member addressing continuing care needs for patients, the nutritionist uses the information received from an evaluation of these areas in an assessment process to develop a nutritional plan that can maintain the optimal nutritional health of the patient in the home and community or in an alternative care facility.

To assist other members of the primary continuing care team, the nutritionist communicates through interactive, reciprocal exchanges and by careful documentation in the medical record to provide the patient and the family with a comprehensive continuing care plan.

Speech-Language Therapist

Whenever the patient's continuing care plan determines that a consultation is necessary because there are communication deficits, the speech-language therapist may be called in. The therapist may be involved either in the direct care of the patient or as a consultant to the primary team.

The role of the speech-language therapist varies in different settings. The therapist's primary role in the acute care setting is to diagnose and to treat persons with disorders of articulation, voice, rhythm, and symbolization (language). Counseling and educating the patient and family members about the communication disorder is another role responsibility. Speech-language therapists also make referrals to other disciplines when necessary and follow through with referrals to alternative care facilities and home health care agencies. When the patient's care plan deems that a speech-language therapist consultation is necessary, the therapist first assesses the patient's level of communication; then, the patient's potential for improvement in communicative functioning is determined, and recommendations are made to the primary team.

The ability to communicate differentiates human beings from other animals. When this capability is lost or impaired, persons are removed from the circle of human life. This isolating potential for the patient and family makes early intervention by the speech-language therapist extremely important. The recommendations of the speech-language therapist are, therefore, another important component needed to complete the continuing care plan, which is designed by factors from all the participating disciplines.

Ambulatory Clinic Nurse

In many acute care settings, an ambulatory care outpatient department is associated with the institution. It may even be a major department. In a primary care health care system, the ambulatory care nurse is often involved as an active member of the primary continuing care team. Many patients have follow-up visits in the ambulatory care department after discharge from the acute care setting. The ambulatory clinic nurse receives a referral from the in-house staff and automatically takes the patient as a primary client. The nurse continues the plan of care that was initiated in the acute care unit and follows the patient after discharge.

When an ambulatory outpatient is admitted to the acute care unit, the ambulatory nurse is helpful in evaluating, with the primary team, the continuing care needs of the patient. Plans need to be reassessed and often changed for each patient. Again, communication and collaboration are key components to successful continuity of care for patients and their families. The ambulatory nurse does not function in isolation but collaborates with other personnel so that patients have the chance to receive the best services available to meet their continuing care health needs.

Resource Team

Continuing Care Nurse Specialist

As a member of the resource team in the model for continuing care planning, the continuing care nurse specialist is a consultant to the primary team as they deal with the continuing care planning needs for the patient. The nurse specialist assumes the responsibility for the assessment, the planning, the implementation, and the evaluation of an organized program within the acute care setting. This program primarily assists the nursing staff to maximize their role in continuing care planning. The continuing care nurse specialist fulfills role responsibilities through consultation with the nursing staff and in their educational development about the continuing care field.

Through multidisciplinary collaboration, the continuing care nurse specialist is available to other services and departments of the hospital to assist them in developing

and strengthening systems within the acute care setting. Such collaboration encourages early, systematic planning for continuing care.

The continuing care nurse specialist participates also in unit-based primary care rounds. By participating in the rounds, the nurse specialist assists the continuing care primary team in the following areas:

- to assess patients' needs for continuing care
- to increase the primary care team's awareness of community health services
- to educate and update the primary care team on regulations, reimbursement systems, and criteria for levels of care
- to identify the most appropriate setting in which to meet patients' needs
- to foster continuity in the establishment of goals, objectives, and a plan for the continuing care needs of the patient

In addition to the role responsibilities that have been described, the continuing care nurse specialist is the community liaison with the nursing departments in the alternative care facilities, the Visiting Nurses' Association, and the home care agencies to which patients are referred upon discharge from the acute care setting. In this role, the nurse specialist evaluates the facilities for their appropriateness for the patient, and thereby promotes interinstitution collaboration for effective patient transfer and high quality continuity of care. The nurse specialist also investigates and follows up (in collaboration with the Social Service Department, patients, and their families) any dissatisfaction that may arise about continuing care arrangements.

An important component of the role of the continuing care nurse specialist is the follow-up and evaluation program in the continuing care planning model. The nurse specialist must develop a program for continuing care evaluation for the primary nurses so that they are able to evaluate the effectiveness of their plan for continuing care.

The continuing care nurse specialist is, therefore, a key link in the continuing care planning model. Without this specialized base of knowledge, in conjunction with multidisciplinary contributions and interdisciplinary collaboration, a successful discharge plan cannot occur. The continuing care nurse specialist is in a unique position on the resource team to clarify, to coordinate, and to evaluate the discharge planning process within an acute care setting.

Other Nurse Specialists

Other nurse specialists' roles not only have an impact on the interactive patient care activities in an acute care setting, but they interact with the primary care continuing care team. Because nurse specialists have been trained and educated in a variety of nursing specialty areas, they, too, possess the capability to assist the primary clinical nurse with planning the nursing care for individual patients and to assist in clinical decision making. Nurse specialists have been trained in a variety of areas, including the following:

- obstetrics, gynecology, and neonatology nursing
- psychiatric nursing
- neurological nursing
- medical nursing
- surgical nursing
- oncology nursing
- geriatric nursing
- cardiovascular nursing
- rehabilitation nursing
- operating room and allied areas of nursing
- ambulatory nursing
- quality assurance nursing

Other areas of nursing expertise include enterostomal therapists, diabetes nurses, and patient education resource nurses. These specialists participate in the development of effective patient care plans and programs according to their specialty and upon the request of the primary care team or through a referral by another resource team member.

Social Service Resource Specialists

A social service resource specialist works within the Social Service Department and assists primarily the social worker in working with patients and their families about their needs and the available community resources. Many patients need extra household help when they go home. They may need to have transportation arranged for them for follow-up outpatient clinic appointments. The worker explores with the patient and family members the availability of resources and what they see as resources. The resource specialist also assists the social workers as they work with the family to gather financial data for Medicaid applications or to look into other insurance reimbursement coverage. Housing is also explored. Often a patient is not able to return to past living arrangements because of a disaster, an eviction, or some other inopportune happening. The resource specialist then helps the patients to obtain housing so that continuing care needs are not interrupted.

The resource specialists have an important role on the continuing care resource team because they also help to put the continuing care planning puzzle together. The needs and social situations of the patient must be assessed early to ascertain the supports that are available and are needed. Thus, the resource specialist is a major link to the primary team.

Social Service Placement Specialists

The social service placement specialist is a person who has been trained in nursing home placement search and in chronic and rehabilitation hospital transfers. They communicate daily with the social worker, the continuing care nurse specialist, and the utilization review coordinator. Contact is made with physicians and primary nurses when that is necessary to gather information that can clarify the status of the patient. They are in daily contact with the larger community, actively seeking placement and transfer options for patients. They are also familiar with the criteria for levels of care and Medicare or Medicaid reimbursement issues. On a rotating basis, they make nursing home evaluation visits with the social worker and the continuing care nurse specialist.

The social service placement specialist then is another important component of the resource team; without this specialist, alternative care placement activities would rest in the hands of other disciplines. This service assists the patient and the family with developing an active, timely, and efficient discharge plan.

Administration

Administrators, too, have an important role in planning, organizing, complementing, and evaluating a continuing care program. There must be a commitment to the program throughout the hospital organization. The success or failure of the program may well depend on the strength of the commitment from the institution. The administration, as a member of the resource team, often provides leadership over and above that which the primary continuing care team can do—particularly in the area of legal matters and difficult transfers and placements. The administration, when their involvement is requested, must ensure that open communication transpires between all appropriate and involved departments. Communication must be fluid and open with the medical staff about continuing care issues and regulations. This communication includes an active involvement with the patient and the family when that is deemed necessary.

To have an effective continuing care planning program requires that a hospital administrator, when called upon, be involved and active on the resource team. Administrative involvement ensures that a continuing care planning program is integrated into the institutional structure and that the appropriate mechanisms of multidisciplinary communication for implementation and ongoing evaluation have been established.

Utilization Review Specialist

The utilization review specialist is also an important member of the resource team. This specialist is an essential and crucial component in the continuing care planning process.

The acute care institution is concerned with the patient's welfare, but it must be concerned also with the fiscal environment and, particularly, with the length of stay of each admission. The utilization review specialist reviews the hospital record of each patient upon admission to determine according to established criteria the medical necessity of an inpatient stay. The expected length of stay is determined by looking at the patient's working diagnosis and at other relevant factors.

The utilization review specialist also assigns an appropriate level of care for patients awaiting short- or long-term alternative care placements. Collaborating with the continuing care nurse specialist, with the social worker, and with the placement specialist on placement referrals and assisting the primary team to initiate appropriate discharge planning is another important function of the utilization review specialist.

The specialist must oversee third party reimbursement from a utilization-of-benefits perspective. Consequently, problems arise when the utilization review specialist notifies the physician and the patient that the hospital stay can no longer be covered by third party reimbursement, and that the patient must be discharged or be responsible for the hospital bill. Obviously, the continuing care program bears the brunt of a lot of anger expressed by the physician and the patient when this announcement is made. Early continuing care planning and a close working relationship with the utilization review specialist is, therefore, essential. Because the specialist can be helpful in the planning process, it is of the utmost importance that the specialist be included in the working plans of the primary continuing care planning team. Surprise termination of benefits can be avoided if communication is open and ongoing.

Pharmacist

The pharmacist becomes a resource to the primary team when a patient needs medication monitoring in the home. In an era that uses high technology in home care, pharmacists are essential to the planning process for home enteral therapy programs, home intravenous therapy, home antibiotic therapy, home chemotherapy, and home pain management. The pharmacist must be consulted about these high technology home care needs.

Community Team

Hospitalization through convalescence in the acute care hospital is no longer probable or possible. The community team, in general, is the group of health care providers who, at the point of discharge from the acute care setting, take over the continuing care plan that was developed for the patient in the acute care setting by the primary continuing care team. Generally, the greatest need for continuing care planning for alternatives to acute care hospital sites is among patients who have been hospitalized for catastrophic illness and among the elderly who have complex medical and chronic conditions. These conditions often require not only a change in life style but additional community support services to maintain them at an optimal level of functioning in mobility and ADL.

The community team consists of nurses; social workers; physicians; occupational, physical, and speech therapists; and nutritionists who care for the patient and the family in a variety of settings. The variety of settings may include the following:

- recuperative centers
- chronic hospitals
- rehabilitation hospitals
- skilled nursing facilities
- intermediate care facilities
- Visiting Nurses' Associations
- home care agencies
- private home care agencies
- community support services

An in-depth description of the array of services available through a community team is discussed in Chapter 8.

It is extremely important for the primary continuing care planning team to communicate with the community, because the community team frequently has information about the patient and the family that can be most helpful in the planning process. Many times patients have been followed in the community by the team before entering into the acute care setting. It is important, then, to plan for the continuing care needs of the patient and the family with the community team.

The community team bears the essence of the open system depicted in this continuing care planning model. An open system maximizes the contributions of all available health personnel according to their professional skills and knowledge. It encourages an open exchange of ideas among all health disciplines. The open system also looks for feedback (both positive and negative) from all teams—primary, resource, community—in order to improve and to develop further a system sensitive to any inputs from within and without. Changes can then be made according to the needs of the patient; the family; and the primary, resource, and community teams.

In summary, an open system fosters the development of multiple kinds of patient-professional relationships and permits the comparison of different kinds of health services available throughout the acute care settings, the community, and the alternative care facilities.

NURSING PROCESS WITHIN THE CONTINUING CARE PLANNING MODEL: AN INTRODUCTORY DESCRIPTION

The nursing process is central to all nursing actions. It is the essence of nursing as it is applied in any setting, in any frame of reference, and within any philosophy. It provides a structured base from which nursing actions can begin.

Yura and Walsh state "Involvement in the nursing process assumes concern for persons, problems, places, and health."[6] According to them, the following premises are pertinent to involvement:

1. A person is a human being endowed with worth and dignity.

2. A person has basic human needs that must be met.

3. Problems result when needs are partially met or unmet—due to limitations in physical, emotional, spiritual, social, and economical capability and the availability of resources.

4. Inability to fulfill one's basic human needs may entail the intervention of another individual who can help a person meet his needs or fill the need directly until such time as the person can resume that responsibility for himself.

5. A person or family presenting themselves for health care desires a client-centered approach that enhances their value and seeks solutions to their health and nursing care problems in the most effective, yet economic manner.

6. The nurse is interested in rendering high quality service to persons and families, no matter what their life style, economic status, or cultural or religious beliefs might be.

7. To utilize the nursing process and develop goal-directed nursing care plans, the nurse must have up-to-date knowledge of theories from the physical, biological, social, and behavioral sciences and must have mastered a knowledge of nursing as well.

8. The practice of nursing involves the ability to focus on another person and requires the full attention and energy of the nurse when she is engaged in the practice of nursing.

9. The heart of the nurse-client interaction is the development of a helping relationship in which the nurse fosters the client's personal development and growth through empathetic understanding, faith in the client's growth potential, respecting and caring for and about the client in an unconditional manner,

willingly being available and freely being one's genuine self.

10. Successful nursing practice results from continued study—both formal and informal—and from an ongoing evaluation of one's self-development and nursing practice, with plans to maximize strengths and minimize limitations.

11. The person or family demonstrates a willingness to share information, feelings, and concerns so that problems can be identified and solutions sought.

12. The nurse strives to meet her own self-development through the practice of nursing.

13. Every citizen has the right to quality health and nursing care rendered with interest, competence and compassion.

14. Nurse practitioners need to focus on preventing disease, maintaining wellness, and rendering care to the sick.

There are four components of the nursing process: (1) assessment, (2) planning, (3) implementation, and (4) evaluation. Although they will be discussed in detail in Chapters 3 to 6, it is desirable that they be treated briefly here in order to set the nursing process within the context of the continuing care planning model.

Assessment Process

Assessment is a continuous process that becomes more accurate as knowledge of the patient deepens. An assessment is continuous, systematic, critical, and orderly. It is a method of collecting, validating, analyzing, and interpreting information about the patient's ability to understand his illness, his coping ability, his desires, his beliefs, and his plans. Input from patients, professionals and families form the data base. The more complete the data base, the more likely that the variety of needs can be accurately identified. A plan for discharge must begin on the day the patient is admitted into the hospital.

Planning Process

When sufficient data about the health care needs of the patient or family have been gathered, the necessity of developing a discharge plan begins. Planning involves the patient and the family in addressing their individual needs and desires for a continuing care plan. The first requirement is an awareness of the available resources and of the patient's eligibility for the use of these resources. Health care providers today must be flexible and creative, especially since the demands for continuing care services are rapidly increasing while resources seem to be decreasing.

Just as the assessment phase requires input from all parties, so, too, does the planning phase.

Implementation Process

Implementing a continuing care plan implies that the assessment and planning processes have been accomplished and are acceptable to those concerned. Implementation involves arranging for services at home and acquiring the necessary equipment and supplies. It may involve transferring the patient to another facility. Of particular importance is the communication of significant information to those persons responsible for posthospital care so that they can arrange to meet the patient's needs in a timely and effective manner. This communication ensures continuity of care for the patient and the family.

Evaluation Process

When evaluating a continuing care plan, it is paramount to determine whether the major concern is to ensure that the patient's needs are being met. Mechanisms are needed for determining from patients or their families whether the care and the services provided are satisfactory and delivered in a timely fashion. Appropriate feedback from community agencies and facilities about the patient's status should also be expected. Evaluating the appropriateness of a continuing care plan can help to ensure the effectiveness of the future planning process for other patients who may have similar needs.

CONCLUSION

It is important to recognize that an effective continuing care planning team is in a position to assess the total needs of the patient and to be influential in working with regulators, reimbursers, physicians, administrators, and others to ensure that the appropriate use of a variety of resources is accomplished. What is needed is ongoing education about health care services; closer communication between legislative, regulatory, and provider agencies; and the development of systems to facilitate the flow of patient care information among providers of health care.

"What's everybody's business is nobody's business!" That statement may be trite, but it is true—especially when we consider the continuity of nursing service through the home, the hospital, and the alternative care facilities. When no one person in the agency or institution carries the authority and the responsibility for seeing to it that the care of the patient continues on a planned basis as that patient moves from one health care facility to another, continuing care seldom becomes a reality. Continuing care is a knowledge-based specialty; when the care is interrupted, a patient is denied a basic right.

REFERENCES

1. M. Hazzard and D. Kergin, "An Overview of System Theory," *Nursing Clinics of North America* 6, 392 (September 1971).
2. Sister Callista Roy, "Adaptation: A Basis for Nursing Practice," *Nursing Outlook* 19, 257 (April 1971).
3. Joan P. Riehl and Sister Callista Roy, *Conceptual Models for Nursing Practice* (Prentice Hall, New York, 1974), p. 138.
4. *Ibid*. p. 139.
5. Jean O. Peteet, "Discharge Planning: A Physical Therapist's Perspective," in *Continuing Care*, Kathleen M. McKeehan, Ed. (Mosby, St. Louis, 1981), pp. 146–147.
6. Helen Yura and Mary B. Walsh, *The Nursing Process: Assessing, Planning, Implementing, Evaluating* (Appleton-Century-Crofts, New York, 1973), pp. 70, 71, 72.

3. Continuing Care Process: Assessment

The next four chapters give definition and direction to the development and use of individualized nursing care plans for implementation in the continuing care process. The nursing care plans developed specifically for this book have been chosen because they represent the identified high risk categories under the diagnosis related groups (DRG) prospective payment system. Within the health care system today, the acute care intervention must be completed within a specific allotted time frame. It is critical that the nursing staff be always knowledgeable about the individual patient, the patient's ongoing status, and the continuing care plan.

This chapter covers assessment, functional health patterns typology, nursing diagnosis (as an integral part of the nursing process), documentation, definition of an admission functional health pattern assessment, and definition of full functional health pattern assessment.

ASSESSMENT

Assessment is the first phase in planning nursing care. It begins with the nursing history and ends with the nursing diagnosis. The nurse assesses and designs interventions to move the total patient toward the goal of improved health.

The purpose of this phase is to identify and obtain data about the patient or the family in order to identify problems relating to health and illness. The nurse's function, therefore, is to identify the patient's behavior in each of the adaptive modes and to recognize the patient's position on the illness-health continuum. This assessment, which can be carried out rapidly, uses both objective data and subjective reports from the patient, the family, or significant others. Focal, contextual, and residual factors influencing the behavior are also assessed.

Moreover, nursing is concerned with the basic human needs that affect the total person rather than one aspect, one problem, or a limited portion of the health care need. It is essential then that the nurse consider health as encompassing simultaneously the social, physical, and psychological facets of the patient. Health is not an either/ or situation. Seldom does a person's health degenerate or disintegrate instantaneously. There are usually clues of pending health problems with a set of symptoms developing gradually. Conversely, neither is health regained instantaneously. A person is not sick at 8 AM and well at 9 AM. (This is an exaggeration, but a point is being made.) Many people make a distinction between sickness and health that is based upon their ability to "go to work." Likewise, acute care nurses often fall into the trap of considering the patient sick until the hour of discharge and well thereafter. Such judgments ignore this transition period and its continuing care needs.

In this and other areas of the nursing process, data collection is an important component. Mitchell and Walter view the assessment involved in the nursing process as the diagnostic phase. They describe it as an organized process that all scientifically based practitioners use to determine (1) whether a patient needs help, (2) what kind of help is needed, and (3) whether the help has been effective.[1] The data collected about the patient and the significant others include a vast amount of information. The data are collected through a comprehensive and individualized nursing history, diagnostic studies, appropriate laboratory data, and a physical examination. The following resources can be used in a total assessment:

- patient and family
- significant others
- other members of the primary team
- patient needs
- other health care agencies (ie, those that have been involved in the patient's care—Visiting Nurses' Association, neighborhood health centers, skilled care facilities, and so forth)

The data-collection tool is defined according to the conceptual frame of reference within the philosophy of nursing practice and the policies of the health care facility. For this book, the functional health patterns typology is used for organizing the assessment data (ie, nursing history), laboratory data, and physical examination for grouping nursing diagnoses.

FUNCTIONAL HEALTH PATTERNS TYPOLOGY

The functional health pattern assessment tool is presented in this book as a tool that facilitates the collection and the organization of information collected by the nurse during the admission nursing history and the physical examination assessment phase of the continuing care process. The tool, designed to collect basic nursing data in any specialty area, is applicable to any age group. This format provides the basis for nursing diagnosis. The 11 functional health patterns used in the tool to organize assessment data conform with the 11 groupings of diagnostic categories, and thereby facilitate the process of moving from nursing assessment to nursing diagnosis.

The following is a description of the 11 functional health patterns used in the assessment tool.

Health Perception–Health Management Pattern

This pattern describes the patient's general health status and how it is perceived by the patient. Also described are self-care practices and their relevance to current activities and for future planning. Included as well is the person's level of health care behavior as it is shown in the patient's compliance with preventive health practices, nursing or medical orders, and follow-up care.

Nutritional-Metabolic Pattern

The nutritional-metabolic pattern is concerned with the appetite patterns and the daily intake of the patient.

Weight loss or gain is an important consideration in this pattern. Also included in this portion of the assessment is the patient's skin condition, temperature, hair, nails, mucous membranes, and dental status.

Elimination Pattern

This pattern particularizes the activity of excretory functions (bowel, bladder, skin). Included in this pattern assessment is an attempt by the nurse to identify the patient's perceived regularity of excretory function and whether the patient uses bowel regimes for bowel elimination. Any changes or disturbances in time-pattern of excretion, quality or quantity, and any devices used to control excretion must be questioned during the nursing history interview.

Activity-Exercise Pattern

The activity-exercise pattern addresses all activities of daily living, such as personal care, mobility status, identifying the use of assistive devices, feeding (ie, by self, by self with help, must be fed, by tube feedings, by intravenous therapy), elimination control, and mental status. Emphasis is also placed on home maintenance, meal preparation, shopping, and transportation issues. Factors that interfere with the desired or expected activity-exercise pattern and leisure activity are also considered. It is important to note the activities that are of high importance to each patient.

Cognitive-Perceptual Pattern

This pattern describes sensory-perceptual and cognitive issues. Hearing and visual difficulties and the use of assistive devices, such as hearing aids and eyeglasses, are assessed. It is important to note any signs and symptoms of pain as well as individual pain management, be it self or medically managed. Cognitive functional abilities delineate orientation, memory, language, recognition, calculations, and decision making.

Sleep-Rest Pattern

The sleep-rest pattern details patterns of sleep, rest, and relaxation periods. The quality and the quantity of sleep are addressed as reported by the patient. Included in this pattern are the aids, such as medication, music, or individualized routines, that a person uses for the induction of sleep.

Self-Perception–Self-Concept Pattern

The self-perception–self-concept pattern details the person's emotional state, affect, or mood. In this functional health area, behavioral clues are observed through the patient's dress, attentiveness, appropriateness, perception of abilities (cognitive, affective, or physical), body image, pattern of body posture and movement, eye contact, and voice and speech pattern.

Role-Relationship Pattern

This pattern is concerned with the family structure and the significant other relationships. Role conflicts are also included here. Work and social relationships with responsibilities are described as perceived by the patient. The person's living situation, the neighborhood, and whether or not the patient is dependent or independent in self-care are assessed in this functional health pattern.

Sexuality-Reproductive Pattern

The sexuality-reproductive pattern assesses patterns of satisfaction or dissatisfaction with sexual relations. Also included are the female's reproductive history, pre- and postmenopausal problems, perceived problems, and birth control measures.

Coping–Stress Tolerance Pattern

The coping–stress tolerance pattern depicts recent changes in the life or life style and the effectiveness of the person's coping ability and stress tolerance in relation to the capacity of the patient to resist the challenge to self-integrity, to the modes of handling stress, and to family and other support systems. This pattern also assesses the person's ability to control and manage life situations.

Value-Belief Pattern

This functional health pattern describes the religious background and practices of the interviewee in terms of values, goals, and beliefs that provide a guide for making choices or decisions. Included in this area are the ethnic and cultural norms and mores perceived as important in life, as well as the conflicts in values, beliefs, or expectations that are health-related.

NURSING DIAGNOSIS

Nursing diagnosis is an integral part of the nursing process. If it is not used in the nursing process, diagnosis is merely an intellectual exercise. *Nursing diagnosis* is the standard nomenclature for describing health problems amenable to treatment by nurses. The goal of a nursing diagnosis is different from that of a medical diagnosis. The nurse examines, questions, observes, and directs efforts toward diagnosing the presenting symptoms of the patient. The physician is concerned with diagnosing the cause of the illness so that the underlying pathologic process can be treated. The nursing diagnosis is therefore different from

the physician's; it provides the basis for nursing orders essential to the patient's welfare. (Medical diagnoses, such as cancer of the pancreas, do not speak to the needs of the individual patient when the person leaves the hospital. However, a nursing diagnosis, such as "self-care deficit related to side effects of chemotherapy" or "impaired physical mobility related to bone metastasis" communicates the patient's specific problem.) Nursing communicates these orders among the nursing staff and revises them as needed according to the nursing diagnosis. Nursing and medical diagnoses, along with the nurses' and physicians' orders, provide the therapeutic care plan for the patient. The collaborative effort of the primary team to provide a care plan for each patient is complementary and beneficial to the patient, who is the sole and ultimate recipient of the continuing care planning efforts of the primary team. Figure 3-1 is a flow chart demonstrating the use of nursing diagnoses in the nursing process. It demonstrates the use of the functional health pattern typology framework.

DOCUMENTATION

Nursing has the professional accountability and responsibility for the patient care that is delivered. With the ever increasing expansion of nursing accountability, nursing practice must provide detailed documentation of care. (Legally and professionally the nursing care documented is defined as nursing care given. Conversely, it is important to note that *care not documented is care not given*.) Documentation is a communication tool. It is quality assurance; it is validation that the patient has been served and that outcomes have been achieved. Furthermore, if pertinent information is documented, documentation becomes a timesaver.

Documentation may also serve as a management tool. By identifying issues and documenting them, nurses can make decisions. Moreover, documentation serves a legal purpose: if services are not provided, a legal suit could be drawn. Note, too, that if a service was provided and not documented, a court of law views it as *not* provided. Documentation is essential because the regulatory agencies are monitoring bodies. Documentation is also helpful for statistical and planning purposes. Ask, "How many referrals have been made in the last six months?" If the referrals are not documented and recorded in some fashion, the assumption is that no referrals have been made.

Documentation has a purpose—especially in a time of early discharging activity. It is critical that all areas of concern (ie, teaching, health needs, equipment needs, and orders) be documented and communicated in a timely continuing care process.

Figure 3-1 Steps in Nursing Process

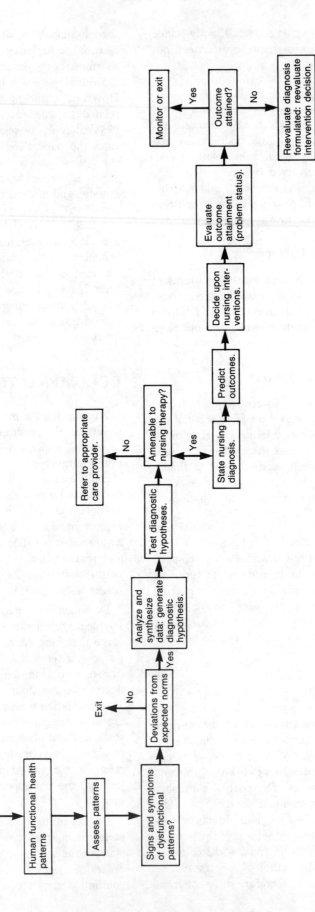

Source: Reprinted from *Manual of Nursing Diagnosis* by M. Gordon with permission of McGraw-Hill Book Company, © 1982.

ADMISSION FUNCTIONAL HEALTH PATTERN ASSESSMENTS

An admission functional health pattern assessment is designed to expedite the assessment process while still maintaining the quality care the patient deserves in an era of decreasing hospital length of stay. This assessment form is discussed in Chapter 7 and is implemented in the nursing care plans in Appendix A.

FULL FUNCTIONAL HEALTH PATTERN ASSESSMENTS

A full functional health pattern assessment is a tool designed to enable the nurse to do a complete nursing

history that leads to a nursing diagnosis. The diagnosis should lead in turn to a design of a nursing care plan appropriate for an individual patient. The format is described in Chapter 7 and is implemented in the nursing care plans in Appendix A.

REFERENCE

1. P. Mitchell and J. Walter, "A Conceptual Framework," in *Dynamics of Problem-Oriented Approaches: Patient Care and Documentation*, J. Walker *et al.*, Eds. (Lippincott, New York, 1976), p. 17.

4. Continuing Care Process: Plan

When sufficient data about the health care needs of the patient and the family have been gathered, discharge planning must begin. The first requirement in the planning phase is an awareness of the available resources and of the patient's eligibility for the use of these resources through the third party reimbursement status. Health care providers must be flexible and creative today, especially since the demand for continuing care services is rapidly increasing while resources seem to be decreasing. Like the assessment phase, the planning phase requires input from all involved health care providers.

This chapter deals with planning and with the nursing care plan and nursing orders.

PLANNING

Nursing Diagnosis

The planning phase begins with the nursing diagnosis—the most important result of the assessment phase and all the information gathered within. It emerges after the data base is formulated and serves as a guide for the patient's plan of care (or design for action). Nurses determine the goals and outcomes and articulate them in plans. Nursing care plans are formulated from decisions. Decisions, then, guide actions because they are selected choices that are followed by actions.

The purposes of the planning phase of the continuing care process can be delineated as follows:

- to assign priorities to the diagnosed nursing problems
- to identify problems that must be resolved by nursing, the patient, family members (or significant others), other primary continuing care team members, and the collaborative primary team
- to indicate specific nursing orders
- to identify long-term, intermediate, and short-term goals for the specified nursing orders
- to state expected behavioral outcomes of these specified nursing orders for the patient
- to write the nursing diagnosis, the expected outcomes, and a nursing care plan with nursing orders (see Exhibit 4-1)

In all cases, the patient should be involved as much as possible in the planning for continuing care needs in the hospital and posthospital periods of intervention. If the patient is unable to assist because of the presenting health status, the family or the significant other must be involved. It is most important that the nurse identify (with the help of the patient or family members) whether the patient has had any previous community service support. Community support may include service provided by a Visiting Nurse Association; a home health agency; a home care program; homemaker, home health aide support; adult day care; hospice; Meals-on-Wheels; and Alcoholics Anonymous. These are a few examples of the community support resources that are important to the continuing care plan. It is also important to identify whether the patient is a nursing home resident.

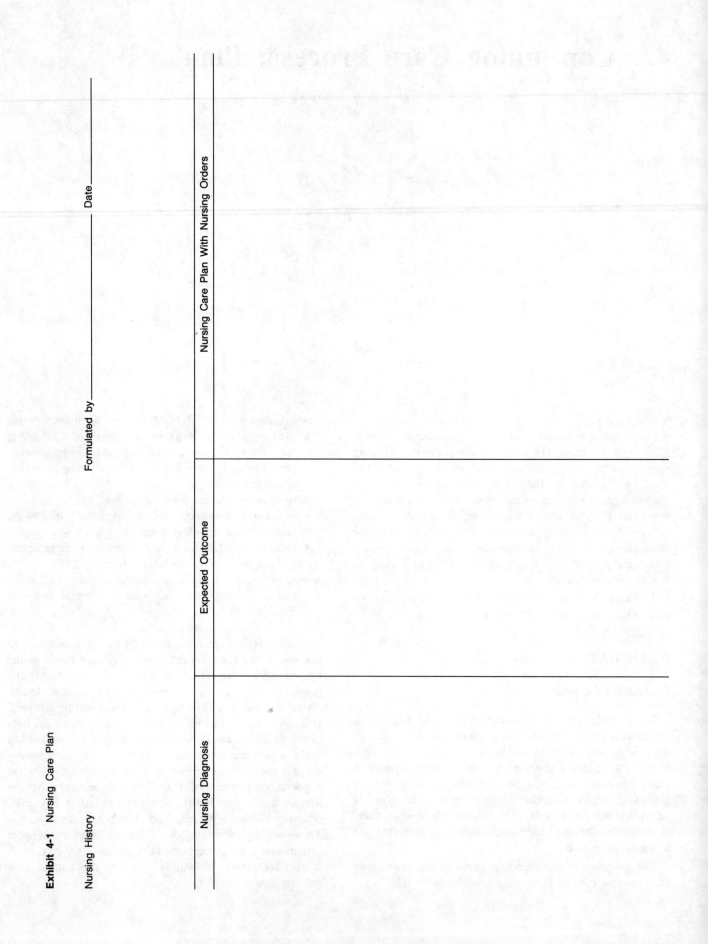

Exhibit 4-1 Nursing Care Plan

Nursing History

Formulated by _____ Date _____

Nursing Diagnosis	Expected Outcome	Nursing Care Plan With Nursing Orders

Expected Outcomes

Outcomes involve different time spans. The *long-term goal*, which is oriented to the future, is an overall direction for specified actions that are a result of the nursing process. The *intermediate goal* is also attained over an extended time, but these outcomes have a shorter range and affect more specifically the nature of the interaction and activities of the patient and the nurse. The *short-term goal* is one that can be accomplished in a short time and is specific to the nursing action for use in the nursing process.

Goals and outcomes for the patient include preventive and rehabilitative motives, as well as crisis interventions determined by the presenting wellness-illness status. Above all, the patient must be viewed as the major factor in the decision-making process. Nursing goals and outcomes must be separated from patient goals and outcomes. Each must be evaluated in the light of its chances for attainment. Moreover, respect must be given to the patient regardless of a difference in goals and outcomes. The nurse must listen to, sort, and reinforce any attempts patients initiate as they make decisions that move them toward optimal health.

The nurse-patient goals and outcomes are only a part of the overall health care outcomes for the patient. Each health care discipline involved in assisting in the continuing care planning process has individual outcomes that contribute to the overall goals. However, these multidisciplinary outcomes must not conflict; moreover, they must be understood and used by the total primary continuing care team.

The primary care team is held accountable for providing the conditions under which patients become well or remain well or achieve a higher level of wellness.

NURSING CARE PLAN AND NURSING ORDERS

After the assessment has been completed, the dysfunctional health patterns identified, the nursing diagnoses

stated, and the outcomes formulated, the next step is to select actions that can be expected to achieve the outcomes. The result of this process is called the nursing plan with nursing orders.

Nursing care plans, which have many purposes, provide for individualized care, continuity of care, communication of care, evaluation of care, comprehensive care, coordination of care, and team spirit. *Nursing orders* are prescriptions for specific behaviors expected from the primary nurse and other members of the primary continuing care team. The expectation is that the prescribed behavior will benefit the patient and the family or the significant other in a predictable way as it is related to the nursing diagnosis and the identified accepted goal or outcome. The intent of the nursing order is to individualize care and to work toward meeting the patient's continuing care needs.

The development of the nursing care plan is a knowledge-based, creative, and intellectual activity. A written, documented nursing care plan is a tool that provides a guide for individualized nursing care of the patient. A commitment must be made to a plan using the nursing orders, because expert nursing care is the key to maintenance, rehabilitation, and preventive health care. Time taken to prepare a nursing history and assessment, a nursing diagnosis, and a nursing care plan that includes nursing orders is time well spent. A clearly written and stated nursing care plan is the most effective means of assuring patients that their problems are being addressed and that their basic human needs are being fulfilled.

The planning process ends when the nursing care plan with nursing orders has been formulated. Because this documented care plan is an excellent communication tool for sharing the plan of care with all primary continuing care team members, it should be designed so that it is immediately usable. It should also ensure that all nursing orders are meaningful, measurable, and focused on resolving the patient's health care problems.

Nursing care plans with nursing orders is illustrated in the appendixes of this book. The nursing care plans in this text have been developed according to the assessments of identified high-risk DRG categories.

5. Continuing Care Process: Implementation

Implementing a continuing care plan implies that the assessment and planning processes have been accomplished and are acceptable to those involved. Implementation entails arranging for services to the patient at home and acquiring the necessary equipment and supplies. It may also involve transferring the patient to another facility. Of particular importance is the communication of significant information to those persons responsible for posthospital care, so that arrangements can be made to meet the patient's needs in a timely and effective manner. This action ensures continuity of care for the patient.

In this chapter, the implementation process of a continuing care plan, community referral forms, and nursing discharge summaries are discussed.

IMPLEMENTATION PROCESS

The implementation phase of the nursing process is the method by which the nurse (using intellectual, interpersonal, and technical skills) prepares the patient for discharge from the acute care setting. Decision making, observation, and communication are additional significant skills needed to enhance the success of the implementation process within the nursing care plan. The expectation is that the prescribed nursing plan and orders can benefit the patient and the family or significant other. These actions, which have the intent of individualizing care, are geared toward meeting the patient's needs.

The medical plan of care is reviewed as nurses implement the orders. It is important, however, for the nurse to recognize that there are two plans: a nursing care plan and a medical care plan. The patient will not suffer from neglect by nursing care if nursing recognizes the importance of collaboration so that both plans are integrated.

Interpretation

Nursing interpretation of the medical care plan takes place, for example, when a patient is taught the importance of wearing support hose to aid in the prevention of blood-clot formation. Integration of the medical and the nursing care plans takes place when the nurse discusses with a patient taking a diuretic the need of dietary supplements because a diuretic may cause a potassium depletion. Instruction may take place about drugs, such as aspirin, that may be contraindicated because the patient is on anticoagulant therapy. Nursing has a body of scientific knowledge that supports these actions for implementation. The nurse's information must be current and accurate, however, so that the implementation action can be deliberate and purposeful.

Communication

Frequently, patients are transferred from one unit to another or from one facility to another. They may also be discharged to other health care providers. Concomitant with this mobility in the continuing care process is the increasing number of persons involved in the care of patients at any one time. With increased mobility communication is imperative. To talk about communicating with the community may seem trite; however, exchange of information is of incredible importance to the patient and the family. Duplication, omissions, and discrepancies can be avoided if the receiving facility and the "new" primary care provider know about the patient's prior care and problems—whether resolved or unresolved. They need to be made aware of the patient's strengths and responses and the nursing care plan implementations that have been successful. All this can be conveyed in a nursing care plan on a referral form (see Appendix A). Time is saved, anxiety is reduced, and efficiency and efficacy are increased when a current and complete plan of care accompanies the patient upon discharge.

Whenever possible, a verbal referral should be made to the receiving primary care provider. Such an exchange of information strengthens the communicative bonds with the community and can ensure continuity of care for the patient. Again, communicating with the community is an integral linkage and networking process in planning for continuity of care.

Conclusion of the implementation phase of the nursing process is initiated when the nurse has documented in the medical record the prescribed nursing orders, their results, and the patient's reaction to them. The implementation phase concludes when the intervention by the other continuing care primary team members have documented their specific actions and interactions with the patient in the medical record. The medical record must show an ongoing record of discharge planning activities by all primary team members.

DOCUMENTATION

Community Referral Forms

In order for continuing care planning to be effective, a standardized referral form must be implemented. This form is a tool to be used in transferring information about a patient from one facility to another or to home health care agencies. The forms may vary from state to state; it is important only that they be state mandated and that they provide reliable and relevant information to be shared so that the patient can receive high quality continuity of care—a basic patient right.

The referral forms displayed in Appendix A have been developed from the information on the functional health pattern assessments and the nursing care plans identified from the high-risk DRG diagnoses.

Nursing Discharge Summaries

A nursing discharge summary must be documented in the medical record at the time of discharge. The following items should be documented:

- discharge site
- significant other involved in care
- condition at discharge (physical or emotional)
- medications
- diet
- ADL
- special teaching or treatments
- follow-up plans

Complete guidelines for writing a nursing discharge summary are given in Chapter 7.

A general interagency referral form may also be used as a discharge summary. This is not to say that both cannot be done at the same time; however, because the information on the referral form does summarize the plan of care for the patient, a summary may be a duplication of documentation.

These two methods of documentation—the referral form and the discharge summary—provide a mechanism for assuring continuity of care. This documentation can also inform, in an orderly manner, the primary continuing care team and the community team of the care being given and a measure of the progress.

6. Continuing Care Process: Evaluation

The major concern of the health care professional must be to ensure that the patient's needs are met. To this end, mechanisms must be developed for determining by responses from patients or their families whether the care and services provided were satisfactory and were delivered in a timely, efficient, and effective manner. Appropriate feedback from the community agencies and facilities about the patient's status should also be expected. Evaluating the appropriateness of a discharge plan certainly enables care providers to improve the future planning process for other patients who may have similar needs.

In this chapter, the evaluation process of continuing care, documentation, and evaluation activities in continuing care planning are considered.

EVALUATION PROCESS

The fourth component of the nursing process is evaluation. It is based on the evidence of the effectiveness of the services provided and on the patient's response to the interventions of the continuing care plan. The evaluation is based not only on the primary continuing care team's activities but also on the patient-family responses. Because patient responses are assumed to reflect the quality of health care given at the time of the acute care intervention, a patient-centered approach to evaluation is important and relevant. It can also be frustrating, because it is difficult to establish objective criteria for desired outcomes. Indeed, evaluating a discharge plan is rarely a clear-cut, pure look at the primary continuing care team's intervention and

(most particularly) at the evaluation of the nursing care plan.

The nursing care plan contains the framework for evaluation: when the nursing process begins, the evaluation process begins. Moreover, evaluation is an ongoing process that occurs each time a nurse updates the nursing care plan. Because the patient's situation changes rapidly on a daily basis, frequent evaluations must be made. Initial conclusions provide the basis for anticipating outcomes and projecting a course of action; therefore, it is essential that achieved outcomes be evaluated at intervals and that the necessary changes be made in the nursing care plan. Various methods of evaluation are used in nursing. Nevertheless, the most important factor is that, whatever the method of evaluation, it must be tailored to the goals being evaluated.

Again, just as there are overlapping areas of responsibility for assessment and diagnosis among the primary continuing care team members, so in an evaluation of a continuing care plan, there is shared professional activity and responsibility. A valid basis exists for the primary nurse's focusing on the nursing care evaluation. The primary nurse is the coordinator for evaluating the patient's responses to the ADL, and the ADL are primarily influenced by the patient's health status at any given assessment interval.

To avoid unnecessary speculation and superfluous discussions in team conference time, the primary nurse may routinely choose to test the patient's health problem suggestions quickly by asking a series of interrelated questions, which can be conveniently diagrammed (see Figure 6-1).

Discharge planning is crucial because it assures continuity of care and assists patients to find the best solutions to their health care problems. Problem-solving techniques are important to the assessment process, the planning process, the implementation process, and the evaluation process where results of the intervention can be measured.

The evaluation phase, again, is a time for reassessment of the patient and the progress (or lack of progress) toward the stated goals and objectives. It is one of the most valuable steps of the process; yet, unfortunately, it is too frequently slighted. Nursing must take the time to consider why successful intervention was, in fact, successful. More frequently, however, decisions are made merely to modify actions that are not working. Ideally, evaluations should produce information about objectives that need to be terminated, continued, or modified. Included as a final written evaluation are the discharge and transfer notes. These summary statements about the patient's status and care are designed to assist the receiving facility or agency as the primary health care provider with a brief but comprehensive review of the patient's experience while being cared for in the acute care setting. Evaluation at the conclusion of the problem-solving nursing process should include a summarization of that which has occurred and the results of any previous evaluations. The evaluating and recording of the patterns of nursing care (together with patient responses) are essential in the nursing component of health care.

DOCUMENTATION

The rising cost of health care services and the increasing demand for such services make imperative a careful scrutiny of the quality of the care for which the patient pays.

Documentation of patient care—one of the first skills an aspiring health care professional learns—all too easily becomes the tedious paperwork that gets shuffled to the bottom of the priority list. The provision of quality health care depends, however, upon keeping an accurate description of the patient's hospital course—complete in every pertinent detail, up-to-date, and readily accessible. Filling this bill compounds the complexity of establishing documentation that can complement the delivery of patient care and can satisfy administrative need for planning and evaluation of continuing care planning—not to mention a potential holdup in the court of law.

The documentation process consists of three areas: (1) purpose, (2) process, including documentation within that process, and (3) follow up.

Purpose

The purpose of documentation is communication. It is important to document in the medical record the patient's responses to the acute care interventions by the primary continuing care team. Sometimes, however, nursing is more concerned with documenting what has been done for the patient and does little with the patient's responses to the intervention; yet the patient's responses are important to the evaluation phase of the nursing process. Likewise, as the intensity of care increases for the hospitalized patient population, nursing has a tendency to concentrate on the direct care of the patients and to neglect other areas of patient care—such as continuing care, which is easier to delay for the moment because the intervention is not immediate.

In these days of alternative health care financing and delivery systems, it is even more crucial for the health care provider to recognize the importance of documentation. Because of this development, the need for accurate, timely assessments by the primary continuing care team and immediate action in discharge planning is equaled only by the need for accurate, succinct documentation. It is important to remember that approval of continuing care for the patient may depend on what is documented in the medical record. In addition, the way the hospital is reimbursed for the services it provides may likewise depend on what is documented.

Documentation is a legal requirement. If services are not offered or are offered and not provided, a legal suit could be drawn. It is necessary, consequently, to document services that are set up for the patient at the time of discharge. Moreover, in the case of legal judgments, lack of documentation of care and services means that care was *not* given and services were *not* provided. In other words, nothing exists in the eyes of the law unless it is documented. Regulatory agencies also monitor the institution and the health care professionals on the basis of documentation within the medical record.

Documentation serves additionally as a management tool. Communication within the medical record of the patient assists the primary continuing care team to identify needs and issues and then to make expert clinical and

Figure 6-1 Questions to Test Patient's Responses to the ADL

Is this plan—

realistic? ⟶ obtainable? ⟶ economical?

functional? ⟶ efficient? ⟶ organized?

flexible? ⟶ effective? ⟶ productive?

nagerial decisions. Documentation is also used for stical and planning purposes. It is the communication management tool used by quality assurance and ation review departments to assist the primary con- g care planning team and hospital administrators in rging patients as early as possible. (Each extra day costs for the hospital for which reimbursement is unlikely.) When pertinent information is succinctly documented, documentation becomes a timesaver and a validator of the patient who has been served and of the method by which outcomes can be measured and evaluated.

Process

The process within documentation is the nursing process. The assessment phase for continuing care planning must take into consideration the patient's socio-economic status, the nursing and medical histories, the patient's functional status (see Chapter 7 for an assessment tool), the patient's homebound status, and the community service the patient is presently receiving. These elements must be documented in the initial admission assessment so that discharge planning can begin on the day of admission.

The planning phase must also be documented in the medical record. This phase, which includes the goals and objectives for the patient, pays particular attention to the timeliness of the plan, the appropriateness of the level of care for which the patient is striving, and the determination of available resources. Information about the patient's source of reimbursement for the services to be provided and an understanding of the regulations that can have an impact on the health care delivery system are essential in continuing care planning.

Documentation within the implementation phase for continuing care planning shows active communication with the community. A nursing home or a Visiting Nurses' Association that is chosen to continue a plan of care for the patient needs documentation within the medical record and communication through documentation by written referrals and discharge summaries. Continuing care depends upon the way the health care professionals document the response of patients to their care. Evidence of patient and family teaching are essential to the process of documentation within the implementation phase.

Follow Up

The follow-up process of documentation is the evaluation phase of the nursing process. Follow up for the purpose of evaluating the continuing care plan is to ensure that the patient's needs are being met. In the follow-up process, some questions must be asked about the continuing care needs of the patient. What goals—immediate, intermediate, or long-range—must be met? Which are being met? If goals have been met, what are the plans to reassess them periodically and to maintain a problem-free status? Were the provided continuing care services communicated effectively, and did the feedback verify this? Follow-up phone calls to the patient or to the family are documented along with phone calls received from patients about their continuing care needs. By documentation in the follow-up process, evaluation of the continuing care plan becomes a continual reassessment of the plan and an opportunity to make partial or complete revisions. Again, documentation is important because it validates the care given to the patient and the outcomes of the continuing care plan.

EVALUATION ACTIVITIES

The activities in continuing care planning can be evaluated in several ways. Such evaluation helps to maintain high standards of care. However, if continuing care planning is to achieve these standards, it must be supported by systematic documentation. One method by which to achieve such documentation is through a uniform referral form (see Chapter 7). While communicating continuing care needs to receiving facilities, agencies, or other health care professions, health care providers can use this form to evaluate the care given and the plan designed for the patient. The evaluation process occurs during the determination of whether the desired outcomes have been met.

After the discharge from the hospital into the community has taken place, other methods for making an evaluation can be used. For example, an interview of the patient and family by telephone can assess whether the plan of care is being followed or whether a need had not been identified during the hospitalization. Questionnaires can also be sent out to the patient and the family to assess whether all the continuing care needs have been met. This method, however, is probably the weakest, because the patient or the family may not put a high priority on mail. Frequently, the questions, when answered, do not give enough information for making informed judgments.

Home visits by the primary care team are the ideal evaluation activity. However, it is important to have a viable program set up. Moreover, the program must be supported by the hospital administration because of the legal implications involved. Home visits by the community team are valuable to the primary continuing care team when the community health professional reports back with a summary of the findings.

Another evaluation technique is a chart audit. (All professional disciplines can do an audit.) *Audit* usually suggests a formal or official examination and verification of accounts. For example, a nursing audit is a review by a nurse of the patient's care or records to determine the extent to which that care and those records meet established standards. Areas of nursing that can be audited are nursing care plans, nursing continuing care planning, and the resulting patient care. A retrospective type of review, in which the patient's legal record-of-care is audited, can also be made.

CONCLUSIONS

Evaluation is important to the health care provider because it can identify ideas and ideals for providing continuing care to other patients with similar needs. Adjustments in the plan are the rule rather than the exception; the availability of community resources and the needs, attitudes, and desires of patients tend to change.

On the essence of the nursing process evaluation, Yura and Walsh have the last word: "Evaluation is always expressed in terms of achieving expected behavioral manifestations within the client. The entire focus of the nursing process is goal directed."[1]

REFERENCES

1. H. Yura and Mary B. Walsh, *The Nursing Process: Assessing, Planning, Implementing, Evaluating* (Appleton-Century-Crofts, New York, 1973), pp. 135, 136.

7. Strategies and Tools for Use in the Continuing Care Planning Process

As hospitals discharge patients earlier in response to changes in health care reimbursement policies, continuing care planning efforts by the health care provider—particularly those of the discharge planners—must be undertaken with new strategies to ensure the continuity of care for their patients.

A discharge from the acute care hospital is increasingly becoming a time of crisis for patients because they are more acutely ill and feel unready to return to the home and community setting. As a result, continuing care planning must begin on admission, and special attention must be paid to the needs of the aged, those who live alone, the chronically disabled, and those without transportation. These are the high-risk patients who need intensive and immediate continuing care planning.

Several successful planning formats, assessment tools, evaluation protocols, and appropriate educational programs for use in a continuing care program are described in this chapter. Included are tools, strategies, and programs that can be used in five phases of the continuing care process: (1) assessment, (2) planning, (3) implementation, (4) evaluation, and (5) education.

ASSESSMENT

The assessment phase of problem solving is perhaps the most crucial because it involves the accumulation of pertinent, accurate data with sufficient scope and depth by which to identify patient needs and to determine barriers to need-fulfillment. This assessment is done both verbally

and nonverbally through observation of the patient's behavior. The nursing history is particularly helpful in that it is an organized series of questions designed to obtain specific information about a patient. A nursing history, which is obtained on the day of admission or within the first 24 hours of admission to the hospital or health care facility, can help to initiate a trusting relationship between the patient and the nurse. While the nurse is obtaining the necessary data, the patient feels that his individuality is respected and that he will receive the care necessary for his well-being.

The final step of assessment occurs after the data base has been collected. Based on the available data and on the nurse's theoretical knowledge, patient needs are established and given a priority. Remember that, whenever possible, the patient is expected to engage actively in the problem-solving process by defining his own needs. Using keen judgment and sensitivity, the nurse then draws conclusions about why the stated needs are not being met. This difference between what should be and what is, combined with a judgment of why, creates a nursing diagnosis. After nursing diagnoses are determined, the planning process begins.

The tools depicted in Exhibits 7-1 through 7-6* can assist the nurse in the assessment phase of the nursing process in continuing care planning. For example, Exhibit 7-1 is a sample nursing assessment worksheet. This

---

*All exhibits appear at the end of this chapter.

39

worksheet enables the nurse to gather assessment data in an orderly fashion and then to document that information in the medical record under an admission note and a nursing assessment.

Exhibit 7-2 is a nursing assessment worksheet guide that identifies several key questions a nurse may use during an interview with a patient on admission. It complements Exhibit 7-1.

Exhibit 7-3 is a format used for an admission assessment. It applies the functional health pattern as a framework for data collection. This format is intended, however, to assist the nurse with an abbreviated format for the initial admission assessment while still using the functional health pattern approach. It includes a general summary area, which includes important admission data, followed by the functional health patterns. The last portion of the format addresses the anticipated discharge status and the initial summarizing statement of the assessment; the nursing diagnosis is entered here. The format also summarizes a general plan for the patient while in the active intervention stages of health care. This tool is important as a timesaver within the early discharge arena of today. The importance of this data collection is realized only when it is documented in the medical record.

Exhibit 7-4 can assist the nurse when doing a complete nursing history, using the functional health pattern assessment (FHPA) in depth. The sample questions can assist in the interviewing process. The 11 FHPA areas are as follows:

1. health perception–health management
2. nutritional-metabolic
3. elimination
4. activity-exercise
5. cognitive-perceptual
6. sleep-rest
7. self-perception–self-concept
8. role-relationship
9. sexuality-reproductive
10. coping–stress
11. values-belief

The sample questions for each pattern area can assist the nurse in doing an in-depth assessment. Some pattern areas may not be valuable for assessing the nursing problem and the diagnosis at hand; therefore, these are rendered not applicable (NA). When the assessment is completed it must be documented in the medical record under the above diagnostic pattern category.

Exhibit 7-5 is an example of a "tickler" card for the nurse to use as a guideline for the nursing process. This 3×5 card is intended to be carried in the uniform pocket for quick and immediate reference.

The patient admission questionnaire (Exhibit 7-6) is a tool used to assist the patient, the family, and the nurse as they begin to look at and to identify basic needs and concerns for continuing care planning. It is expected to be a timesaver when gathering basic information. It is assistive in the scope of early discharge planning and is given to the patient on the day of admission or in a preadmission screening program.

A current list of nursing diagnoses accepted for clinical testing by the North American Nursing Diagnosis Association (NANDA) is given in Exhibit 7-7. The Nursing diagnoses are the terms used to summarize assessment data. The diagnoses, which represent clinical judgments made by professional nurses, are conditions primarily resolved by nursing care methods.

Exhibit 7-8 depicts an initial discharge planning sheet, which is placed in the front of the medical record. This form enables the primary team to evaluate the potential discharge status of the patient. It has been developed to assist in decreasing the length of stay through identification of immediate discharge needs and the actions that must be taken. It is also a communication tool.

PLANNING

The planning component involves the development of a nursing care plan. For each nursing diagnosis, patient objectives or behavioral outcomes are stated and alternative approaches are developed and selected. Patient objectives serve as guidelines or directional markers, signifying behaviors that will be observed in the patient if the problems are resolved. Stated in terms of the results that are intended to be achieved, they are specific and measurable, so that progress can be readily identified and the evaluation process simplified. An important component of creating realistic objectives is the time factor; there must be enough time to accomplish that which is desired.

In the nursing profession, objectives serve to organize activities and to unify the reasons for individual action. When each member of the helping team is aware of the objectives that are being sought, sharing of ideas is more likely to occur about patient care needs. This process reduces the chance that each primary health care team member will intervene in his or her own particular manner, thus preventing the outcomes of continuity of care.

Tools and Strategies

The nursing care plan (Exhibit 4-1), which provides a nursing history (diagnosis, expected outcomes, and nursing care plan with orders), is a useful tool for the primary nurse. These worksheets are usually kept with the nursing kardex and are updated as necessary. This nursing history also serves as a communication tool between nurses.

The Elderly Decision Model for Matching Client Need with Community Services: Skilled Services (Figure 7-1) is

Figure 7-1 Elderly Decision Model for Matching Client Need With Community Services: Skilled Services

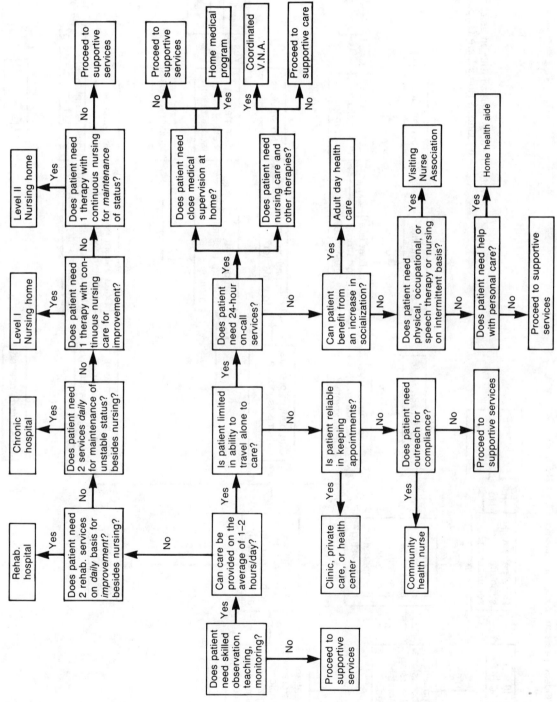

Source: © Francine Fritsch Gikow. Reproduced by permission.

Figure 7-2 Elderly Decision Model for Matching Client Need With Community Services: Supportive Services

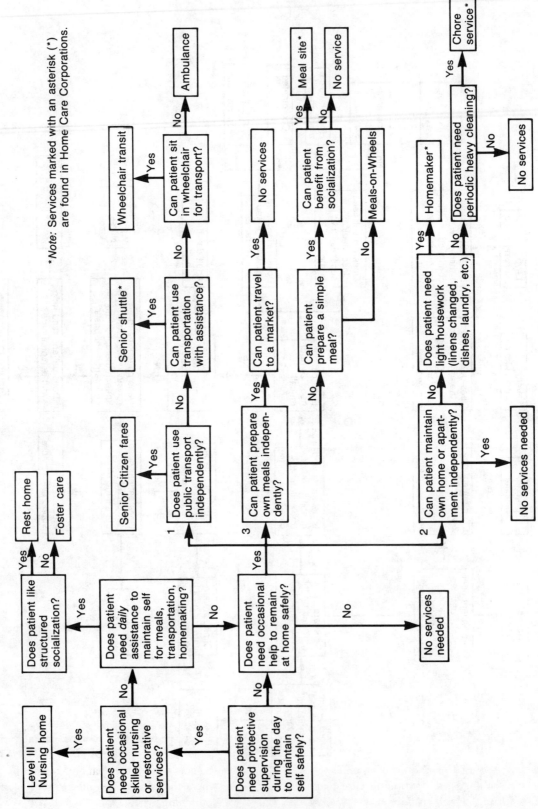

Note: Services marked with an asterisk (*) are found in Home Care Corporations.

Source: © Francine Fritsch Gikow. Reproduced by permission.

intended to assist the continuing care planning team in setting up services for the patient through a visual decision-making process. The model depicted in Figure 7-2 is used in the same way, except that it is for supportive services. A coding format (Exhibit 7-9) is useful in assessing the continuing care needs of the patient in terms of functional levels and matching available community support systems.

A screening chart (Exhibit 7-10) printed on a 5 × 8 card is designed to assist the continuing care nurse coordinator or nurse specialist in determining the appropriate level of care patients require so that they are evaluated by the appropriate alternative care agency or facility. These levels are the levels of ADL. The finally determined level is based on regulations set by the state and federal governments.

The continuing care referral form (Exhibit 7-11) is a consultation form intended to be used by continuing care coordinators or nurse specialists when they are consulted about a patient's discharge plan. It also serves as a record-keeping mechanism for reporting statistics of activities in the continuing care program or department.

In order to provide continuity for the patient in continuing care planning, it is also important to receive information from community agencies. Patients often have well-integrated community health plans and primary care providers before they are admitted into the acute care setting.

Frequently, information about their home health care can be elicited from patients, but they may not have any clue as to the agency providing the care. Therefore, it is helpful for the acute care facility to receive a notification from the home health agency about the services already being provided and the specific names of the community health care providers. It is also helpful to contact the community health care provider when discharge plans are being developed. The community team is helpful in assisting in the discharge plans. (See Exhibits 7-12 and 7-13 for examples of such notifications from the community to the acute care hospital.)

Using the prospective payment health care system with DRGs, Exhibit 7-14 displays a decision matrix that helps to identify courses of action that can assist in decreasing the length of stay. The matrix also identifies the four categories of high risk that are potential problem areas under this health care system and that have an impact on the continuing care field.

Programs

Continuing Care Rounds

Continuing care rounds are multidisciplinary team meetings that are useful to the continuing care planning process. In this forum, which usually meets weekly on each unit, the primary continuing care team reviews the current status of the patients on the particular unit. The key to successful continuing care rounds is that they focus on patient care needs, goals, objectives, and the matching of services to fulfill those needs.

Family Meetings

Family meetings are formal meetings, usually initiated and set up by the primary nurse or the social workers with the patient or family members, to discuss multiple, complex continuing care needs of the patient. The goal is to create and to implement a discharge plan that meets as many as possible of the specific needs and requests of both patient and family. The community team and a member of the resource team are frequently involved.

A family meeting must serve at least one purpose, and the group members must work toward that purpose if the meeting is to be effective and productive. A *group* is defined here as two or more individuals united for a common purpose—identifying continuing care needs for a patient. A family meeting must also be viewed as a group oriented toward decision making and problem solving that uses the basic communication skills of sharing, listening, and questioning.

In order for a family meeting group to accomplish its purpose and objectives, it must follow six group task functions that facilitate problem solving:

1. Initiate
   - Suggest the agenda for the meeting.
   - Pose questions and define the discharge problem and need.
   - Redirect and reenergize the discussion, as needed, throughout the meeting.
2. Seek Information and Opinion: Request facts, ideas, resources, and suggestions to assure firmly based group action and decision.
3. Give Information and Opinion: Offer facts, ideas, beliefs, resources, and suggestions relevant to the concerns or needs at hand.
4. Clarify and Elaborate
   - Restate ideas to validate understanding.
   - Interpret or explain in order to help others clarify their thinking.
   - Expand upon or coordinate ideas to enhance their meaning and relevancy.
5. Summarize
   - Restate ideas or suggestions for review.
   - Combine ideas and state them in a single, integrated form.
   - Review where the patient or family has been, where they are now, and goals or plans for their continuing care.
6. Seek Consensus

- Check with the patient or family and primary continuing care team on whether they are nearing agreement or decision.
- State conclusions for the patient or family and primary team and seek their acceptance or rejection of the plan.

Functions that facilitate the family meeting process and that focus on the group members more directly than on the group purpose are the maintenance functions. These functions include gatekeeping, encouraging, and harmonizing. *Gatekeeping* facilitates the communication process by encouraging and inviting participation from those members who share less readily and by monitoring those who dominate the discussion. *Encouraging* involves accepting, supporting, and praising group members and their contributions. It requires sensitivity, perception, empathy, responsiveness, and friendliness and includes appropriate feedback. *Harmonizing* is the attempt to mediate differences or to resolve conflicts among group members, thereby reducing tensions, frustration, anger, and fighting.

Although the role of an effective leader is a complex one, three basic principles can provide success in leadership: (1) shared leadership, (2) effective communication, and (3) promotion of growth.

Successful leadership is shared by the membership, not assumed by one individual. Moreover, shared leadership happens when any intervention by the leader or a group member moves the group forward toward three goals: (1) the accomplishment of the task, (2) the resolution of internal group problems, and (3) the ability of the members to work together effectively as a group.

Leadership not only involves effective communication skills but also requires keen observation and perceptive listening. Attention to verbal and nonverbal cues, overt and covert behaviors, as well as the feelings and emotions of members is mandatory.

Leadership furthermore involves promoting growth of the group and of its members. A supportive environment that diminishes the sense of risk and competition encourages trust and cooperation.

Leading successful groups is a challenge and an art. Special skills can be learned, and experience can be gained. Sensitivity and concern, however, cannot be learned; they are given.

Primary Nursing Rounds

Primary nursing rounds are a weekly forum at which the unit-based nursing staff addresses patient care issues and continuing care needs. These rounds provide an informal setting for the nursing staff to interact with one another about concerns they have for their patient.

The primary nurse is accountable to the patient for providing knowledgeable and comprehensive nursing care from the time of admission through the discharge process. To ensure this high quality care, primary nursing rounds offer the primary nurse an arena in which to present information and to engage in dialogue with colleagues about nursing care problems. The primary nurse can thereby plan for the patient's needs and provide continuity of care.

AND Meetings

One more program must be noted—the meeting labeled Administratively Necessary Days (AND). Held weekly, the AND is a meeting at which the administration, utilization review, social services, nursing, and inpatient accounts deal with the "difficult-to-discharge" patient. The difficulty may be due to insurance benefits, regulation issues, conservator and guardianship needs, nursing home bed availability, or difficult problems and needs (medical, nursing, or social). The goal of this meeting is to enable these disciplines to provide a discharge plan based on ideas and suggestions from all the field specialists. Often a problem can be avoided because immediate attention is given to the issue and support is forthcoming—particularly from the administration. The AND meeting can also serve as an educational experience inasmuch as the group is actively addressing the many facets of the continuing care planning process.

IMPLEMENTATION

In the implementation phase, the nursing care plan and nursing orders are initiated. Observation, critical thinking, and written and verbal documentation are key concepts needed to execute this phase of the continuing care process. Nursing documentation in the medical record should be a continual record of the patient's care and progress. Notes should be objective and factual rather than subjective. They are more than a commentary. Moreover, it is imperative that the notes include nursing activities and actions done for the patient and the responses to such care. With the recent increase in the number of malpractice suits filed against nurses and other health care providers, accurate and comprehensive documentation is vital. After the nursing care has been given and documented, the final evaluation process occurs.

Tools and Strategies

Nursing Communication Forms

While patients are in the acute care setting, they often leave the unit for other diagnostic workup within the hospital. So that care can be continued and the physician's and nursing's orders implemented, a nursing communication card is suggested. This card has basic information about the patient's status and care. An example of a radiology nursing communication card is given in Exhibit 7-15. This card is filled out by the patient's primary nurse on the unit and goes with the patient to the Radiology Department. The information makes it much easier to plan the patient's care and to make modifications that are necessary during the radiology procedure. Exhibit 7-16 depicts another nursing communication form intended for the alternative care facility that is sending a patient into the acute care setting for an outpatient radiographic procedure. Again, this form assists in the continuity of patient care, modifications in radiographic procedure, and safety for the patient while away from the primary care facility—a time when confusion can be overwhelming to the elderly patient in particular. In return, the nurse from the acute care setting communicates back to the alternative care facility about the procedure and the patient's response to it (Exhibit 7-17). This is continuity of care, which every patient deserves as a basic right.

Discharge-Related Forms

Various implementation tools are also needed when the patient is discharged from the acute care hospital. These run the gamut from discharge statement forms to nursing discharge resumes. A discharge statement form (Exhibit 7-18) is designed to assist health care providers with general information and a summary about the patient at the time of discharge. It is also helpful to medical-record coders and to regulatory personnel for billing and auditing.

Another form, the patient medication minder (Exhibit 7-19), is a strategy, as well as a tool, that can be used in patient education to reinforce the medication regimen to be followed by the patient at home. The actual pill is frequently taped to the form under *Name/Dose*, so that the patient can identify the medication by sight as well as by name and dosage.

The uniform referral form (Exhibit 7-20), like that used in the Commonwealth of Massachusetts, is a state-mandated form that must be completed before a discharge can take place between the acute care hospital and a receiving agency or facility (eg, a Visiting Nurse Association, a home health care agency, rehabilitation and chronic facilities, and all levels of nursing home facilities). Reimbursement for services provided by the alternate care facilities and home health agencies will not be paid unless this form is on file. It is made out in triplicate. The original sheet goes with the patient, the second sheet (yellow) becomes part of the permanent hospital record, and the third sheet (pink) is used by the Continuing Care Department for statistical and monitoring purposes. To achieve high standards of continuing care planning and continuity of patient care, a systematic documentation process must be supported.

The use of an alternative care facility discharge envelope (Exhibit 7-21) assures the receiving facility that all transfer documents are with the patient coming from the acute care institution. Moreover, it offers the acute care hospital a checklist for identifying nursing information that is needed to complete the discharge process in a timely and efficient manner. The envelope is orange so that it can be easily identified and located during the transfer.

Exhibit 7-22 provides useful guidelines for a nursing discharge summary (the information given in question form is to be used as a guide). Information pertinent to the individual patient is especially important to document. All patients must have a nursing discharge summary in the medical record. Exhibit 7-23 is an example of a completed nursing discharge summary.

Exhibit 7-24 is an example of a format used to assure that the medical record has a completed nursing discharge resume in every chart. The form is made out in duplicate. The original becomes part of the medical record; the other is retained on the nursing unit for reference.

Durable Medical Equipment Orders

The implementation phase also includes the ordering of durable medical equipment (DME) for patients and clients.

With so many companies providing DME, it is difficult to monitor the quality of services for patients. The equipment and supplier segment of the home health care industry is expected to grow from $1.5 billion dollars in the 1980s to $7 billion by the 1990s. This growth represents an increase of more than 35 percent a year. As a result, many large corporations and independent entrepreneurs are entering the home health care equipment business. This intense competition in the DME industry has had a positive impact because it encourages companies to offer quality equipment and service to homebound patients at competitive prices.

There are many indicators of a high-quality home health care equipment company. These should be thoroughly investigated before a DME company is selected.

Understanding how Medicare, Medicaid, and other third-party insurances reimburse DME suppliers is an important step in choosing a company. Because the reasonable charges for DME are similar for suppliers in the same geographic area, the focus in making a decision must be on the supplier's reimbursement expertise and the service levels. The following questions are some of those that should be asked of a DME company:

- Do you do the third-party billing?
- How do you handle the 20 percent coinsurance?
- Do you ask for cash on delivery?
- What is your procedure on rent-to-purchase options? Do you inform the patient of this option?

- If the patient chooses to purchase the item, is there a budget plan? Is a warranty provided? What about equipment service?
- If the patient's decision is to rent the item, how long is the DME piece rented before conversion to purchase? Is any of the rent applicable to the purchase cost?
- How does the company handle claim rejections?
- How do you keep track of inventory?
- What is your procedure and the time frame for emergency deliveries?
- Do you provide a prescreening service in the home for space availability?
- What is your evaluation process for quality assurance?
- Do you carry product liability insurance?
- Describe your emergency service coverage.
- Do you provide loaner units when original equipment is taken out of the patient's home for repair?
- What is the geographic service area?
- Where is the central warehouse?
- What is the time span from telephone referral to delivery?

As a general rule, companies have had to include certain services as standard. The basic services are the following:

- A complete line of the newest, carefully inspected home health care equipment
- Acceptance of direct assignment of Medicare, Medicaid, and private insurance plans
- Courteous and prompt free delivery available 24 hours a day, 7 days a week, *by trained personnel*

It is up to the suppliers to provide quality products in good repair. A quality control monitoring system must be part of a monthly routine.

A good indication of a company's understanding of the rules and regulations governing reimbursement is demonstrated by how many questions they ask on the phone and the quality of their questions when a referral is made. Acceptance of the assignment of the claim by the DME supplier is essential.

With DRGs placing increased demands on continuing care plans for earlier patient discharge, the speed with which the DME company can respond to these demands is a crucial factor to be considered in the evaluation of a provider. The competency of the delivery force is an important indication of the company's commitment to patient service. Well-trained delivery technicians help to reduce the patient's and the family's anxiety toward home health care.

Some companies go beyond the basics and provide other services. These services may include the following:

- Credentialed respiratory therapists and enteral nutritionists who are available to instruct the patient or the family in the use and care of equipment
- Free delivery, home inspection, and 24-hour free home trial
- Special consideration for indigent patients

Many suppliers have developed full-service packages for patients who require respiratory or enteral therapy at home. Because programs can differ greatly in their quality, they should be reviewed on an individual basis. Some companies rely on part-time clinical consultants to make one-time visits; others employ full-time staff and offer routine patient follow up. A good DME supplier is also willing to send out a qualified person to evaluate the patient's needs and living conditions when it is difficult to determine which equipment is indicated. A few DME suppliers even offer 24-hour free trial periods.

Patients without Medicare or third party insurance are the biggest challenges in continuing care planning. A company's willingness to show flexibility and to make special considerations for the less fortunate patient is a good demonstration of their "people" sensitivity. Some DME suppliers retain older, outdated equipment in functional condition for these specific instances. The Medicare program allows DME suppliers to waive the 20 percent copayment for indigent patients. This privilege should be assessed on an individual basis. However, it is frequently used by some suppliers as a marketing ploy.

The final measure of a company's total service package is reflected in its marketing approach. A DME supplier who strives to be perceived as a peer professional maintains a sales force of highly trained persons to answer questions on reimbursement and to provide in-service training on new technological developments.

In the final analysis, however, it is the responsibility of health care providers as patient advocates and professionals to assess the quality of the services provided by DME suppliers.

EVALUATION

The evaluation phase is a time for reassessment of patients and their progress (or lack of progress) toward the stated objectives. It is one of the most valuable steps of the process, but, unfortunately, it is too frequently slighted. Time is rarely taken to consider why objectives were successful. More frequently, decisions are made to modify actions that are not working well. Ideally, the evaluation process should produce information about objectives that need to be terminated, continued, or modified. The evaluation process should occur throughout the problem-solving process as well as at the conclusion of that process. It is far better to note the efficiency and effectiveness of the continuing care plan during the implementation phase than after the results. Then immediate attention can be given to the changes that need to be made.

A plethora of evaluation forms is available for use in a variety of settings. The following questionnaires may be useful to elicit responses about the discharge planning process.

A postdischarge patient questionnaire (Exhibit 7-25) is given to patients on the day of discharge. Patients may complete it before they leave the hospital or may take it with them and return it within one week to the Continuing Care Department. It may be completed by the patient, a family member, or a significant other. If a family member or a significant other fills it out, it should be done with assistance from the patient.

A questionnaire to be filled out by the primary nurse is also needed in the evaluation process (see Exhibit 7-26). For the nurse, this response can serve as an evaluation of the continuing care planning process; the continuing care coordinator can use it to identify continuing care educational needs. Coupled with Exhibit 7-25, it is useful for comparing the nurses's and the patient's perceptions of the discharge planning process. When problem areas are identified, they must be modified so that the patients who follow will experience an improved discharge plan when they leave the acute care setting. The practice of professional health care must be constantly evaluated and changes must be made to achieve and to maintain high standards of quality health care for the consumer.

The audit criteria form (Exhibit 7-27) is an audit tool designed to assess continuing care documentation in the medical record. It uses the nursing process as a basic framework for the 11 functional health pattern areas. In order to maintain high standards of nursing practice, audits of the medical record must be ongoing. A nursing quality assurance program is helpful within an institution to monitor these activities.

Exhibit 7-28 is an example of an evaluation form to be used in assessing a home health care agency. These services include Visiting Nurse Associations, community health agencies, and hospital-based home care programs. This form can be kept on file and retrieved when necessary. It can be useful to have this information readily accessible for continuing care planning.

A form for assessing a long-term care facility (Exhibit 7-29) is useful when doing on-site facility evaluations. Having this information readily accessible to professionals involved in discharge placement planning assists them in giving adequate, observed information to the patient and family members. Although helping families through the discharge to an alternative care facility is often difficult, this information can ease the problems.

An example of a community agency summary evaluation sheet, Exhibit 7-30, provides the community agency with a way to evaluate each patient who is being cared for

or has been cared for. The acute care hospital uses this summary to evaluate the outcome of the continuing care plans and to gain insight into the care provided by the community agency. The acute care hospital of the agency must receive these summary evaluation forms in order to assure that high standards of health care are being practiced and that continuity of care is provided to the individual patient.

Exhibit 7-31 is an example of a telephone call evaluation format. This method is an excellent way to call the patient or the family and to inquire about their status and progress since the time of discharge. The nurse is provided with an opportunity to identify (with the client and family) needs that were not met at the time of planning for the patient's continuing care. It also gives patients a time to ask the nurse about any concerns or any questions they may have. Often a readmission into the acute care facility can be avoided because of this telephone evaluation interview.

EDUCATION

Pollack and McKeehan, in their chapter on "Designing Teaching Strategies for Education Programs on Discharge Planning in Continuing Care," state that "the goal of any discharge planning program should be to adequately educate primary care providers to apply the principles of discharge planning in their own delivery of health care. It is these providers who are responsible for direct patient care."[1]

Several ways exist for primary care providers to be educated. The informal education takes place during hallway or "sidewalk" consults. A great deal of learning can take place in this way. The telephone is another vehicle through which the educational process can occur. Somewhat more formally, teaching may occur during the consultative process. The opportunity to learn is always available. To use each experience as one in which learning can take place must be an option afforded both the educator and the learner.

Unit-Based Education Format

Formal continuing care education is important. Implementing a program and monitoring the activity in continuing care is enhanced basically through the information given in this type of process. The following example of a general and basic unit-based continuing care program can be adapted to meet the institution's needs (Exhibits 7-32 to 7-35). It includes the purpose, the goals, the program objectives, the topics and their specific content, the teaching methods and strategies, and the activities and materials used in this program. Exhibit 7-36 is an example of an evaluation method and tools for evaluation to be used in coordination with this specific continuing care educational format.

Series Education Format

Within individual institutions or particular settings, it is often not feasible to do all unit-based continuing care education. If this is a factor to consider, opt for a hospital-wide program. Exhibit 7-37 is an example of a series of educational programs offered to all staff members who are involved in the patient care activities. Program topics may be chosen around identified needs in continuing care or important issues for information sharing.

Nursing grand rounds is a format used primarily in nursing education. It is suggested that these be held once a month in a convenient location and at a specified time. The lunch hour is recommended because the nurse can eat lunch during the presentation. The hour is spent in listening to a patient case presentation. The monthly presentations focus on different fields of interest. Surgical and medical nursing and rehabilitation, geriatric, continuing care, cardiac, renal, and orthopedic nursing are examples of patient case presentations. Audio-visual material and handouts enhance the presentation. An opportunity must always exist for questions and discussion. Often resource and community teams present the program along with the primary nursing presenters. The opportunity also exists to use a patient or the family in this format.

The acute care institution is in an excellent position to offer educational programs to the community. The hospital staff become recipients of all-day programs or workshops, for which Continuing Education credits are offered. The topics offered depend upon the need. In continuing care, such topics might be "DRG-Based Continuing Care Planning"; "Nursing in Continuing Care: Ideas and Ideals"; and "Continuing Care Update."

A seminar series is a format that can be offered for nursing home personnel. Along with being an educational program format, it is an excellent manner in which to network with staff from alternative care facilities. Exhibit 7-38 is an example of a seminar series.

Programs within the hospital can be established that particularly support those families, for example, having difficulty with the nursing home process. A sampling of the topics for discussion could include community support services, financial considerations regarding nursing home placement, explanation of nursing home levels, and explanation of changing family dynamics. Other areas to consider in setting up these support programs include the patient and the family after open heart surgery, bereavement groups, and long-term predelivery hospitalization groups.

Because hospitals must discharge patients earlier, discharge planners must undertake new strategies to ensure the continuity of care for their patients. This chapter has identified several tools and strategies to achieve this goal.

REFERENCES

1. B.A. Pollack and K.M. McKeehan, "Designing Teaching Strategies for Education Programs on Discharge Planning in Continuing Care," in *Continuing Care: A Multidisciplinary Approach to Discharge Planning*, K.M. McKeehan, Ed. (Mosby, St. Louis, 1981), p. 28.

Exhibit 7-1 Nursing Assessment Worksheet

BETH ISRAEL HOSPITAL
Nursing Services

Nursing Services Worksheet

Patient_____
Name_____
Date_____

HISTORY

Reason for hospitalization:

Other medical problem(s):

Social, cultural, economic history:

Source of health care in community:

Significant others (include age, relationship, pertinent data, who patient lives with):

Medications taken PTA:

Allergies:

Functional data on admission:

  Food habits:

  Sleep habits:

  Personal hygiene:

  Elimination:

  Female reproductive status:

  Recreation and hobbies:

  Other:

PHYSICAL ASSESSMENT DATA

Patient status on admission (weight, height, temperature, general description):

Vision (acuity, glasses/contacts):

Ears (hearing of normal conversation, hearing aids):

Mouth (teeth/dentures, condition of mucosa, speech, ability to chew and swallow):

Neuro/mental status (level of consciousness, orientation to time, PERRL, ability for spontaneous speech, emotional expression, comprehension):

Skin (cleanliness, color, temperature, edema, abnormalities):

Respiratory (rate, normal/abnormal breath sounds, rhythm, depth, cough, dyspnea):

Cardiovascular (pulse-rate, character, presence of peripheral pulses if indicated; blood pressure readings in L and R arms and positional blood pressure, if indicated):

Mobility (extremity loss, gait, abnormality of movement, deformities, appliances):

NURSING PROBLEMS

PLAN

Anticipated discharge date:_____

Source: Beth Israel Hospital.

Exhibit 7-2   Nursing Assessment Guide

BETH ISRAEL HOSPITAL
Nursing Services

Nursing Assessment Worksheet Guide

INTRODUCTORY STATEMENT

I would like to ask you a few questions about yourself and your usual daily activities at home to help us make your care as individual as possible while you are here in the hospital.

REASON FOR HOSPITALIZATION

What health problem led you to come to the hospital at this time?

How long have you had this problem?

What do you know about your illness?

What are your expectations of this hospitalization?

What things worry you at this time?

OTHER MEDICAL PROBLEMS

Have you ever been hospitalized before?

If yes, for what purpose?

Do you have any medical problems besides the problem for which you are being admitted?

SOCIAL, CULTURAL, ECONOMIC HISTORY

Do you live in your own home? An apartment?

How many stairs must you climb?

What is your occupation? Are you retired?

What was the date of your last employment?

Has your illness affected your family or your usual way of life?

What is your ethnic background?

Do you have any religious practices you would like us to honor?

Will the cost of this hospitalization cause any problems for you financially?

SIGNIFICANT OTHERS

Who do you live with?

Tell me about the members of your family (friends).

Will anyone at home need assistance while you are in the hospital?

While you are in the hospital, do you expect to have anyone visit you?

If yes, who?

Do you have someone able to care for you when you are discharged, if you should need help?

MEDICATIONS TAKEN PTA

Have you been taking medication or treatments before your admission to the hospital?

If yes, what is the drug or treatment, the dosage, the usual times you take them?

Can you explain the purpose of the drugs (treatment)?

What medicines do you take that can be purchased over the counter?

ALLERGIES

Are there any drugs or foods that you cannot take?

If yes, what is the drug or food?

What happens when you take them?

FUNCTIONAL DATA ON ADMISSION

Food Habits

Do you have any restrictions on your diet; for example, are you diabetic or do you have to follow a low-sodium diet because of high blood pressure?

Tell me about your eating habits at home; for example, do you eat all three meals, skip breakfast, have a big lunch?

Tell me exactly what you ate the day before you came into the hospital.

Is there anything you particularly like or dislike?

Sleep Habits

Do you have any trouble sleeping?

If yes, what helps you?

Tell me about your usual sleeping pattern.

Level of Activity

Are you able to get around the house, do errands, and take care of your personal needs independently, or do you need assistance?

If you need help, explain what you need.

Personal Hygiene

Tell me about your usual routine for daily hygiene.

Do you prefer a bath or a shower? When? How often?

Do you need assistance in grooming?

What do you do for mouth care, denture care?

Exhibit 7-2   continued

Do you use any special soaps, lotions, or other items that you may need here?

Elimination

We will be checking to make sure that your voiding and elimination patterns remain as close to normal as possible while you are hospitalized, so we would like to know your usual pattern; for example, do you have any problem passing your urine or stool?

Do you have daily bowel movements?

Do you use a laxative?

If yes, what kind and how often?

Female Reproductive Status

What was the date of your last menstrual period?

When do you expect your next period?

Have you used, or are you using any particular method of birth control?

Do you have any menstrual problems?

Any postmenopausal problems?

When was the date of your last PAP smear?

Do you examine your own breasts?

If yes, how often?

Recreation and Hobbies

What do you normally do for recreation or to pass time?

Tell me about your special interests or hobbies.

Other

Do you smoke?

If yes, what do you smoke?

If cigarettes, how many packs per day?

Do you partake of alcoholic beverages?

If yes, what kind? How often?

Can you tell me of any special requests that you would like us to honor while you are here?

PHYSICAL ASSESSMENT DATA

Patient Status on Admission

Subjective data from patient or family:

Height

Weight

Temperature

General appearance

Vision

Include use of prosthesis (glasses, contacts), pattern of care, and effectiveness.

May include the following descriptors and information, if appropriate: inflammation, date of last eye exam, use of medication, discharge, or muscular control.

Ears

Include voice and tone needed for patient to distinguish sound (low, moderate, loud).

Include whether hearing is partial or complete and whether the patient is able to lip-read.

Include whether patient wears hearing aid.

Mouth

Indicate if patient has teeth/dentures. Describe condition of teeth.

Include color, turgor, and intactness of mucous membranes.

Include any unusual speech pattern, such as lisping, stutter, or use of esophageal speech.

Include patient's ability to chew and swallow.

Also include date of last dental exam.

Indicate the presence of lip sores and breath smell.

Neuro/Mental Status

Include state of consciousness (ie, alert and quick to respond to stimuli, drowsy, semiconscious, or difficult to arouse).

Orientation—to time, place, and person. May also include ability to recall past or present events.

Include pupillary status (ie, pupils equal, round, and reactive to light).

Emotional expression—appropriateness of behavior and affect.

Spontaneous speech.

Comprehension.

Skin

Include cleanliness, presence of unusual discoloration, pallor, rubor cyanosis, and jaundice.

Include whether broken, intact, any sensitivity to heat or cold.

May include the following descriptors: rashes, decubiti, itching, lesions, pigmentation.

Include descriptors about hair: color, texture, cleanliness, distribution.

Include information about nails: color, length, cleanliness.

Include other abnormalities; for example, indicate presence, location, and degree of edema.

Exhibit 7-2 continued

Respiratory

Include rate changes, depth, rhythm (regular or irregular, such as Cheyne Stokes).

Indicate whether the chest is clear or abnormal.

Dyspnea—include any use of the accessory respiratory muscles and the presence of sounds, such as stridor or wheezes.

Respiratory aids—include type, such as medihalers and any abnormal respiratory opening, such as a tracheostomy.

Cardiovascular

Pulse—record pulse obtained, indicating if regular or irregular. Indicate site pulse was obtained by checking the appropriate space (apical or radial).

If irregular, describe.

Blood pressure—minimum requirement, blood pressure taken in both arms lying, sitting, or standing; indicate the position selected.

Record postural signs if patient has a complaint of dizziness or another symptom that would warrant this.

Peripheral pulses—obtain *if* indicated, and record their absence or presence.

Source: Beth Israel Hospital.

Mobility

May include whether patient ambulates with assistance or with a supportive aid, such as a person, crutches, braces, walker.

Include the location and level of extremity loss and the type of prosthesis, if indicated.

Describe whether movement is coordinated, uncoordinated, convulsive, spastic, or tremorous.

Describe any deformities, such as contractures.

Describe gait (ie, coordination and balance).

Appliance (self-explanatory).

NURSING PROBLEMS AND PLAN

Use the space provided to work out the nursing problems identified from the assessment data and the corresponding plan of care.

ANTICIPATED DISCHARGE DATE

Include a general time frame and the place to which the patient is expected to return.

Exhibit 7-3   Admission Assessment Criteria

BETH ISRAEL HOSPITAL
Nursing Services

FHPA—Admission Assessment Criteria

GENERAL SUMMARY

Level of consciousness   Vital signs, height, weight
Allergies   Persons accompanying patient
Time of admission   Pertinent clinical data
Admitted from   Valuables, glasses, dentures, prothesis

PATTERN AREAS

Health Perception–Health Management   *Cognitive-Perceptual*

General health (PMH AND PSH)   Prosthesis and disposition

Smoking, ETOH   Language spoken

Reason for admission   Sensory perceptions (pain, vision, etc.)

Medications   Level of orientation

Health care provider   Name wishes to be called by

Self-Perception–Self-Concept   *Activity-Exercise*

Perception of illness   Exercise pattern

Expectations of hospitalization   Assistive devices

Impact of illness on self/others   *Nutrition-Metabolic*

Roles-Relationship   Diet

Name of person to be notified in case of an emergency   Weight loss/gain

Living situation/support system   Skin status

Occupation   *Elimination*

Coping-Stress   Bowel and bladder patterns

Major stresses   *Sleep-Rest*

Usual coping mechanism   Sleep patterns

                                                Values-Beliefs

                                                Religious practice/needs

                                                Sexuality-Reproductive

                                                Pertinent pattern information

ANTICIPATED DISCHARGE STATUS

ASSESSMENT

PLAN

Source: Beth Israel Hospital.

Exhibit 7-4   Complete Nursing History using FHPA

1. Health perception–health management pattern

   a. How has general health been?

   b. Any colds in past year?

   c. Most important things to do to keep healthy? Think these things make a difference to health? (Include family cold remedies, if appropriate.) Use of cigarettes, alcohol, drugs? Breast self-exam?

   d. In past, been easy to find ways to follow things doctors or nurses suggest?

   e. If appropriate: What do you think caused this illness? Actions taken when symptoms perceived? Results of this action?

   f. If appropriate: Things important to you while you're here? How can we be most helpful?

2. Nutritional-metabolic pattern

   a. Typical daily food intake? (Describe.) Supplements?

   b. Typical daily fluid intake? (Describe.)

   c. Weight loss/gain? (Amount)

   d. Appetite?

   e. Food or eating: Discomfort? Diet restrictions?

   f. Heal well or poorly?

   g. Skin problems: Lesions, dryness?

   h. Dental problems?

3. Elimination pattern

   a. Bowel elimination pattern. (Describe.) Frequency? Character? Discomfort?

   b. Urinary elimination pattern. (Describe.) Frequency? Problem in control?

   c. Excess perspiration? Odor problems?

4. Activity-exercise pattern

   a. Sufficient energy for desired/required activities?

   b. Exercise pattern? Type? Regularity?

   c. Spare time (leisure) activities? Child: Play activities?

   d. Perceived ability for (code for level)

      Feeding_____

      Bathing_____

      Toileting_____

      Bed Mobility_____

      Dressing_____

      Grooming_____

      General Mobility_____

      Cooking_____

      Home Maintenance_____

      Shopping_____

Functional Levels Code:

Level 0: Full self-care

Level I: Requires use of equipment or device

Level II: Requires assistance or supervision from another person

Level III: Requires assistance or supervision from another person and equipment or device

Level IV: Is dependent and does not participate

5. Sleep-rest pattern

   a. Generally rested and ready for daily activities after sleep?

   b. Sleep onset problem? Aids? Dreams (nightmares)? Early awakening?

6. Cognitive-perceptual pattern

   a. Hearing difficulty? Aid?

   b. Vision? Wear glasses? Last checked?

   c. Any change in memory lately?

   d. Easiest way for you to learn things? Any difficulty learning?

   e. Any discomfort? Pain? How do you manage it?

7. Self-perception–self-concept pattern

   a. How would you describe yourself? Most of the time, feel (not so) good about yourself?

   b. Changes in your body or the things you can do? Problem to you?

   c. Changes in way you feel about yourself or your body (since illness started)?

   d. Do things frequently make you angry? Annoyed? Fearful? Anxious? Depressed? What helps?

8. Roles-relationship pattern

   a. Live alone? Family? Family structure (diagram)?

   b. Any family problems you have difficulty handling (nuclear/extended)?

   c. How does family usually handle problems?

   d. Family depend on you for things? How managing?

   e. If appropriate: How family/others feel about your illness/hospitalization?

   f. If appropriate: Problems with children? Difficulty handling?

   g. Belong to social groups? Close friends? Feel lonely (frequency)?

   h. Things generally go well for you at work? (School)? If appropriate: Income sufficient for needs?

   i. Feel part of (or isolated in) neighborhood where living?

Exhibit 7-4   continued

9. Sexuality-reproductive pattern

   a. If appropriate: Any changes or problems in sexual relations?

   b. If appropriate: Use of contraceptives? Problems?

   c. Female: When menstruation started? Last menstrual period? Menstrual problems? Para? Gravida?

10. Coping-stress pattern

    a. Tense a lot of the time? What helps? Use any medicines, drugs, alcohol?

    b. Who's most helpful in talking things over? Available to you now?

    c. Any big changes in your life in the last year or two?

d. When (if) have big problems (any problems) in your life, how do you handle them?

e. Most of the time, is this (are these) way(s) successful?

11. Value-belief pattern

    a. Generally get things you want out of life?

    b. Religion important in your life? If appropriate: Does this help when difficulties arise?

    c. If appropriate: Will being here interfere with any religious practices?

12. Other

    a. Any other things that we haven't talked about that you'd like to mention?
    b. Questions?

Source: Reprinted from *Manual of Nursing Diagnosis* by M. Gordon with permission of McGraw-Hill Book Company, © 1982.

Exhibit 7-5 Nursing Process Guideline Card

BETH ISRAEL HOSPITAL
Nursing Services

Nursing Process: Guidelines

I. **Primary Nurse Identification**

A. To patient/significant other
B. On Primary Nursing Board
C. On cover of patient's chart

II. **Admissions Data**

A. Date and time
B. Reason for admission/patient complaint
C. Vital signs
D. Level of consciousness/alertness
E. Allergies
F. Medications PTA

III. **Nursing Assessment**

A. History
  1. Reason for hospitalization
  2. Other medical problems
  3. Social, cultural, economic history
  4. Source of health care in the community
  5. Significant others

B. Functional Data

  1. Food habits
  2. Sleep habits

  3. Level of activity
  4. Personal hygiene
  5. Elimination
  6. Reproductive status
  7. Recreation & Hobbies

C. Physical Assessment Data

  1. Patient status on admission
  2. Vision
  3. Ears
  4. Mouth
  5. Neuro/mental status
  6. Skin
  7. Respiratory
  8. Cardiovascular
  9. Mobility
  10. GI/GU

IV. **Problem List with Etiology and Nursing Care Plan Documentation in:**

A. Medical record
B. Nursing kardex

V. **Progress Notes**

A. Ongoing evaluation of interventions
B. Formulation of nursing plan for new problems

Source: Beth Israel Hospital.

Exhibit 7-6 Patient Admission Questionnaire

Name _____ **Date** _____ **Room** _____

1. Where will you go when you leave the hospital?

2. How will you get there?

3. Do you have family or close friends who live with you and assist with your transportation, shopping, cooking, etc?
Yes _____ No _____

4. If the answer to the above is no, indicate what is needed by circling the letters below:

   a. Housing   e. Transportation
   b. Food and shopping   f. Housework
   c. Personal care   g. Special equipment
   d. Meal preparation   h. Other

5. Additional comments or concerns about going home:

   _____
   Primary Nurse

   _____
   Physician

Exhibit 7-7 Nursing Diagnoses Accepted by NANDA

**List of Nursing Diagnoses Accepted for Clinical Testing
by the North American Nursing Diagnosis Association, April 1982**

Activity Intolerance

Airway Clearance, Ineffective

Anxiety

Bowel elimination, alterations in: Constipation

Bowel elimination, alterations in: Diarrhea

Bowel elimination, alterations in: Incontinence

Breathing Patterns, Ineffective

Cardiac Output, Alterations in: Decreased

Comfort, Alterations in: Pain

Communication, Impaired Verbal

Coping, Ineffective Individual

Coping, Ineffective Family: Compromised

Coping, Ineffective Family: Disabling

Coping, Family: Potential for Growth

Diversion Activity, Deficit

Family Process, Alteration in

Fear

Fluid Volume Deficit, Actual

Fluid Volume Deficit, Potential

Fluid Volume, Alterations in: Excess

Gas Exchange, Impaired

Grieving, Anticipatory

Grieving, Dysfunctional

Health Maintenance, Alterations in

Home Maintenance Management, Impaired

Injury, Potential for

Knowledge Deficit (specify)

Mobility, Impaired Physical

Non-compliance (specify)

Nutrition, Alterations in: Less Than Body Requirements

Nutrition, Alterations in: More Than Body Requirements

Nutrition, Alterations in: Potential for More Than Body Requirements

Oral Mucous Membranes, Alteration in

Parenting, Alteration in: Actual

Parenting, Alterations in: Potential

Powerlessness

Rape-Trauma Syndrome

Self-Care Deficit (specify level: Feeding, Bathing/hygiene, Dressing/grooming, Toileting)

Self-Concept, Disturbance in

Sensory Perceptual Alterations

Sexual Dysfunction

Skin Integrity, Impairment of: Actual

Skin Integrity, Impairment of: Potential

Sleep Pattern Disturbance

Social Isolation

Spiritual Distress (Distress of the Human Spirit)

Thought Processes, Alteration in

Tissue Perfusion, Alteration in

Urinary Elimination, Alterations in

Violence, Potential for

Source: Reprinted from "Classification of Nursing Diagnosis: Proceedings of the Third and Fourth National Conferences" by M.J. Kim and D.A. Moritz with permission of McGraw-Hill Book Company, © 1982.

Exhibit 7-8 Initial Discharge Planning Sheet

Patient Admitted From:

RISK FACTORS:

AGE - 70 YRS +	YES	NO
LIVES ALONE	YES	NO
HEALTH INSURANCE	YES	NO
SUPPORT SYSTEM	YES	NO

DISCHARGE PLANS:

PROJECTED LEVEL OF CARE

LEVEL PRIOR TO ADMISSION _____

EXPECTED DISCHARGE STATUS

_____

M.D.

PROJECTED DISCHARGE DATE-

INSTRUCTIONS/CONCERNS: (ie. Rehabilitation, skilled Nursing Needs, etc.)
                                                                Initials

PRIMARY NURSE

ANY ANTICIPATED PROBLEMS AT DISCHARGE (if yes, state why)
                                                                Initials

SOCIAL WORK

CONSULT REQUESTED BY _____ DATE _____

SPECIAL PROBLEMS _____

PATIENT SCREENED BY	ACCEPTED	REJECTED	ANTICIPATED DATE OF DISCHARGE
1			
2			
3			

OTHER COMMENTS

Source: Beth Israel Hospital

Exhibit 7-9 Anticipated Discharge Status

FUNCTIONAL LEVELS

0 = Completely independent   Home

1 = Requires use of equipment   Home
     or device

2 = Requires assistance from   Family, VNA, home care,
     another person   Adult day care

3 = Requires assistance from   Home health care, VNA,
     another person(s) and   rehabilitation hospital, short-
     equipment or device   term nursing home

4 = Is dependent, does not   Alternative care facility:
     participate in activity   chronic hospital, nursing
                             home—long-term

Exhibit 7-10 Screening Chart to Determine Level of Care Needed

Patient's Name   Unit   Primary Nurse

Diagnosis: _____

Care:	Complete	Partial	Self		
Mobility:	None	Bedrest	Bed/Chair	Unassisted	Assist _____
Feeding:	Self With Help	Must be fed	NG	GT	IVs
Bowels:	Continent/Inc.	Inc. at times	Colostomy		
Bladder:	Continent/Inc.	Inc. at times	Condom	FC	Irrigations
Mental Status:	Alert	Depressed	Confused	Restraints	

Skilled Nursing Needs:

Comments:

Level:

_____

Continuing Care Nurse Specialist

Exhibit 7-11 Consultation Firm Referral

BETH ISRAEL HOSPITAL
Nursing Services

Continuing Care Referral

Date: Unit No.:

R.N.:   Physician:

Patient's Name: Significant Other:

   Address   Address:

   Telephone: Telephone:

Diagnosis:

Reason for Referral:

____ Visiting nurse/home health aide   ____ Levels of care/third party payers

____ Medical equipment (including inhalation equipment)   ____ Homemaker

____ Senior citizen nutrition program   ____ Home evaluation

____ Health education   ____ Transportation

____ Alternative care   ____ Discharge plans

____ Home care   ____ Other

____ Chronic/rehabilitation

Comments:

Signature _____

Exhibit 7-12 Notice of Hospitalization

Patient's name _____   Check if patient may present a d/c problem

Town & agency _____   Yes ____ No ____

Hospital _____

                                                                                          Disciplines Active

Date admitted _____

                                                                                        Nsg ____

                                                                                        PT ____

                                                                                        OT ____

Signed _____   ST ____

                                                                                        SW ____

Date _____   HHA ____

                                                                                        HM ____

Exhibit 7-13 Letter About Services Already Provided to Patient

Dear Continuing Care Department,

    A patient of ours, _____ , was admitted to your hospital on _____ .
Home Health Care has been involved at home with this person. We are providing you with the following list of providers to facilitate the *discharge planning*. Please contact the primary nurse with any specific questions.

Primary nurse _____

Home health aide _____ hrs/wk

Physician _____

Social worker _____

Home care corporation _____

Case manager _____

Homemaker _____

                             Sincerely,

                             _____

Other information:

Exhibit 7-14 Continuing Care Planning Decision Matrix

High-Risk DRGs	*High-Risk Patients*	*Placement Risks*	*Educational Risks*
1. Usually associated with placement or intensive "after" acute needs	1. Variant within DRG[†] 2. Patient history	1. Any length-of-stay increase due to a lack of services/ resources	1. Intensive patient educational needs
2. LOS* rather than DRG[†] frame increases		2. Highly unusual resource needs	2. Family education 3. High readmits
3. Difficult clinical management			

ACTIONS

1. Preadmission policy	1. Generic screening	1. Analyze patterns	1. QA[§] on readmissions
2. Integrated involvement: community resources	2. UR[††] and RN case finding	2. Cultivate resources	2. Heighten teaching/patient education awareness
3. Staff education	3. If needed, strengthen social services	3. Attend meetings	3. Decrease patient dependence
	4. Staff education		

Notes: * Length of stay
      † Diagnostic related groups
     †† Utilization review
     § Quality assurance

Source: Beth Israel Hospital.

Exhibit 7-15 Nursing Communication Card

BETH ISRAEL HOSPITAL

Radiology—Nursing Communication

1. I.D. Band ___
2. Alert ___   Confused ___
    Unresponsive ___   Combative ___
3. Ambulatory ___   Stands alone ___
                       Walks alone ___
4. Blind ___ Amputee ___ Language barrier ___
    Deaf ____ Other _____

    Patient Having: CT _____
5. NPO ___   US _____
6. Allergies _____   X-RAY _____
7. Precautions _____
8. Significant medical diagnosis
    Seizures ___ Diabetes ___ Angina ___ Other _____
9. Current IV _____
10. Current oxygen flow rate _____
11. Recent significant medication _____
12. Other _____

_____ RN

Source: Developed by Charlotte Feital, Beth Israel Hospital, Boston, Mass.

Exhibit 7-16 Communication Form from Alternative Care Facility to Acute Care Facility

From: *Alternative Care Facility* To: *Beth Israel Hospital*
   Nursing Communication   *Radiology Department*

Appointment for: X-Ray ☐   CT ☐   US ☐   L2 ☐   Nuc Med ☐   Date_____

Describe (in detail) preparation given for exam _____

_____

Patient identification   Armband I.D.? Y ☐   N ☐
Name:_____   B.I. Unit No. _____   _____   _____

Sex: _____   DOB_____   Soc. Sec. No. _____   _____   _____

Address: (Street) _____   Apt. No._____

(City) _____   (State) _____   (Zip) _____   Tel. No. (   )_____

Facility_____   Person to contact_____

Telephone_____   Telephone_____

Doctor_____   Transport Co._____

Telephone_____   Telephone_____

PATIENT MEDICAL STATUS

Date: _____   Vital signs: BP_____   P_____   R_____   T_____   WT_____

Mental status: Alert_____   Depressed_____   Confused_____   Combative_____

Mobility: None_____   Bedrest_____   Bed/chair_____   Unassisted_____   Assist_____

Blind_____   Deaf_____   Amputee _____

Language barrier_____? Language_____

Diet:_____

NPO Yes_____   No_____

Allergies:_____

Precautions:_____

Seizures:_____   Date of last one:_____

Diabetes:_____   Management:_____

Angina:_____   Chest pain protocol:_____

Primary medical diagnosis:_____

Recent significant medication:_____

Any other pertinent information:

Date:_____   Signature:_____RN

Source: Developed by Charlotte Feital, Ruth Jurist–Levy, and Nancy Zarle, Beth Israel Hospital, Boston, Mass.

Exhibit 7-17 Communication Form from Acute Care Facility to Alternative Care Facility

To: *Alternative Care Facility*
    Nursing Communication

From: *Beth Israel Hospital*
    Radiology Department

Patient Name _____ Unit No. _____

Report:

Signed _____RN/RT

Radiologist to Contact: _____

    Telephone No.: _____

Other Instructions:

Source: Developed by Charlotte Feital, Ruth Jurist-Levy, and Nancy Zarle, Beth Israel Hospital, Boston, Mass.

Exhibit 7-18   Discharge Statement Form

FORM NO. 270-128
259701 8/85

BETH ISRAEL HOSPITAL
BOSTON
DISCHARGE STATEMENT

ADMITTING DIAGNOSIS _____

ALLERGIES _____

DISCHARGE DATE _____   PRIMARY NURSE

DIAGNOSES

PRINCIPAL DIAGNOSIS – Condition which, after study, was found to have specifically caused hospitalization.

_____

SECONDARY DIAGNOSES – Either pre-existing or arising during hospitalization.

1. _____   5. _____

2. _____   6. _____

3. _____   7. _____

4. _____   8. _____

PROCEDURES

PRINCIPAL PROCEDURE _____	SURGEON	DATE

SECONDARY PROCEDURES _____

1. _____

2. _____

3. _____

4. _____

5. _____

DRG _____   QA INITIALS

TREAT-MENTS

RELEVANT FINDINGS AND OTHER TREATMENTS AND PROCEDURES –

_____

_____

DISCHARGE DATA

                                        DESCRIBE

DISCHARGE CONDITION – ☐ WALKING   ☐ WALKING W/ASSISTANCE   ☐ EXPIRED   ☐ OTHER:

DISCHARGE TO – ☐ HOME   ☐ BI HOMECARE   ☐ VNA (HHA)   ☐ OTHER HOMECARE   ☐ EXPIRED   ☐ OTHER FACILITY*
*NAME OF OTHER FACILITY: ☐ AMA

DISCHARGE INSTRUCTIONS –   (DIET, FOLLOW-UP VISIT, MEDICATION, ACTIVITY)

_____

STATE-MENT

I certify that the narrative description of the principal and secondary diagnoses and the major procedures performed are accurate and complete to the best of my knowledge.

_____ M.D. _____
(SIGNATURE OF ATTENDING PHYSICIAN)   (DATE SIGNED)

Exhibit 7-19 Patient Medication Minder

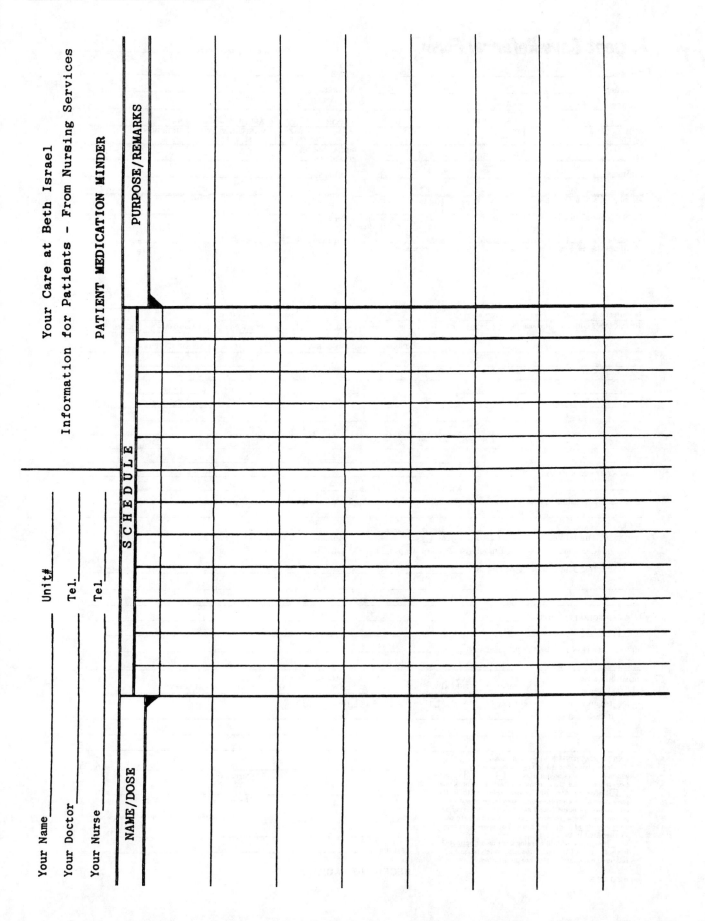

Exhibit 7-20 Uniform Referral Form

Patient Care Referral Form

Patient's Hospital Record # _____

FROM: _____

PATIENT NAME _____

Unit/Clinic _____

ADDRESS: _____

ADDRESS _____

_____ TEL. _____

	TEL.			FLOOR		APT. #	BIRTHDATE
ADM. DATE		DISCH. DATE		AGE	SEX M F	MARITAL STATUS S M W D SEP.	RELIGION

TO: _____

RELATIVE OR GUARDIAN: _____

ADDRESS: _____

ADDRESS: _____

_____ TEL. _____

_____ TEL. _____

MEDICARE NO. & LETTER	PLAN A B	BLUE CROSS NO.	SOC. SEC. NO.	OTHER
CLINIC APPOINTMENTS	DATE	TIME	Agency Worker Office Address Telephone	

DIAGNOSIS (S) Surgery Performed and Date, Allergies or Infections

Is Patient ____ Family ____ aware of diagnosis? | Date of last physical _____

PHYSICIAN'S ORDERS: (Include specific orders for Diet, Lab Tests, Speech, and O.T.) | TRANSPORT BY: ☐ Ambulance ☐ Car

MEDICATION	STRENGTH AND FREQUENCY	DATE & TIME OF LAST DOSE

TREATMENTS & FREQUENCY: _____

DIET: _____

PHYSICAL THERAPY: Restrict Activity ☐ Yes ☐ No   Sensation Impaired ☐ Yes ☐ No

Precautions   Weight Bearing Status - Non-Weight ☐   Partial-Weight ☐   Full-Weight ☐

SPECIFIC TREATMENT & FREQUENCY: _____

ANTICIPATED GOALS: _____

REHABILITATION POTENTIAL IS: _____

HOME HEALTH SERVICES: ☐ NURSING ☐ OCC. THERAPY ☐ SPEECH THERAPY ☐ SOCIAL WORK ☐ H.H. AIDE ☐ OTHER - SPECIFY

The above services require Level of Care: ☐ I ☐ II ☐ III ☐ IV

If Chronic Hospital, why? _____

CERTIFICATION: ★(when applicable)
Services above needed to treat condition for which patient was hospitalized ☐ Yes ☐ No
I certify that the above named patient is: (check one)
☐ Under my care (or has been referred to another physician having professional knowledge of patient's condition); is home bound except when receiving outpatient services; requires skilled nursing care on an intermittent basis or physical or speech therapy as specified in the orders.
☐ Requires skilled nursing care on a continuing basis for any of the conditions for which he/she received care during this hospitalization.

_____ M.D.
Signature

_____ M.D.
Print Name

Tel. _____ Date _____   Will follow ☐ Yes ☐ No - If no, who? _____

_____ M.D.

ADDRESS: _____ TEL. _____

RECEIVING FACILITY

620-15B

Exhibit 7-20 continued

Page 2
Patient Care Referral Form

NURSING: Self Care Status Check Functional Level		Inde-pendent	Needs Assist-ance	Unable
Ambulation	Bed-Chair			
	Walking			
	Stairs			
	Wheelchair			
	Crutches			
	Walker			
	Cane			
Activities	Bathe self			
	Dress self			
	Feed self			
	Brushing teeth			
	Shaving			
	Toilet			
	Commode			
	Bedpan/Urinal			

Bowel & Bladder Program   ☐ Yes   ☐ No

Incontinence: Bladder ☐   Bowel ☐
Date of Last Enema

Catheter: Type
Date last changed:

Weight	Height	Date
Anointed Yes ☐ No ☐		Date

Check if Pertinent: (describe at right) ▷

DISABILITIES
- ☐ Amputation
- ☐ Paralysis
- ☐ Contractures
- ☐ Decubitus
- ☐ Other

IMPAIRMENTS
- ☐ Speech
- ☐ Hearing
- ☐ Vision
- ☐ Sensation
- ☐ Other

COMMUNICATION
- ☐ Can Write
- ☐ Talks
- ☐ Understands Speaking
- ☐ Understands English
- ☐ If no, Other Language?
- ☐ Reads
- ☐ Non-Verbal

BEHAVIOR
- ☐ Alert
- ☐ Forgetful
- ☐ Noisy
- ☐ Confused
- ☐ Withdrawn
- ☐ Wanders
- ☐ Other

REQUIRES

Mark "S" if sent; "N" if needed

- ☐ Colostomy Care
- ☐ Cane
- ☐ Crutches
- ☐ Walker
- ☐ Wheelchair
- ☐ Other
- ☐ Dentures
- ☐ Eye Glasses
- ☐ Hearing Aid
- ☐ Prosthesis
- ☐ Side Rails

Name _____

Record # _____

Transfer to: _____

PATIENT CARE PLAN

(Explain details of care, medications, treatments, teaching, habits, preferences, and goals.)

Medications: Note time last dose given on day of discharge.

Signature of Nurse

Telephone _____ Date _____

NUTRITION: (discuss food preferences, understanding of diet, teaching needs and goals)   Diet enclosed ☐ Yes ☐ No

Nutritionist Signature   Telephone   Date

RECEIVING FACILITY

Exhibit 7-20 continued

Page 3

Patient Care Referral Form

Name: _____

SOCIAL SERVICE:

Record # _____

Prior to hospitalization, patient lived:

☐ Alone   ☐ Nursing Home

☐ With Family   ☐ With Friends

☐ Other _____

Transfer to: _____

_____

SOCIAL INFORMATION (including patient's personality, attitude toward illness and family constellation and inter-relationships)

Identified Problems:

Plan (include short and long range plans)

Will referring unit social worker plan to follow patient: Yes ☐   No ☐

Name	Signature & Title	Phone	Date

THERAPIES (P.T., O.T., Speech)   Instructions enclosed: Yes ☐   No ☐

Signature of Therapist	Phone	Date

DMC 71

Source: Beth Israel Hospital.

RECEIVING FACILITY

APPROVED BY THE MASSACHUSETTS DEPARTMENT OF PUBLIC HEALTH

Exhibit 7-21 Alternative Care Facility Discharge Envelope

Beth Israel Hospital
330 Brookline Avenue. Boston. MA 02215 / (617) 735-2000

Alternative Care Facility Discharge Envelope

LOCATION			
E U	PA	O P D	INP

NAME

UNIT NO

SEX   AGE

FISCAL NO

Facility:_____

Discharge Doctor _____ MD

Primary Nurse _____ RN   Telephone _____

Instructions
Unit Coordinator: Be sure all forms listed are complete, signed and in envelope
RN: Check forms in envelope, check that patient has all personal property
RN AND Unit Coordinator: Sign envelope when discharge process is complete

Item	Yes	No	Comment
Referral — Page 1			
Referral — Page 2			
Referral — Page 3			
Medical Summary			
Follow Up Appointment Clinic or Private			
Prescription(s)			
Medication Minder			
Discharge Diet Instructions			
Personal Items			
Teeth			
Glasses/Contacts			
Hearing Aid			
Cane/Walker			
Clothing			
Other			
Valuables from Safe			

#_____

Additional Instructions _____

Unit Coord. _____

Nurse _____ RN

660-20B

Source: Beth Israel Hospital.

Exhibit 7-22 Discharge Summary Guidelines

By the time of the discharge, the primary nurse will ensure that a discharge summary is documented in the patient's record.

Criteria

1. There will be a discharge summary title.
2. The *date* and *time* of discharge summary will be recorded.
3. Documentation will indicate the patient's/significant other's knowledge about each of the following (label and underline subtitles):

● Discharge site	Where is patient being discharged?
● Significant other involved in care	Who is available to assist patient with posthospital care?
● Condition at discharge—physical/emotional	What is significant about the patient's physical/emotional status?
● Medications	Has the patient been instructed about name, dosage, schedule of administration, action, side effects?
● Diet	On what type of diet is the patient being discharged? Has the patient received necessary instruction about food selection, buying, and preparation? What is the patient's response to dietary limitation?
● ADL	Will the patient be able to resume normal activities of bathing, eating, dressing, etc, without assistance? If assistance is needed, how will those needs be met? Special devices, etc?
● Special teaching or treatment	Does the patient have special needs/treatments that will be continued upon discharge (colostomy care, dressing changes)? Has patient or s/o been properly instructed? Discuss specifics of treatment plan that are significant for follow-up.
● Follow-up plans	Who will provide follow-up care (physician, clinic, nurse)? What plans have been made for the next appointment?

4. Additional information is noted if necessary.

_____ RN

Exhibit 7-23 Sample Nursing Discharge Summary

Mr. J is a 62-year-old male admitted with cholylithiasis for elective cholycystectomy. He has a history of high BP for which he takes Aldomet and NAS diet. He had an uncomplicated cholycystectomy and is now being discharged 6 days after surgery.

Date	Discharge Summary	
4–1–80 10:00 AM	Discharge site:	Home in Brookline
	Significant other involved in care:	Wife
	Condition at discharge:	Anxious to go home.
	Medications:	Codeine 30 mg po q 3h prn for pain Aldomet 250 mg po TID (as PTA)
		He understands how and when to take meds, and he understands their side effects. Discharge BP 152/88.
	Diet:	NAS (as PTA) Dietary consult for sample menus and food lists because patient was "cheating" PTA.
	ADL:	Patient may return to normal activities. He understands he should do no heavy work or lifting (more than 20 lbs.) for 6 weeks. He may drive and walk stairs. Return to work pending doctor's orders. No bathing until after follow-up appointment.
	Special treatments:	Wound steristripped (stitches out yesterday). Dry 4x4 over old Penrose site. Patient given 4x4's and paper type to change dressing daily until follow-up appointment. He knows he should notify doctor if he has any discharge from wound, redness, pain, or swelling.
	Follow-up Plans:	Team II clinic appointment for one week from today. Patient given appointment slip with prescriptions.
		N. Nurse, RN, PN

Source: Beth Israel Hospital.

Exhibit 7-24 Nursing Discharge Resume Form

Nursing Discharge Resume
Admitted from:
Discharge date:

DISCHARGE SITE

Discharge to:

☐ Home ☐ Home with assistance ☐ Alternative care facility

Living situation:

☐ Lives alone ☐ Nursing ☐ PT ☐ OT ☐ Chronic
☐ Lives with family/ ☐ Speech ☐ Social Service ☐ Rehab
significant other ☐ HHA ☐ HM ☐ IV Therapy Level

☐ Other ☐ Other _____ ☐ I ☐ II ☐ III ☐ IV

Name of agency or facility discharged to: _____

FUNCTIONAL STATUS

Activity: ☐ Ambulatory ☐ Ambulatory with assitive device ☐ Nonambulatory

ADL Status: ☐ Self-care ☐ Partial Care ☐ Complete care ☐ Other _____

Mental Status: ☐ Alert ☐ Oriented ☐ Confused ☐ Lethargic ☐ Unresponsive ☐ Agitated

DISCHARGE INSTRUCTIONS

Discharge diet: _____

Medications (List name, dose, and frequency): _____

_____

_____

Equipment:

Patient education: (Check if instructions given)
☐ Medications ☐ Treatments (ie, Dressings) ☐ Nutrition
☐ Written instructions ☐ Discharge program

Follow-up appointment: ☐ Clinic _____ ☐ Private _____

NURSING SUMMARY STATEMENT

Nursing Summary Statement: (Briefly describe significant nursing problems and other clinical problems.) _____

_____

_____

_____

_____

_____

_____

_____

_____

_____

_____

_____ RN   DATE: _____

Source: Beth Israel Hospital.

Exhibit 7-25 Postdischarge Patient Questionnaire

BETH ISRAEL HOSPITAL
Nursing Services
Quality Assurance

Postdischarge Patient Questionnaire

Code: Age:

Reason for hospitalization:

Please check the best answer.

Did your nurse explain what to expect when you leave Beth Israel? yes_____ no_____

Were the nurse's explanations clear to you? yes_____ no_____

Did the nurse answer your questions? yes _____ no_____

Did the nurse help you and family/friend to understand what to expect? yes_____ no_____

Please answer the following questions in as much detail as you can provide. Use the back of this page if necessary.

- How have you felt since leaving the hospital?
- What kind of help have you needed? Who provides that help?
- What kinds of responsibilities or social activities do you participate in?
- What was the best advice you received from your nurse?
- Has anything unexpected occurred? Please explain.
- What was the most difficult aspect of returning home?
- What advice would you give to another person in your situation?

Please check the column that describes your current activity best.

	Always	Usually	Sometimes	Never
I feel "good" about myself and my progress.				
I am comfortable enough to go about my usual activities without severe pain.				
I know where to get help when I need it.				
I use the help that was recommended by my nurse.				
I am able to meet my spiritual needs satisfactorily.				
I visit and do things with other people.				
My home is safe and reasonably well cared for.				
I have adequate clothing.				
I am able to get foods for my diet.				
I eat food recommended for my diet each day.				
I take my medicines according to the doses and times recommended.				
My bowels and bladder work well, without problems.				
I exercise regularly within the recommended limits.		/		
I am able to feed, bathe, and meet my hygiene needs each day.				
I feel reasonably well rested when I awaken from sleep.				
I am able to follow the doctors' and nurses' suggestions.				

Questionnaire completed by patient ☐   family member ☐   friend ☐

Source: Developed by Celeste Hurley and Nancy Zarle, Beth Israel Hospital, Boston, Mass.

Exhibit 7-26 Primary Nurse Questionnaire

BETH ISRAEL HOSPITAL
Nursing Services
Quality Assurance

Primary Nurse Questionnaire

Code:

Highest degree earned: *Years experience*

Diploma _____ BS _____   Total _____

    AD _____ MS _____   At B.I. _____

Please answer these questions as clearly as possible. Use the back of this page if necessary.

- What is your patient's living situation?

- When and how did you begin discharge planning?

- What consultative services or other resources did you use?

- What patient education did you provide?

- Did you feel adequately prepared to provide the education?

- How did your patient demonstrate understanding of your explanation?

- Do you feel your patient was satisfied with his preparation for discharge? Explain.

- How did you help the family/s.o. understand ways to help the patient?

- How did family/s.o. demonstrate understanding of your teaching?

- At the time of discharge, what kind of help did your patient need? How did you make that decision? To whom did you communicate the need?

- What, in your opinion, is the best piece of advice you gave the patient? The family/s.o.?

- What do you anticipate will be the most difficult part of the postdischarge transition for the patient?

- What, if any, problems do you anticipate the patient/family/s.o. will have during the first week postdischarge?

Exhibit 7-26   continued

- What did you tell the patient/family/s.o. concerning these potential problems?

Additional Comments:

What percent of TOTAL patient care time would you estimate was spent on
- Planning and coordinating preparations for discharge? _____%
- Teaching (patient, family/friend)? _____%

Please check the column that best describes your continuing care activities for this patient.

	Adequate	Inadequate	NA
Consults/team planning			
Referrals to community supports			
Provision of essential supplies			
Communicating information (phone, verbal reports, documentation)			
Teaching: Diet			
Medications			
Activities (limits, ADLs)			
Self-health care procedures			
Pain management			
Risk reduction			
Recognizing need for assistance			
Access to community supports			
Family coping			
Shaping attitudes/beliefs			

Source: Developed by Celeste Hurley and Nancy Zarle, Beth Israel Hospital, Boston, Mass.

Exhibit 7-27 Audit Criteria Form

BETH ISRAEL HOSPITAL

Nursing Services

Continuing Care Documentation Audit Criteria

Code _____ Date _____

Unit _____ Rater _____

Key: C = Complete   A = Absent

I = Incomplete   NA= Not applicable

ASSESSMENT

Does nursing admission include notation of the following FHPAs?

	C	I	A	NA	Comments
1. Health perception–health management pattern: a. General health status					
b. Self-care practices					
c. Health behaviors					
2. Nutritional–metabolic pattern: a. Appetite/daily intake					
b. Weight loss/gain					
c. Dental status (dentures)					
d. Skin condition					
e. Temperature					
3. Elimination pattern:					
a. Bowel elimination pattern					
b. Urinary elimination pattern					
4. Activity-exercise pattern:					
a. P, R, BP					
b. Assistive devices					
c. Perceived ability for (please check) ____ feeding ____ bathing ____ toileting ____ bed mobility ____ dressing ____ grooming ____ general mobility ____ meal preparation ____ home maintenance ____ shopping ____ transportation ____					
5. Sleep-rest pattern: a. Sleep onset problems					
b. Rest periods					
c. Aids (med., music)					
6. Cognitive-perceptual pattern: a. Hearing difficulty (hearing aid)					
b. Visual difficulty (eyeglasses)					

Exhibit 7-27   continued

	C	I	A	NA	Comments
c. Signs and symptoms of pain					
d. Pain management					
e. Intellect (ie, memory, orientation, recognition, calculation)					
7. Self-perception–self-concept pattern: a. Emotional state (affect or mood, self-esteem)					
b. Behavior clues—dress, appropriateness, attentiveness					
8. Roles-relationship pattern: a. Family structure/significant others (include any role conflicts)					
b. Living situation (living alone, neighborhood)					
c. Dependent or independent/self-care					
9. Sexuality-reproductive pattern: a. Sexual relations (problems, changes)					
b. Birth control measures					
c. OB/GYN History (ie, menses, L&D status)					
10. Coping–stress tolerance pattern: a. Recent changes in life/life-style					
b. Coping mechanisms (ie, sharing med., ETOH, drugs)					
11. Value-belief pattern: a. Religious background/practices					
b. Ethnic and cultural norms/mores					
PLAN Does the nursing administration assessment include notation of the following?					
1. Previous service provided by— a. Visiting Nurse Association					
b. Home health agency					
c. Home care program					
d. Homemaker/home health aide					
e. Other community support service (ie hospice, Adult Day Care, FISH, Meals on Wheels, AAA, etc)					
f. Physician					
2. Nursing Home Resident 3. Initial goal/plan for discharge a. Home					
b. Home with supports					
c. Alternative care facility					
d. Other					

Exhibit 7-27 continued

	C	I	A	NA	Comments
IMPLEMENTATION Has collaboration (intervention by the following health team members) been documented in the patient record?					
1. Nursing (ie, PN, AN, nurse specialists)					
2. Medicine					
3. Social Services					
4. Physical medicine (ie, PT, OR, RT, speech)					
5. Nutritionists					
Does the nursing care plan include documentation of updated discharge plans?					
EVALUATION					
1. Does the medical record include either					
a. a 3-page Patient Care Referral Form or					
b. a discharge summary?					
2. Does the 3-page referral form include					
a. completed handwritten demographic data (pg 1)?					
b. nursing problems and care plan (pg 2)?					
3. Does the discharge summary include					
a. discharge site					
b. significant other involved in care					
c. condition at discharge					
d. medications					
e. diet					
f. ADL					
g. treatments					
h. teaching					
i. outpatient follow up?					

Source: Developed by Nancy Zarle, Beth Israel Hospital, Boston, Mass.

Exhibit 7-28 Home Health Care Evaluation Form

Home Health Care Agency: Evaluation

Agency:

Geographical Area Served:

 # Patients Served in Past Year:

Staff: RN ( )   H.H.A. ( )   O.T. ( )   SW ( )

         LPN ( )   P.T. ( )   S.T. ( )

<u>Yes</u>   <u>No</u>

Hours Available for Care: **Staff Development Opportunities:**

Reimbursement Sources: **Skilled Programs:**
                                          Chemotherapy
     Pain management
     IV therapy
     Enteral
     COPD
     Antibiotics
     Hydration

Services Provided:

Nursing	( )
Home health aide	( )
Nutrition	( )
Hospice	( )
Physical therapy	( )
Occupational therapy	( )
Speech therapy	( )
Social worker	( )
Other:	( )
_____	( )
_____	( )
_____	( )

Available and/or Contracted Services:

Homemaker hours
Caseworker (community)
Private Care
Day Care - Adult
 Infant/toddlers
Meals on Wheels
DME company
Respite care program
Volunteers
Community program/education

NOTES/COMMENTS:

Source: Developed by Nancy Zarle, Beth Israel Hospital, Boston, Mass.

Exhibit 7-29 Long-Term Care Facility Assessment Form

Name _____ Date Visited _____

Address _____ Phone Number _____

Level   I   II   III   IV   Chronic Rehab   No. of beds _____

Room Rates _____ Owner _____

Public Transportation _____

_____

Administrator _____ Director of Nursing _____

Contact Person _____ Application necessary?   Yes____No____

Percentage of patients accepted on Medicaid _____% Will accept younger patients?   Yes____ No____

Please check if the following are offered:

Ostomy care	_____	Psychiatry	_____	Social worker:	_____
Bowel/blad prog	_____	Dental	_____	MSW: Consult _____ Staff	_____
Tube feedings:	_____	Calendar of activs	_____	Counseling	_____
NG ___ G ___ J	_____	Community vols	_____	Screening	_____
IVs	_____	Transportation	_____	Family work	_____
Indwelling caths	_____	Resident council	_____	Medicaid eligibility	_____
Hyperalimentation	_____	Speech therapy	_____	Groups:	_____
Ventilators	_____	PT _____ OT	_____	Describe:	_____

Facility Accepts: Wanderers _____   Psych. pts _____   Past ETOH history _____

Management problems _____   Dialysis patients _____

Comments: _____

_____

_____

Nursing inservice/staff edu _____

Nursing coverage (agency?) _____

Medical Director _____ Hospital Backup _____

Are patients able to retain their own physician?   Yes_____   No_____

Physical description of facility _____

Types of rooms: Private _____   2 Bed _____   3 Bed _____   4 Bed _____

Elevators: Yes _____   No _____

Personal belongings allowed?   Yes _____   No _____

Does facility smell of urine?   Yes _____   No _____

Exhibit 7-29   continued

Comments

Appearance of patients

Facility's strengths

Facility's limitations

_____

_____

Evaluators

Source: Developed by Jane Matlaw and Nancy Zarle, Beth Israel Hospital, Boston, Mass.

Exhibit 7-30 Summary Evaluation Form

PATIENT PROGRESS REPORT

To (Facility/Agency): _____ Patient: _____ Age: _____

Date of Discharge: _____ Medical Record # _____

Attending Physician: _____ Diagnosis: _____

In order to improve our discharge planning program, the Continuing Care Social Work Services Department is interested in obtaining follow-up information on the appropriateness of the discharge plan and the progress on the patient's well being.

We would appreciate if you would complete and return this form within three weeks of the patient's admission to your care. Thank You.

	Yes	No	Not Applicable	Comment
The client was informed relative to the discharge plan	___	___	___	___
The family/significant others were informed relative to the discharge plans.	___	___	___	___
Relevant economic information was transmitted (e.g., Medicare, etc.).	___	___	___	___
A medical discharge summary was received.	___	___	___	___

Please rate adequacy of information received:

	High Value	Mod. High Value	Average Value	Mod Low Value	Low Value	N/A	Comment
Medical Information							
Nursing Information							
Dietary							
Psycho-Social Information							
Physical Therapy							
Occupational Therapy							
Speech Therapy							

Do you feel the patient/family needed additional teaching or counseling prior to discharge from this facility?

Yes _____ No _____ If yes, what _____

Is the pateint improving?

Yes _____ No _____ In what way? _____
_____

If not, why? _____

Do you feel the discharge plan was appropriate?

Yes _____ No _____ If no, why _____

Has the client been discharged from your agency?

Yes _____ No _____ If yes, when, where and why _____
_____

For Discharge to Nursing Homes Only

The planned level of care is accurate.

Yes _____ No _____ If no, why _____

What services are you providing?

Social Service _____ P.T. _____ O.T. _____ Speech _____

For Discharge to Home Care

What services are you providing?   Date of first visit _____

Nursing _____ Home Health Aide _____ P.T. _____ O.T. _____ Speech _____

Meals on Wheels _____ Homemaker _____ Social Services _____

Did the patient have the necessary equipment for the home?

Yes _____ No _____ If no, what was needed _____
_____

Additional comments: _____
_____
_____
_____

_____   _____
Date   Signature

BRCCN, 1983
Boston Regional Continuing Care Nurses

Exhibit 7-31 Guidelines for Patient Interview by Telephone

BETH ISRAEL HOSPITAL

Guidelines for Patient Evaluation Interview

1. *Physical well-being at home*
   - How have you felt physically since leaving the hospital?
   - Is that different from how you felt in the hospital?

2. *Help needed with administering medication*
   - What kind of help have you needed while you have been taking your medication at home?
   - Who helped you?

3. *Alteration in ADL*
   - How have your normal activities at home been changed?
   - In what way have they changed?

4. *Problems experienced at home*
   - Did anything happen at home, related to your health problem, that you felt you were unprepared for (eg, problems with activities, dressings, catheter, medications)?
   - Why did you feel unprepared?

5. *Patient teaching*
   - Did you feel your teaching in the hospital adequately prepared you for your discharge home?
   - If not, why?
   - What changes would you make now that you have done this (eg, what would you add, delete, or reinforce)?

6. *Recommendations*
   - What recommendations would you give to another person going home after a hospitalization?

7. *Level of satisfaction*
   - Overall, were you satisfied or dissatisfied with your discharge plans?
   - Why?

Exhibit 7-32 A Unit-Based Continuing Care Planning Program

Purpose

The purpose of the Unit-Based Continuing Care Planning Program is to broaden the knowledge base and to enhance the ability of the nursing staff to assess and plan effectively for patient needs for continuing care.

Goals

The participants, at the completion of the planning program, will strive to realize the following goals:

- A philosophy of commitment to the concept of continuing care
- An understanding and acceptance that continuity of care includes the patient's nonmedical as well as medical problems
- The existence or development of a multiteam approach
- A commitment to match the patient's needs with available and appropriate resources
- A firm belief that the patient and the family are the most important members of the planning team

Program Objectives

At the conclusion of the program, the participant will be able to do the following:

- Identify assessment factors upon admission that influence discharge planning
- Develop an awareness of available community resources and patient support services
- Identify factors in determining functional levels for care
- Assess patient needs for appropriate discharge planning and referral
- Develop an awareness of the Medicare and Medicaid rules and regulations that afford patients access to supportive services
- Analyze a case study and write a discharge plan

Exhibit 7-33 Continuing Care Planning Workshop: Topics and Specific Content

I.   Gain an Overview
      A. What is continuing care?
      B. What is discharge planning and its importance in continuing care?
      C. Evaluation of plan—phone call, visit

II.   Identify the Resources Involved
      What and where are the available resources for discharge planning, and how does one mobilize them (ie, social worker, physical therapist, occupational therapist, chest therapist, dietician, nurse specialist, home care, Visiting Nurse Association, community resources, equipment, transportation, homemaker, home health aide)?

III. Identify the Forces
      A. Levels of care; state requirements
      B. Third party payers
         1. Medicare and Medicaid regulations
         2. Private insurance
         3. Blue Cross and Blue Shield
      C. Utilization review, PRO, discharge audit, etc.
      D. Documentation—legal implications

IV.   Design a Continuing Care Plan
      A. Interagency referrals
      B. Referral forms
      C. Nursing assessment, patient care plans, and their importance to continuing care planning
      D. Discharge charting
      E. Case study and designing a discharge plan

Exhibit 7-34 Continuing Care Planning Program: Teaching Methods and Strategies

A four-day program will take place on a specific unit for the purpose of enhancing the knowledge base of the nursing staff as it relates to continuing care.

The program will cover four broad areas. Each specific area will be discussed at a 45 minute session each day. There will be one session from 11 AM to 11:45 AM and another session from 3:30 PM to 4:15 PM. The hours for the workshop are flexible, according to the needs of the individual units.

Information will be presented to the staff by the continuing care coordinator or nurse specialist who will use a didactic teaching method with visual aids. Nursing staff will be involved at the end of each session in a question-and-answer period. At the conclusion of the four workshop sessions, the participants will discuss a case study and design a continuing care plan specific to that case.

The continuing care coordinator or nurse specialist will remain on the specific unit for a second week for individual and unit-based consultation and to assist with continuing care and discharge planning.

Exhibit 7-35 Continuing Care Planning Program: Activities and Materials

The following activities take place before the program on each individual unit:
- The continuing care coordinator or nurse specialist meets with the medical and surgical directors to set unit priority for the workshop.
- The continuing care coordinator or nurse specialist meets with the head nurse to finalize plans for the unit-based workshop.
- An announcement is sent to the unit with specific dates, time, and workshop topics.
- Copies are made of specific articles and a general bibliography for the nursing staff to read before workshop sessions.

Exhibit 7-36 Continuing Care Planning Program: Evaluation Method

Strategy No. 1: Sentence Completion
  (To be written in workshop session No. 1)

Strategy No. 2: Values Continuum
  (To be completed in workshop session No. 4)

Evaluation of workshop
  (To be completed in workshop session No. 4)

Strategy No. 1: Sentence Completion

1. I remember having used continuing care planning for _____
   _____
   _____

2. Continuing care planning should begin when _____
   _____
   _____

3. Past experience with continuing care planning taught me that _____
   _____
   _____
   _____

4. The most significant people to include in the continuing care planning process are ____
   _____
   _____

5. Continuing care planning should include patients who _____
   _____
   _____

Strategy No. 2: Values Continuum

1. My role as a nurse is

   more important _____ equal to _____ less important
   (than) the role of the social worker in *coordinating* continuing care planning with patients.

2. My role as a nurse is

   more important _____ equal to _____ less important
   (than) the role of the social worker in *coordinating* continuing care planning with families.

3. My role as a nurse is

   more important _____ equal to _____ less important
   (than) the role of the social worker in *planning* continuing care planning with patients.

4. My role as a nurse is

   more important _____ equal to _____ less important
   (than) the role of the social worker in *planning* continuing care planning with families.

5. My role as a nurse is

   more important _____ equal to _____ less important
   (than) the role of the physician in *coordinating* continuing care planning with patients.

Exhibit 7-36   continued

6. My role as a nurse is

_____

more important   equal to   less important
(than) the role of the dietician in *planning* continuing care planning with patients.

Evaluation of Workshop

1. Please indicate the sessions you attended by checking the appropriate box.

	Yes	No
I. Gain an Overview	—	—
II. Identify the Resources Involved	—	—
III. Identify the Forces	—	—
IV. Design a Continuing Care Plan	—	—

2. Did you find the sessions useful? Please indicate the appropriate box.

	Yes	No
I. Gain an Overview	—	—
II. Identify the Resources Involved	—	—
III. Identify the Forces	—	—
IV. Design a Continuing Care Plan	—	—

3. Did the workshop sessions enhance your knowledge base in the area of continuing care or discharge planning? *Please* comment!

4. Was the timing of the sessions agreeable with your schedule? If not, what suggestions could you make?

5. Please indicate any issues/areas/topics in continuing care that you would be interested in discussing in the future.

6. Please feel free to make further comments regarding the workshop, ie, teaching, content, speakers. (Use back of page.)

Exhibit 7-37 Hospital-wide Series Program

Continuing Care Update Series
1984/1985
Tuesdays, 10:30 AM to 11:30 AM

Date	Program Topic	Location
September 11	Case Management Screening Program/Networking With the Placement Office	
October 16	The Elder Abuse Assessment Team	
November 20	The Role of the Utilization Review Coordinator in Continuing Care	
December 11	Regulation Update: Medicare and Medicaid	
January 15	The Home Antibiotic Program: Home TPN Program and CAPD	
February 19	High-Risk Criteria and Goal Setting in Continuing Care	
March 12	The Commission on Affairs of the Elderly	
April 23	Home Care Corporations	
May 28	Continuing Care Assessment Strategies and Documentation	
June 25	Adult Day Care or Foster Care Programs	
July 23	Hospice Care and Regulations	
August 13	Patient Education in Continuing Care Planning	

RESERVATIONS ARE NOT REQUIRED.
ALL INTERESTED STAFF ARE WELCOME TO ATTEND.

Exhibit 7-38 Seminar Series Format

Seminar Series for Nursing Home Personnel

I. Patient Care
    A. Guest Speaker: "Geriatric Medicine"
    B. Presentation
       1. Topics:
          • "Dementia & Alzheimer's Disease"
          • "Drug Management in the Elderly"
       2. Discussion

II. Patient Care II
    A. Guest Speaker: "Linking the hospital and LTCF"
    B. Presentation: "Elder Abuse"
    C. Presentation
       1. Topic: "A Model for the Acute Care Hospital"
       2. Discussion

III. Reimbursement Issues and Approaches to Resolution
    A. Guest Speaker
    B. Panel Reaction/Presentations
       1. Perspectives:
          • Administrative
          • Fiscal
          • Patient/Family
       2. Discussion

Source: Developed by Jane Matlaw and Nancy Zarle, Beth Israel Hospital, Boston, Mass.

8. Array of Services

Many patients are being discharged from hospitals earlier than ever before; yet they have greater continuing care needs. The primary continuing care planning team must therefore be aware of a broader range of services available to the patient. Because of the decreased length of stay, it will be necessary to arrange more services for the patient—and within a very short time. Moreover, many more patients will be needing these services. Health care professionals from all the specialty fields, particularly nursing and social service, must become more informed about how patients can receive these services from the community.

In this chapter, the array of services available to the patient are described—from the most restrictive services (institutional setting), through the less restrictive services (community setting), to the least restrictive services (home setting). Figure 8-1 visually depicts this presentation.

INSTITUTIONAL SETTING

The acute care hospital is viewed in the health care system as the facility that provides the most intensive level of care to the ill consumer.

Acute Care Hospital

The acute care hospital is used only for acute, complicated, or highly technologic health problems. When a person is hospitalized, daily acute care services are provided. (They are generally reimbursed by insurance bene-

fits.) By the time it is determined that the acute care intervention is no longer needed, the continuing care plan must be in place and the patient must be moved to another setting—institutional, community, or home.

Chronic Care Hospital

Continuing patient care in a chronic care hospital assists patients who have slowly progressing diseases, terminal or irreversible pathological conditions, illnesses of long duration, or conditions with permanent or residual disabilities. Skilled nursing services provide observation and supervision on a daily basis. Additional medical attention is available on a 24-hour basis, and special rehabilitation services are provided. The goal of a chronic care hospital is to attempt to slow the disease process, to prevent complications, and to teach the patient how to function with disabilities as effectively as possible.

Rehabilitation Hospital

A rehabilitation hospital is an institutional care facility for patients who require an intensive program of restorative therapy after an injury, illness, or disease. The goals of a rehabilitation program are to prevent permanent disability; to restore the ability to function as normally as possible; and to maximize the patient's physical, mental, social, vocational, and economic usefulness. As a result of the rehabilitation program, the patient is expected to return home or to a family's home after discharge.

91

Figure 8-1 Available Continuing Care Services

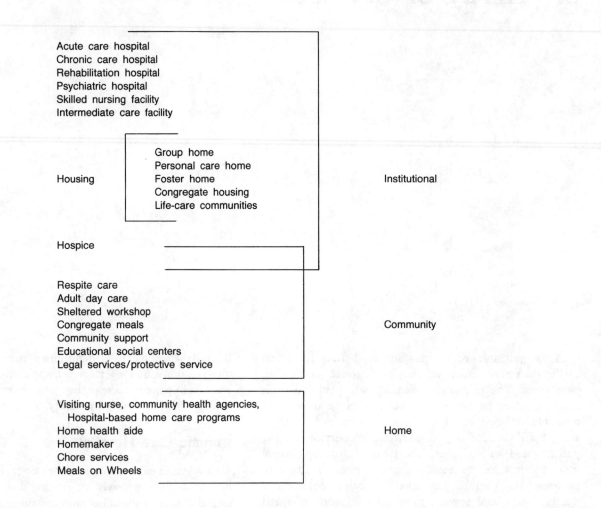

ARRAY OF SERVICES   SETTING

Most Restrictive

Acute care hospital
Chronic care hospital
Rehabilitation hospital
Psychiatric hospital
Skilled nursing facility
Intermediate care facility

Housing
    Group home
    Personal care home
    Foster home   Institutional
    Congregate housing
    Life-care communities

Hospice

Respite care
Adult day care
Sheltered workshop
Congregate meals   Community
Community support
Educational social centers
Legal services/protective service

Visiting nurse, community health agencies,
    Hospital-based home care programs
Home health aide   Home
Homemaker
Chore services
Meals on Wheels

Least Restrictive

Psychiatric Hospital

An institutional facility for patients with functional psychoses (without significant physical illness or disability) and for whom outpatient treatment is not feasible is called a psychiatric hospital. For admission to a psychiatric hospital, a patient must be suffering from an acute or chronic mental illness, a severe brain syndrome with a concomitant disturbing behavior, or alcoholism. The psychiatric hospital provides self-protection, nursing management, and regular medical treatment.

Skilled Nursing Facility

Patients who require a skilled nursing facility must be in need of an intensive, organized program of restorative services and nursing care. At one level of a skilled facility,

the length of stay may be relatively short and could be viewed simply as a recuperative period. In such cases, the patient's rehabilitation potential is usually high. At another level of care, patients may require long-term skilled nursing intervention, or they may have a combination of needs that require unskilled nursing care.

Intermediate Care Facility

Patients being transferred to an intermediate care facility need assistance with the activities of daily living (eg, eating, dressing, and mobility status). Routine nursing supervision occurs in these facilities; skilled nursing is available as it is needed. Physician coverage is also available.

Housing

Housing is an institutional setting with an independent, self-care focus.

Group Home. A group home is a nonprofit neighborhood home for active persons who value their independence. Residents generally pay privately for this family-sized group living. Usually, they have their own private rooms with a shared bath and common kitchen facilities.

Personal Care Home. Another type of housing facility is the personal care home. It is based on belief in the basic human right of each person who has severe physical disabilities to live an independent and a productive life in the community. Services provided for clients in this setting include health maintenance skills training, independent living skills training, and personal care attendants hired by the client to assist in the ADL.

Foster Home. An option to placing a client in an intermediate care facility is foster home placement—a service that enables the client to experience and to enjoy a home and a caring family atmosphere. Families who want to provide foster home care are carefully screened and matched with the client. The families receive a monthly stipend for assuming the care of the elderly client.

Congregate Housing. A residence for elderly people that combines a boardinghouse style of living with a sharing of ADL (ie, kitchen and bath facilities) is called congregate housing. There, respect is given for the privacy and individuality of each resident. Each apartment has a private toilet and wash basin. Generally, meals are served in the central dining room, as well as in the shared kitchens on the separate floors. The center of activities for the elderly within the community includes the dining facilities, sheltered workshops, and a social service program. Usually, a full range of support services is available.

Life Care Communities. Complexes that have been labelled *life care communities* usually consist of apartments, townhouses, private houses, mobile homes, or a mixture of these. Included also are an infirmary, a clinic, a nursing home, and recreational and social facilities (a golf course, a swimming pool, an exercise club, and a movie theater). Some communities have physicians in residence and a small hospital. The population may be large enough to support the cultural, social, and shopping facilities of a small town. The recreational and medical costs and facilities are included in the general charges of some communities; they are optional and extra in others. Many life care communities are well guarded against the outside world. A gatehouse at the entrance to the village provides security control, which protects the residents from unwanted visitors and allows them to feel safe and protected at any time of the day or night.

Hospice

The hospice movement attempts to improve the institutional environment for care of the terminally ill patient. There are four basic areas in which the hospice differs from the traditional hospital, and all of these differences improve the psychosocial care of the patient.

1. The focus of the hospice is on the person, which counteracts the dehumanization of hospitals.
2. The hospice encourages, rather than discourages, family interaction.
3. More attention is paid to the proper control of pain in hospices than in the traditional acute care hospitals. Hospice personnel endeavor to allow the patient to function normally to the greatest extent possible while pain is controlled.
4. Hospices are more likely to rely on allied health professionals (the social worker, pharmacist, clergy, and psychologist) than are acute care hospitals.

Because hospice staff have ties to the family, they form a small community for the comfort and ease of the seriously ill patient. Its emphasis provides promising alternatives to certain types of existing hospital care.

COMMUNITY SETTING

The community offers a person support in self-care management and independence.

Hospice

The mission of hospice in the community is to provide support and care for terminally ill persons and their families in the last phases of an incurable disease so that they can live as fully and comfortably as possible. Community hospice programs range from interest and support groups to organizations that provide complete palliative and supportive services. Most community programs provide home care and can arrange for inpatient care when it is needed or desired.

Respite Care

Respite care offers temporary care for elderly persons who are in good health and need supervision or shelter for a time when the regular caretakers or family are unavailable because of vacation or other reasons. This care is usually financed through private payment. Two purposes of respite care services are (1) to relieve the primary caretakers from their everyday responsibilities and (2) to enable participants to experience their ongoing ADL—including special and recreational activities—without disruption to their home and community life style.

Adult Day Care

This program is structured to meet through health care and socialization activities the needs of the frail, the moderately handicapped, and the slightly confused elderly persons. Most of these clients are at risk of being placed in an alternative care facility without intervention. Others, who have recently been discharged from a hospital or long-term care facility, are in need of assistance to make the transition to independent living.

The goal of an adult day care program is not only to promote the physical and mental well-being of the client but also to help the client achieve the highest level of independent functioning. Concomitantly, when applicable, the program may provide relief for the primary caretaker or the family from full-time responsibility.

The emphasis of the program is on health maintenance and education, nursing care, restorative therapies, and nutrition. Other important components of adult day care are the assistance in personal needs (bathing, eating, toileting), planned recreational and social activities, transportation, and social service counseling that is given to clients and their families. These centers are usually located in nursing homes, social agencies, or hospitals. They are in operation at least eight hours each day and five days each week. A registered nurse is available at least four hours each day.

Sheltered Workshops

These community workshops, which offer rehabilitation for the disabled, allow them to return to regular or sheltered employment. Services available to the client are work evaluation, adjustment training, job training, sheltered employment, work tryout, placement, medical services, and psychological and social work services.

Congregate Meals

A program designed to meet the nutritional and social needs of the older ambulatory persons living in the community is called congregate meals. At least one meal per day is served in a congregate housing setting at least five days each week. To be eligible for this program, clients must be at least 60 years old (spouses are eligible regardless of age). Although there are no income requirements, clients must be financially unable to provide proper food and must have insufficient skills or knowledge in selecting and preparing nourishing meals. Limited mobility, impaired capability to shop and cook, and feelings of rejection and loneliness that destroy the incentive to eat are additional requirements for eligibility. Payment for this program is in the form of an optional donation at the meal site.

Community Supportive Services

Supportive services within the community include mental health, medical, and dental. These services may be sought through the government agency—Area Agency on Aging (AAA). This agency is the chief administrative structure in each region of the state for pursuing goals of developing federally funded programs on the community level. At the local level, the councils on aging can support the interested client in obtaining needed services.

Educational and Social Centers

Centers have been established in communities to assist the elderly residents to discover available resources and education opportunities in such areas as health, nutrition, social services, cultural and recreational affairs, employment and volunteer opportunities, transportation, information and referral processes, and discount and security programs. These centers also serve as advocates for the elderly.

Legal and Protective Services

Legal services and protective services are assistance programs available to the elderly for legal aid, information and referral, advocacy, and advice on civil matters (eg, housing, social security, welfare, Medicaid, and consumer issues and problems). Lawyers and paralegal aides are available to provide assistance. When it is necessary, home visits are made. This service is generally free to the elderly population because it is a state-supported service.

HOME SETTING

Home health services provide a broad range of services—skilled nursing, social service, speech therapy, occupational therapy, physical therapy, and home health aide services. The Visiting Nurse Association, community home health agencies, and hospital-based home care programs are examples of agencies that provide these services. Home health services are available to patients recently released from hospitals, the elderly and others with chronic illness, persons who are terminally ill, persons requiring teaching about and monitoring of their medications and treatments, and new mothers and their babies. Health counseling and support are also available. Moreover, some home health agencies operate various types of clinics and screening programs in their local communities and provide health services and education to schools and other community groups.

Home health agencies assist many persons to remain in their homes who might otherwise require more expensive institutional care in hospitals and skilled care facilities.

To receive these services, clients must have a physician's order and an assessment and acceptance by the receiving agency. Fees for this service are based on costs and time; third party reimbursement is a possibility.

Home Health Aide

Home health aides are another important service to the home care team. They provide personal care for those persons who need help with bathing, dressing, ambulation, or eating—all the activities of daily living. The primary nurse in the acute care setting with the help of the patient, the family, and significant others must be responsible for identifying these needs through the process and practice of discharge planning and observation of the overall continuing care needs of the patient.

If a patient requires skilled nursing care in the home, home health aide services are generally arranged by the primary nurse through the Visiting Nurse Association or another home health care agency. If the patient does not require any skilled nursing care, arrangements for a home health aide are made through home health care agencies or a homemaker–home health aide agency.

Homemaker

Homemakers provide basic housekeeping for persons who need help with cleaning, shopping, and cooking meals. They do not usually assist with personal care.

For the patient *under* 60 years old who needs this type of assistance, services are not readily available. The patient's social worker should be contacted so that all available resources can be explored. For the patient who can afford to pay for homemaker services, several private agencies are available.

For the patient *over* 60 years old, homemaker services are provided in a variety of ways by the different states. In the State of Massachusetts, homemaker services are provided through various home care corporations and are financed through the Department of Elder Affairs. However, patients will be asked many questions about their finances before the services are provided. Because the evaluation process and the availability of services may be a problem, it is critically important to identify this particular need as early as possible in the planning process. State agencies will then be able to identify needs in advance and to manage personnel planning appropriately and in as timely a manner as is possible.

Chore Services

A chore service is usually coordinated with the service provided through the Visiting Nurse Associations because it is a federally funded program and there is no charge to eligible persons. The service available is for heavy housecleaning, minor repairs, snow removal, and relocation preparation. A client must be 60 years old and have a limited income in order to be eligible for this program.

Meals-on-Wheels

The Meals-on-Wheels program is designed to meet the nutritional needs of the elderly who are homebound. The meals, which are delivered to the home, usually include one hot meal and one cold meal. Food stamps and optional donations (when possible) are accepted for payment for the meals.

CONCLUSION

Maximizing resources and services in a changing health care scene and in a lean economy is no easy task. The health care provider needs to be well aware of the resources and services available and of the regulations governing their availability. Only then will the patients and clients served have their needs understood and met during a time when continuing care planning is so critical and important.

9.   Conclusions

Continuing care planning, one of the most important concepts of health care today, is introduced early in a nurse's professional education. The discharge process is often regarded as the final, triumphant step for the patient in a long chain of sophisticated medical and nursing care in an acute care setting. Today, with the advent of prospective reimbursement and a new era of competition in the health care field, that planning is receiving greater emphasis. The system now encourages shortened hospital stays because Medicare reimburses hospitals on the basis of fixed rates, regardless of the length of stay. Continuing care planning through the process of discharge planning is crucial, therefore, in assuring patients and their families that their needs will be met in the community when the patient is released from the hospital. (Patients are being discharged quicker and sicker.) Timeliness and the inclusion of appropriate input from those persons in the hospital and in the community milieu assure a smooth transition to the home or to an alternative care facility. A coordinated continuing care plan, then, is the key that ensures the continued effectiveness of the acute medical and nursing regime.

The most sweeping change that has come with the advent of prospective pricing for the acute care setting is in the financing of health care for the aged and disabled. Medicare, which was legislated in the mid-1960s, has been largely responsible for this change. Prospective pricing, which uses the DRG system, is the method chosen by federal agencies to restrain Medicare costs.

For almost two decades, the hospital has been the reservoir—or safety valve—for the impaired elderly who could not be returned home or to the community without support services. Yet, despite demonstration programs and privately funded services, there is not sufficient public support for continuing long-term care services.

The challenge to all those involved in continuing care planning is to make effective use of existing resources while demonstrating the need for additional services. The primary goal of discharge planning has *not* changed under the DRG system. By being involved in the discharge planning process the hospital maintains its fiduciary responsibility while maintaining high standards of patient care.

Maintaining high standards of patient care can be accomplished only by early assessment of the patient's need for continuing care services. Improvement in this process depends on interdepartmental systems and interdisciplinary collaboration. The hospital must reach into the community and extend and deepen relationships with the community-based health and social service agencies. Of course, the purpose of reaching out into the community is to participate in the creation of new services and in the development of improved referral procedures. More effective linking and networking with the public and voluntary agencies is critical.

Moreover, continuing care planning is not a one-person or a single-discipline process or activity. In the area of coordination (and management), the continuing care plan needs considerable attention. The managing of the process and the development of a comprehensive information system are the essential components of continuing care planning.

The appropriate involvement of the patient and significant others is the most important process in discharge planning; nevertheless, the emphasis on the use of hospital resources and the attention paid to costs tend to move the patient away from the center of the care process. Basic patients' rights are involved because choices and decisions are made that will affect the remainder of the person's life. It must be ensured, then, that the patient's freedom of choice is exercised. The patient's involvement is essential for a timely, effective, and efficient discharge to continuing care services at home and with community agencies.

What are the major factors that will draw the shape and direction of the health care delivery system over the next 20 years? There will be a heightened sensitivity to health care costs, which will result in changes in reimbursement factors. Demographics also will change—especially because of the aging population. The acceptance of limits on provider and patient freedom of choice will increase; so will acceptance of limits on new biological and technological developments.

In the next two decades, it is expected that changes will also occur in the health care delivery system in the different health care sites, in treatment and technology, and in the caregiver component. There will be a greater use of hospices, home health care, surgicenters, extended care facilities, "drop-in" hospital ambulatory clinics, and life care communities.

In the treatment and new technology arena, it is expected that some cancer vaccines will be developed. There will also be a greater use of self-diagnosis and drug therapy, an increased use of computers in making diagnoses, and an increase in organ transplants and mechanical implants.

Primary caregivers—health maintenance organizations (HMOs), life care communities, and multiinstitutional health care systems—will increase. The regionalization of hospitals will also increase.

The implications for expert planning in the continuing care field are enormous. The problem of the medically indigent is a growing issue; so is the quality of care for the patient. The responsibility of the health care team in the continuing care planning process is major.

Important to these issues that have been mentioned is the recognition that an effective continuing care planning program (or process) and the professionals within it can be in a pivotal position to assess the total needs of the patient and to influence the regulators, the reimbursers, the administrators, and others to ensure the appropriate use of a variety of resources. The emphasis on reimbursement, rather than on directing people to appropriate care, continues to taint a good idea—our belief that we can care for all. We must be positive. We must become more efficient. We must move above and beyond where we are. Human services are the hands that clasp us into the very circle of society; so we must all be an active part of that circle for the good of all those involved. What is needed is consumer education about health care services, closer communication between regulatory and provider agencies, and the development of systems to facilitate the flow of patient care information among providers of health care.

"What's everybody's business is nobody's business!" has never been more appropriate than when we consider continuity of nursing between home, the hospital, and the alternative care facilities. When no one person in the institution or agency carries the authority and the responsibility for seeing that the care of patients continues on a planned basis as they move from one level of care to another, nursing in continuing care seldom becomes a reality. Continuing care is an important process; when that process is interrupted, a patient is denied a basic right.

Appendix A. Suggested Nursing Care Plans for Nine High-Risk DRG Categories

These nursing care plans were written by the contributing authors to illustrate a shortened version of the Functional Health Pattern Assessment (FHPA) called the Functional Health Pattern Admission Assessment (FHPAA) in addition to a complete FHPA, a nursing care plan, and a patient care referral form. In the final step of the continuing care process, the referral form is written by the primary care team and is sent to the receiving facility or agency. The form may not reflect the nursing orders or actions or the physician's orders stated on the care plan, but it is the most recent update of orders for the community team to follow. Changes may have been made in accord with the medical status of the patient at the time of discharge.

1. Acquired Immune Deficiency Syndrome (AIDS)—Aurelie Cormier, RN, BSN
2. Asthma—Nancy O'Rourke, RN, BSN
3. Burns—Heidi Picard, RN, BSN, and Debora Tobojka, RN, BSN
4. Chronic Obstructive Pulmonary Disease (COPD)—Ellen Kitchen, RN, BSN
5. Diabetes—Nancy Brown, RN, BSN
6. Head trauma—Patricia Casaccio, RN, BSN
7. Hip fracture—Susan Kinnell, RN, BSN
8. Hypertension—Kathleen Smith, RN, BSN
9. Stroke—Evelyn Stelmack, RN, BSN

ACQUIRED IMMUNE DEFICIENCY SYNDROME (AIDS)

FHPAA

General Summary

Mr. J., a 30-year-old bisexual male, was diagnosed with AIDS in May 1982. He was electively admitted on January 29, 1983 at 4 PM with complaints of extreme fatigue and fevers. This was the patient's fourth hospital admission. His vital signs were recorded as follows: Temperature, 39.1°C; pulse rate, 100 beats per minute; respirations, 12/min; and BP, 124/68. He was 6 ft. tall and weighed 140 lb. The patient was allergic to seafood, IVP dye, and perphenazine (trilafon), and suffered from lactose intolerance. He was accompanied to the hospital by a friend.

Pattern Areas

Health Perception–Health Management

The patient has a past medical history (PMH) of exercise-induced asthma; lactose intolerance—diagnosed in June 1981; giardiasis, amebiasis, and positive antinuclear antibodies (ANA)—1970 and 1980; *Pneumocystis Carinii* pneumonia; and Kaposi's sarcoma. His past surgical history (PSH) is negative. He does not smoke, and alcohol history (ETOH) is also negative. The patient was admitted because persistent fevers, weight loss, diarrhea, and weakness made it increasingly difficult for him to care for himself at home.

Medications include the following:

- a-interferon, 18 million units, given three days each week IM
- $FeSo_4$, 325 mg, p.o., BID
- Psyllium hydrophilic muciloid (Metamucil), 1 pkg., p.o., BID
- DTO, 4–5 gtt, p.o., BID
- Chlortrimazole troches, i, p.o., QID
- $CaCO_3$, 420 mg, p.o., TID
- Prochlorperazine (Compazine), 5 mg, p.o., PRN

The health care provider is Dr. T.

Self-Perception–Self-Concept

The patient is upset by his significant weight loss and identifies this as a distressing aspect of his illness. He believes, however, that he can gain control of his illness through meditation and visual imagery. He maintains a positive attitude. His friend feels that the decreasing muscle strength and the weakness have caused increased responsibility for the primary care provider because the patient is less able to care for himself at home.

Roles-Relationship

The patient is a former business professional who is presently unemployed and receiving disability. He lives alone in a five-story brownstone house, which he owns. The friend who accompanied him to the hospital rents an apartment on the two upper levels and assists with the cooking and shopping. The patient derives much of his support from a strong network of friends and family.

Coping-Stress

Two major stressors at this time are the weight loss (which is frightening for the patient) and the increasing inability to care for himself at home. His usual coping mechanisms are relaxation and visual imagery. The patient has been working with a relaxation therapist, but he also finds it helpful to talk with friends and his lover.

Cognitive-Perceptual

The patient, who requests that he be called Bill, is currently alert and oriented. He states that he has become forgetful at times and feels weak and tired most of the time. His friend states that since January 1983, the patient has had transient staring episodes involving speech difficulties and has been conversing inappropriately at times. The patient describes his taste as dull. His hearing, vision, touch, and smell are within normal limits.

Activity-Exercise

A former six-mile-a-day runner, the patient becomes now short of breath on exertion and is fatigued most of the day—especially after any physical activity, including all ADL activities.

Nutritional-Metabolic

Before becoming ill, the patient weighed 171 lb. He now weighs 140 lb and is increasingly anorexic, which is accompanied by nausea and vomiting at times. His diet consists mainly of Ensure Plus, middle eastern sandwiches, and Chinese food.

Elimination

The patient voids without dysuria but denies hematuria, burning, or any discharge. Bowel movements are characterized by loose frequent stools; at times, the patient is incontinent. He is distressed because the diarrhea is severe in the AM and often occurs several times during the day.

Sleep-Rest

The patient sleeps often throughout the day, secondary to fatigue. He has eleven hours of sleep at night.

Values-Beliefs

The patient has no specific religious preference. He describes himself as being pantheistic.

Sexuality-Reproductive

This bisexual man has lived with one partner for five years. He has had ten sexual encounters outside of this relationship.

Anticipated Discharge Status

The goal is that the patient will return home with home health assistance and assistive devices.

Assessment and Plan

The nutritional deficit 2°, nausea, vomiting, and anorexia will be dealt with under the following plan:

- Continue Ensure Plus as tolerated (a goal of 3 to 4 cans each day).
- Weigh patient every AM.
- Count calories for three days.
- Contact the Dietary Department for consultation and recommendations.

To determine the etiology of the diarrhea, the following plan is recommended:

- Obtain a bedside commode.
- Record the frequency and the character of stool, and perform a guaiac test on all BMs.
- Perform perirectal skin care after each stool.
- Contact the physician for antidiarrheal therapy.
- Observe excretion precautions.

The self-care deficit and the deceased activity tolerance of 2° fatigue will be approached by using the following plan:

- Document the patient's perception of those activities he feels he can complete.
- Arrange the room and the bedside table in a way that will minimize exertion.
- Assist the patient with ADLs as necessary.
- Encourage the patient to take short walks with assistance.
- Provide a quiet environment for rest during the day.

FHPA

Pattern Areas

Health Perception–Health Management

The patient describes his general health as being excellent until April 1981 when he began to experience weight loss, nausea and vomiting, anorexia, and fatigue. In May 1982, he developed *Pneumocystis carinii* pneumonia and was diagnosed with AIDS. He also began to develop Kaposi's sarcoma. He was treated with sulfamethoxazole with trimethoprim (Bactrim) and α-interferon. The patient tested positive for hepatitis A and had oral herpes and candidiasis. In October 1982, the patient was treated for pneumonia with Bactrim for 6 days and $4,4^1$-(pentamethylenedioxy) dibenzamidine (Pentamidine) for 13 days. In December 1982, he developed a fever of unknown origin. Cultures of his sputum, blood, and urine were negative. Transient staring episodes occurred.

Nutritional-Metabolic

The patient weighed 171 lb before he became ill; he now weighs 140 lb. Presently nauseous he vomits at times and is becoming increasingly anorexic. The patient's daily diet includes the following:

- Breakfast: 1/2 can of Ensure Plus and a slice of toast
- Midmorning break: one glass of orange juice
- Lunch: middle eastern sandwich and one cup of tea
- Midafternoon break: 1/2 can of Ensure Plus
- Dinner: Chinese food and one cup of tea

Examination of the oral mucosa revealed *Candida* on tongue. The patient's skin showed the presence of multiple Kaposi's sarcoma over the entire body.

Elimination

The patient is voiding in normal amounts and frequency without dysuria. He denies hematuria, burning, or discharge. He is having loose stools, approximately six times each day. He is distressed because the diarrhea is severe in the AM and also occurs several times during the day. The patient is using kaolin with pectin (Kaopectate), 2 tbsp up to 6 times/d to control the diarrhea. This medication was initially effective in decreasing the frequency of the stool but not its character. Before admission, the patient states that Kaopectate has "not helped at all over the past 2 days." The perirectal skin is red and tender to the touch, but there is no skin breakdown.

Activity-Exercise

When the patient was well, he was a six-mile-a-day runner. Now he is short of breath on exertion and is tired and exhausted most of the day. The patient is especially fatigued after normal ADLs, such as walking to the bathroom or showering. He feels that he now needs assistance with his ADLs. Although he used to prepare his meals, he now is unable to do this because of the weakness. For example, the patient's bathroom is located one floor up from his bedroom; he finds it extremely difficult to get there. Spending most of his day in bed, he listens to classical music and talks on the telephone.

Sleep/Rest

The patient spends most of his day resting in bed. Feeling weak and tired, he sleeps off and on during the day. He also sleeps 11 hours at night. He does not take any medications to induce sleep, but he finds that listening to classical music assists him to relax.

Cognitive-Perceptual

The patient requests that he be called Bill. He is alert and oriented at present, but states that he has become forgetful at times. He feels weak and tired most of the time. His friend states that since January 1983, the patient has had transient staring episodes. He also has difficulty with speech and verbalization at times. The patient sometimes converses inappropriately. He describes taste as dull. Hearing, vision, touch, and smell all within normal limits.

Self-Perception–Self-Concept

The patient has strong feelings about himself and believes that he can have control of his illness through meditation and visual imagery. His attitude is positive and hopeful.

Roles-Relationship

The patient is a former business professional who is presently unemployed and receiving disability insurance. He lives alone in a five-story brownstone house, which he owns. A friend rents an apartment on the two upper levels and assists with shopping and meal preparation. The patient has many friends and enjoys a great deal of support from them. His family also is very supportive—especially a twin sister, who lives in a neighboring state and visits every other week.

Sexuality-Reproductive

Bill is bisexual. Although he has lived with one partner for five years, he has had ten sexual encounters outside of this relationship. He is comfortable with his sexuality patterns.

Coping-Stress

The patient is experiencing two major stressors at this time. One is weight loss, and the other is an increasing inability to care for himself at home. His usual coping mechanisms are relaxation and visual imagery. The patient works on a weekly basis with a relaxation therapist in an outpatient clinic setting, but he also finds it helpful to talk with his lover and his friends. He finds these techniques helpful in enabling him to cope with his current situation. He would like to continue these exercises while he is hospitalized.

Values-Beliefs

Bill has no specific religious preference. He describes self as being pantheistic. His philosophical beliefs are of the mind-body interaction.

NURSING CARE PLAN

FORMULATED BY Aurelie Cormier, R.N.   DATE 1/29/83

NURSING HISTORY

Pt is a 30-year-old bisexual man who was diagnosed with AIDS 5/82. Past medical history includes pneumocystis carinii pneumonia, Kaposi's sarcoma, giardia, and amoebiasis. He is electively admitted with chief complaint of weakness, fatigue, N/V, anorexia, incontinence of stool, and persistent fevers. The pt lives alone and is now unable to care for self at home. He has received α-interferon in the past and is now receiving α-interferon 3 times a week.

NURSING DIAGNOSIS	EXPECTED OUTCOME	NURSING CARE PLAN WITH NURSING ORDERS
1. Potential for infection due to immune deficiency.	- Pt will not develop any new infections. - Temp. will remain within normal limits.	1. Protective isolation, private room with bathroom, careful handwashing. 2. Avoid IM injections when possible, rectal temps, enemas, rectal tubes, foley catheters. 3. Daily physical assessment of signs and symptoms of infection: lungs, Gu tract, mouth, rectum, skin, culture as necessary. 4. Notify M.D. of T↑ 100.5 po 5. Mouth care qid 1 Perox-a-mint and Chlortrimazole troches. 6. Perirectal care c̄ warm water and soap after each BM. 7. Assess temp q4° and control as ordered, Tylenol, alcohol baths. 8. Administer α-interferon as ordered.
2. Activity intolerance manifested by weakness and fatigue due to: - inadequate nutrition - anemia - malabsorption - increased metabolic demands	- Able to perform ADL's without shortness of breath or fatigue.	1. Plan activities within limits of pt's tolerance. 2. Arrange environment for optimum convenience of pt, accessibility of commode, emesis basin. 3. Guiac stool, urine emesis, sputum. 4. Assess for SOB, DOE. 5. Reassure pt of continued assistance and support.

NURSING DIAGNOSIS	EXPECTED OUTCOME	NURSING CARE PLAN WITH NURSING ORDERS
3. Alteration in nutrition less than body requirements as seen by: - weight loss of 30# since 6/83 - decreased albumin to 2.7, T.P. 5.1 - decreased Ca 7.7 - N/V, diarrhea	- Pt will put on weight. - Pt will maintain nutritional status by increased po intake. - Normal skin turgor - I/O balanced - No S/S of electrolyte imbalance	1. VS q4°, Iro daily weight. 2. Dietary consult, calorie counts x3 days. 3. Assess N/V, administer antiemetics and antidiarrheas as ordered. Assess need for schedule vs prn order. 4. Ensure plus as dietary supplement. 5. CaCO₃ as ordered. 6. Mouth care q4°.
4. Alteration in bowel elimination as seen by incontinence of stool.	- Pt will have less frequent stools.	1. Quantitate stool. Note quality, color, consistency. Guiac all stool. 2. Administer anti-diarrheas as ordered. 3. Good perianal care c̄ each BM - wash with warm water and soap, sitz baths tid. 4. Assist pt with putting on a dignity pad after each BM.
5. Cognitive impairment manifested by increased periods of forgetfulness, confusion, and staring episodes.	- Pt will maintain safety.	1. Assess neuro status of shift focusing on memory and level of orientation. 2. Monitor vs q4°; assess for H/A, neck stiffness.
6. Partial self care deficit: bathing, toileting, mobility.	- Pt will return home. - Pt will maintain ADL's with assistance of home health aide.	1. Contact Home Care in preparation for discharge planning to arrange for home health aide 5x/week + NSG 3x/week.
7. Potential for avoidance coping.	- Pt will be able to acknowledge feelings and concerns. - Pt and family will be able to recognize and utilize available support systems.	1. Establish consistent caretakers and an environment of trust and confidence. 2. Allow for periods of verbalization when pt can express his thoughts and feelings about his disease. 3. Contact clinic to assist with medication and visual imagery while pt is in the hospital. 4. Allow time each shift for pt to do meditation and visual imagery uninterrupted. 5. Talk with lover, friend, and family members - allow them periods to verbalize their thoughts and feelings.

Patient Care Referral Form

FROM: Beth Israel Hospital

Unit/Clinic 10th floor Medical

ADDRESS 330 Brookline Ave

Boston, MA 02215 TEL. 222-1111

ADM. DATE 1/29 DISCH. DATE 2/11

TO: Beth Israel Home Care

ADDRESS: 330 Brookline Ave., Boston, MA 02215

TEL. 777-0000

Patient's Hospital Record # _____

PATIENT NAME Bill

ADDRESS: 1111 Elm Street

Seaside, MA TEL. 333-3333

FLOOR 1 APT. # 1 BIRTHDATE 2/2/56

AGE 30 SEX M F MARITAL STATUS S M W D SEP. RELIGION NSP

RELATIVE OR GUARDIAN: Friend, 1112 Elm Street, Seaside, MA

ADDRESS: Apt. #2 TEL. 555-5555

MEDICARE NO. & LETTER	PLAN A B	BLUE CROSS NO.	SOC. SEC. NO.	OTHER
Disability			000-11-2222	BC/BS 444444

CLINIC APPOINTMENTS	DATE	TIME	Agency Worker Office Address Telephone

DIAGNOSIS (S) Surgery Performed and Date, Allergies or Infections

1. AIDS, S/P giardiasis, S/P pneumocystis
2. Fever of unknown origin
3. Exercise induced urticaria/asthma
4. Lactulose intolerance

Is Patient Family aware of diagnosis? yes

Date of last physical 2/6/85

PHYSICIAN'S ORDERS: (Include specific orders for Diet, Lab Tests, Speech, and O.T.)

TRANSPORT BY: ☐ Ambulance ☐ Car

MEDICATION	STRENGTH AND FREQUENCY	DATE & TIME OF LAST DOSE
Compazine 10 mg po qid prn n/v		$CaCO_3$ 420 mg po tid
Metamucil 1 pkg po tid in H_2O		Theragran-M 1 po qd
Chlortrimazole troches 1 po tid		Antacids q4° prn gastric
DTO 5-20 gtts po tid pin/diarrhea		distress
$FeSO_4$ 325 mg po tid		
α-interferon 18 milliom U IM MWF (in 1-ccNS)		
Lomotil 2 tabs po qid prn diarrhea		

TREATMENTS & FREQUENCY: Basic hygiene care, assistance c̄ medical diagnosis (especially diarrhea), help washing & meal preparation, periodic blood transfusion, administration of IM α-interferon 3x/week

DIET:

PHYSICAL THERAPY: Restrict Activity ☐ Yes ☐ No Sensation Impaired ☐ Yes ☐ No

Precautions Weight Bearing Status - Non-Weight ☐ Partial-Weight ☐ Full-Weight ☐

SPECIFIC TREATMENT & FREQUENCY: resumption of baseline level of activity; resumption of ADL's

ANTICIPATED GOALS: semi-independent living

REHABILITATION POTENTIAL IS: poor

HOME HEALTH SERVICES: ☒ NURSING ☐ OCC. THERAPY ☐ SPEECH THERAPY ☒ SOCIAL WORK ☒ H.H. AIDE ☐ OTHER - SPECIFY

The above services require Level of Care: ☐ I ☐ II ☐ III ☐ IV

If Chronic Hospital, why? _____

CERTIFICATION: ✱(when applicable)
Services above needed to treat condition for which patient was hospitalized ☐ Yes ☐ No
I certify that the above named patient is: (check one)
☐ Under my care (or has been referred to another physician having professional knowledge of patient's condition); is home bound except when receiving outpatient services; requires skilled nursing care on an intermittent basis or physical or speech therapy as specified in the orders.
☐ Requires skilled nursing care on a continuing basis for any of the conditions for which he/she received care during this hospitalization.

Signature _____ M.D.

R. Jones _____ M.D.

Print Name

Tel. 222-1111 Date 2/7/85 Will follow ☐ Yes ☒ No - If no, who?

Dr. John Smith _____ M.D.

ADDRESS: Beth Israel Hospital TEL. 222-1111

282-956 9/85

APPROVED BY THE MASSACHUSETTS DEPARTMENT OF PUBLIC HEALTH

DISTRIBUTION — **WHITE** — RECEIVING **PINK** — MEDICAL RECORDS **YELLOW** — C.C. SERVICE

Page 2
Patient Care Referral Form

Name ___Bill___

Record # ___00-11-22___

Transfer to: ___1111 Elm Street, Seaside, MA and BI Home Care___

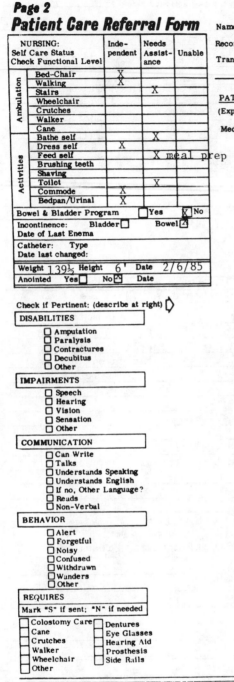

PATIENT CARE PLAN

(Explain details of care, medications, treatments, teaching, habits, preferences, and goals.)

Medications: Note time last dose given on day of discharge.

Bill is a 30-year-old bisexual male who lives in Seaside, MA; admitted 1/29/85. He is a former businessman and is now on disability 2° AIDS. PMH includes pneumocystis carinii pneumonia, Kaposi's sarcoma, +hepatitis Ab, oral herpes, candidiasis, giardia, amoebiasis, exercise induced asthma, and lactose intolerance.

1. Potential for infection due to immune deficiency 2° AIDS dx'd 5/82, now with persistent dry cough and intermittent fevers to 104°po. Had sx's x 8 mos before he was diagnosed. Fever w/u. The mycobacterium in sputum has been found to be resistant to everything. No treatment at this time. Receiving Tylenol and alcohol baths to decrease temperature. Pt to cont. with good mouthcare - brush, rinse with Perox-a-mint, troches qid. Good perirectal care after each BM (pt on blood/secretion/ excretion precautions). Pt is presently on a research protocol using α-interferon 3x/week. Wear gloves when handling urine and stool. Dispose diapers in plastic bags. Wash linens and pt's clothing separately. Don't share eating utensils.

2. Activity intolerance manifested by weakness and fatigue due to inadequate nutrition, anemia, malabsorption and increased metabolic demands. Pt's Hct. ā dx = 36.5. Now his baseline is 28.3. 2/7 pts hct decreased 27.4 - tx c̄ 2 u.PC. Will have blood drawn by Hem/Ouc clinic q week. Pt also experiencing increasing weakness, SOB, and DOE. His sx's have continued to progress to the point where he is so weak he wants to lie in bed most of the day. I have encouraged him to increase his strength by Amb. bid-15 min.-45 min. Pt OOB at meals. Pt will be spending most of his time in his bedroom. It would be helpful

_____
Signature of Nurse

Telephone _____ Date _____

NUTRITION: (discuss food preferences, understanding of diet, teaching needs and goals)   Diet enclosed ☐ Yes ☐ No

Nutritionist Signature _____ Telephone _____ Date _____

White - Receiving Facility   Canary - Medical Records   Pink - C.C. Services

620-22M - 821-640   9/85

Page 2

Patient Care Referral Form

Name _____ Bill _____

Record # _____

Transfer to: _____

_____

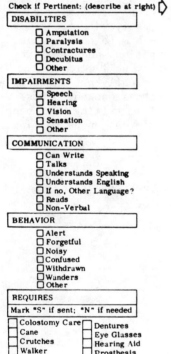

NURSING: Self Care Status Check Functional Level		Inde- pendent	Needs Assist- ance	Unable
Ambulation	Bed-Chair			
	Walking			
	Stairs			
	Wheelchair			
	Crutches			
	Walker			
	Cane			
Activities	Bathe self			
	Dress self			
	Feed self			
	Brushing teeth			
	Shaving			
	Toilet			
	Commode			
	Bedpan/Urinal			

Bowel & Bladder Program	Yes ☐	No ☐

Incontinence: Bladder ☐   Bowel ☐
Date of Last Enema

Catheter: Type
Date last changed:

Weight	Height	Date
Anointed Yes ☐ No ☐		Date

Check if Pertinent: (describe at right) ▷

DISABILITIES
☐ Amputation
☐ Paralysis
☐ Contractures
☐ Decubitus
☐ Other

IMPAIRMENTS
☐ Speech
☐ Hearing
☐ Vision
☐ Sensation
☐ Other

COMMUNICATION
☐ Can Write
☐ Talks
☐ Understands Speaking
☐ Understands English
☐ If no, Other Language?
☐ Reads
☐ Non-Verbal

BEHAVIOR
☐ Alert
☐ Forgetful
☐ Noisy
☐ Confused
☐ Withdrawn
☐ Wanders
☐ Other

REQUIRES
Mark "S" if sent; "N" if needed

☐ Colostomy Care	☐ Dentures
☐ Cane	☐ Eye Glasses
☐ Crutches	☐ Hearing Aid
☐ Walker	☐ Prosthesis
☐ Wheelchair	☐ Side Rails
☐ Other	

PATIENT CARE PLAN

(Explain details of care, medications, treatments, teaching, habits, preferences, and goals.)

Medications: Note time last dose given on day of discharge.

for energy conservation to arrange his room c̄ commode and emesis basin to decrease fatigue.

3. Alteration in nutrition less than body requirements as seen by 30# wgt loss, decrease albumin, decrease Ca, N/V. Wgt loss is a frightening problem. One of his biggest fears is that he'll waste away. He needs meals prepared and served to him. He loves many different types of ethnic foods (Lebanese sandwiches, Chinese food, etc). He also supplements his meals with Ensure. He has been encouraged to have an increased protein and calcium diet. Has a Na of 129 which has slowly been decreasing. Encouraged to limit free water (which he loves) and use salt liberally. His usual wgt before dx was 170#. He now ranges 139-142#. Needs wgt q week. Administer antiemetics as ordered.

4. Alteration in bowel elimination and incontinence of stool. Pt has chronic loose bowels. However in the last 4 mos. he has become incontinent of stool. Now wearing a dignity pad. He also has a hx of hemorrhoids and an anal fissure. Watch stools for S/S of bleeding as these pts are at increased risk of GI bleed 2° K. Sarcoma lining the GI tract. He has had some blood clots in the past which he attributes to his anal fissure. To control his diarrhea he takes Metamucil 1 pkg po BID + DTO 5 gtts po BID. Arrangements to rent a commode for his bedside have been made.

5. Cognitive impairment manifested by increased periods of forgetfulness and confusion neuro w/u this adm. attributes decreased MS to progressive dementia 2° to AIDS. A+0x3, monitor MS.

_____
            Signature of Nurse
Telephone _____ Date _____

NUTRITION: (discuss food preferences, understanding of diet, teaching needs and goals)   Diet enclosed ☐ Yes ☐ No

_____   _____   _____
    Nutritionist Signature   **Telephone**   **Date**

White - Receiving Facility   Canary - Medical Records   Pink - C.C. Services

Page 2
Patient Care Referral Form

Name _____ Bill _____

Record # _____

Transfer to: _____

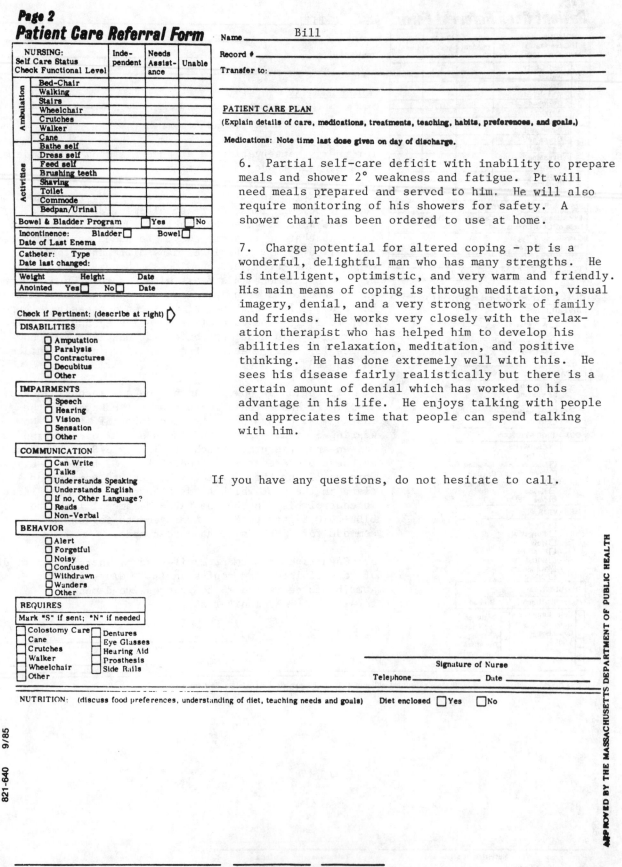

NURSING: Self Care Status Check Functional Level		Independent	Needs Assistance	Unable
Ambulation	Bed-Chair			
	Walking			
	Stairs			
	Wheelchair			
	Crutches			
	Walker			
	Cane			
Activities	Bathe self			
	Dress self			
	Feed self			
	Brushing teeth			
	Shaving			
	Toilet			
	Commode			
	Bedpan/Urinal			

Bowel & Bladder Program	☐ Yes	☐ No

Incontinence: Bladder ☐　Bowel ☐
Date of Last Enema

Catheter:　Type
Date last changed:

Weight	Height	Date
Anointed　Yes ☐　No ☐　Date		

Check if Pertinent: (describe at right) ⬭

DISABILITIES
- ☐ Amputation
- ☐ Paralysis
- ☐ Contractures
- ☐ Decubitus
- ☐ Other

IMPAIRMENTS
- ☐ Speech
- ☐ Hearing
- ☐ Vision
- ☐ Sensation
- ☐ Other

COMMUNICATION
- ☐ Can Write
- ☐ Talks
- ☐ Understands Speaking
- ☐ Understands English
- ☐ If no, Other Language?
- ☐ Reads
- ☐ Non-Verbal

BEHAVIOR
- ☐ Alert
- ☐ Forgetful
- ☐ Noisy
- ☐ Confused
- ☐ Withdrawn
- ☐ Wanders
- ☐ Other

REQUIRES
Mark "S" if sent; "N" if needed

- ☐ Colostomy Care
- ☐ Cane
- ☐ Crutches
- ☐ Walker
- ☐ Wheelchair
- ☐ Other
- ☐ Dentures
- ☐ Eye Glasses
- ☐ Hearing Aid
- ☐ Prosthesis
- ☐ Side Rails

PATIENT CARE PLAN
(Explain details of care, medications, treatments, teaching, habits, preferences, and goals.)

Medications: Note time last dose given on day of discharge.

6. Partial self-care deficit with inability to prepare meals and shower 2° weakness and fatigue. Pt will need meals prepared and served to him. He will also require monitoring of his showers for safety. A shower chair has been ordered to use at home.

7. Charge potential for altered coping - pt is a wonderful, delightful man who has many strengths. He is intelligent, optimistic, and very warm and friendly. His main means of coping is through meditation, visual imagery, denial, and a very strong network of family and friends. He works very closely with the relaxation therapist who has helped him to develop his abilities in relaxation, meditation, and positive thinking. He has done extremely well with this. He sees his disease fairly realistically but there is a certain amount of denial which has worked to his advantage in his life. He enjoys talking with people and appreciates time that people can spend talking with him.

If you have any questions, do not hesitate to call.

_____
Signature of Nurse

Telephone _____ Date _____

NUTRITION:　(discuss food preferences, understanding of diet, teaching needs and goals)　Diet enclosed ☐ Yes　☐ No

_____
Nutritionist Signature　　Telephone　　Date

White - Receiving Facility　　　　Canary - Medical Records　　　　Pink - C.C. Services

821-640　9/85

APPROVED BY THE MASSACHUSETTS DEPARTMENT OF PUBLIC HEALTH

Page 3
Patient Care Referral Form

Name: ___Bill_____

Record # ___00-11-22_____

Transfer to: ___1111 Elm Street, Seaside, MA and BI Home Care___

<u>SOCIAL SERVICE:</u>

Prior to hospitalization, patient lived:
☒ Alone   ☐ Nursing Home
☐ With Family   ☐ With Friends
☐ Other _____

SOCIAL INFORMATION (including patient's personality, attitude toward illness and family constellation and inter-relationships)

Pt is a 30-year-old single bisexual male dx'd with AIDS 5/82.. Pt responded to diagnosis with appropriate disbelief and some level of denial. Pt has coped with illness through expression of feelings, finding positive aspects of his life, being active in own care, and appropriate level of anxiety re uncertainties and fears of illness and prognosis. Pt also copes via working with relaxation therapist who has aided pt with skills in meditation, visual imagery, and positive thinking.

Identified Problems:

Pt lives in 5 story brownstone. He has close and significant relationship with his lover, twin sister, and close friend. All are active in his care and supportive.

Pt has experienced increasing weakness and fatigue, finding it difficult to walk up and down stairs or complete ADL's. Pt is having understandable difficulty dealing with potential loss of independence and fear of uncertainties.

Plan (include short and long range plans)

Cont. to provide supportive interventions; help pt to continue to verbalize fears and concerns, finding ways of adapting support coping style and defenses (i.e. pt's involvement in own care). Pt to be d/c'd with HHA 5x/week.

Will referring unit social worker plan to follow patient: Yes ☐   No ☒

Name	Signature & Title	Phone	Date
Jane Williams		777-8888	2/7/85

THERAPIES (P.T., O.T., Speech)   Instructions enclosed: Yes ☐   No ☐

Signature of Therapist	Phone	Date

RECEIVING FACILITY
DISTRIBUTION: **WHITE**-RECEIVING FACILITY; **CANARY**-MEDICAL RECORD; **PINK**-C.C. SERVICE

620-17M - 681-282   9/85

APPROVED BY THE MASSACHUSETTS DEPARTMENT OF PUBLIC HEALTH

ASTHMA

FHPAA

General Summary

A 49-year-old, alert and oriented $\times 3$ (A+O$\times$3) white man was admitted from home by ambulance to the emergency unit on April 28, 1985. The diagnosis was exacerbation of asthma. The patient had a long-standing history of chronic obstructive pulmonary disease (COPD). His chief complaint (CC) was of increased shortness of breath, fatigue, and a productive cough (white sputum) for one week before admission. Symptoms persisted despite frequent rest periods and the use of metaproterenol sulfate (Alupent Inhaler). On the day of admission, the patient noted increased wheezing, tightness, and the inability to "catch his breath." He notified his physician, and was referred to the emergency unit. The usual precipitants of such an exacerbation were present and included upper respiratory tract infection, stress, and dust. The patient related the exacerbation to having had his apartment painted two weeks before admission and to his continued habit of smoking 1/2 pack of cigarettes each day. The patient has no known allergies.

The patient arrived on the floor at 1 AM by stretcher. He was sitting in a high Fowler's position, leaning forward with hands on thighs, wearing oxygen, audibly wheezing, appearing anxious, with flushed face, and in moderate respiratory distress. Aminophylline was given IV by infusion at 30 mg/h. Examination of the lungs revealed audible wheezing with scattered rhonchi throughout the lung fields and decreased breath sounds at the bases; no rales were noted. Respirations were 36/min without the use of accessory muscles or pursed-lip breathing. The patient denied having chest pain or palpitations. No pedal edema was noted. He stated that shortness of breath persisted, but that it had improved since his admission. His vital signs were recorded as follows: Temp, 36.9°C; pulse rate, 120 beats per minute; respirations, 36/min; and BP, 110/70, He weighed 154 lb, and was 5 ft 9 in tall.

Laboratory studies disclosed the following values: ABGs, O_2, 2 L, Po_2 68, Pco_2 38.7, pH 7.43; hematocrit, 49.9%; hemoglobin, 14.4 g/dl; WBC 1/5.4; Na, 143 mEq/L; K, 4.1 mEq/L; CO_2 31 mmHg; blood glucose 107 mg/dL; BUN, 8 mg/dL; Cr .9 mg/dl; theophylline, 13.1 (normal, 10–20)

The only valuables the patient had with him when admitted were reading glasses and a radio.

Pattern Areas

Health Perception–Health Management

K.D. (or Kevin, as the patient prefers) feels that his respiratory status has progressively deteriorated over the past year; there were three exacerbations that required hospitalization. The patient has always viewed himself as an active, independent man, and so he verbalizes frustration and anxiety over his declining health status, due to asthma. He reports that he tries to pace his activities, to get adequate rest, and to take all medications in order to minimize the symptoms of asthma; but he finds this hard to do. The patient reports also that he was hesitant to come to the hospital; however, now that he is here, he is more relaxed.

The patient's past medical history includes asthma since 1978 (but no history of intubation); cigarette smoking (three packs per day for many years; presently ½ pack per day); ETOH abuse (abstinent for ten years); hepatitis; status past (S/P) left herniorrhaphy (1968); and S/P vein-stripping for varicose veins (1980).

Medications include the following:

- anhydrous theophylline (Theo-Dur), 400 mg, p.o. TID
- prednisone, 60 mg, p.o., QD (Patient has been steroid dependent for one year; prior attempts to taper steroid use led to exacerbations.)
- oxazepam (Serax), 30 mg, p.o., BID, for anxiety
- metaproterenol sulfate (Alupent) by nebulizer, q4h while awake
- magnesium hydroxide with aluminum hydroxide and simethicone (Mylanta), alternating with aluminum hydroxide (Amphojel), QID

The health care provider is Dr. M. of the Boston Community Health Center. The patient has monthly appointments and drives himself to the appointments.

Roles-Relationship

Kevin has been living alone since the death of his mother in February 1985. He verbalizes feelings of grief over the loss of his mother, but reports a strong, supportive relationship with his sister and brother-in-law, who reside nearby. He has never married because he "has never found the right girl." However, he does report several strong friendships established over the past ten years while attending Alcoholics Anonymous meetings.

The patient owns a one-family house with three flights of stairs. The bedrooms are on the third floor; the bathroom is located on the first. He does his own cooking and shopping.

The patient has worked for many years as a machinist. During admission to the hospital in February 1985, he decided to apply for medical disability because of his declining health status. A social worker is involved in the case, and has followed the patient since his last discharge.

Coping-Stress

Kevin reports that he is anxious about his declining health status and views this past year as the hardest. Stressors include worsening asthma, his mother's death, the responsibility of caring for the house, concerns about his financial status, and the "idle" time while he is in the process of being classified as medically disabled. He willingly and openly verbalizes feelings. The patient understands the contraindications of smoking by an asthmatic, but he states that smoking decreases his anxiety and prevents him from drinking. He takes Serax (BID, PRN) for anxiety. He states, "I'm trying my hardest to live with this."

Cognitive-Perceptual

The patient (A+O×3) wears glasses for reading. He has good hearing and can hear a normal conversational tone. He is English-speaking and high-school educated. The patient denies any memory loss.

Activity-Exercise

The patient is independent in his ADLs. However, he reports that dyspnea on exertion (DOE) and fatigue have increased over the past year because of the asthma. He states that he paces activities and takes frequent rest periods. Over the past week, the patient has been unable to care for himself properly. Doing even minimal activity causes severe DOE and fatigue.

Nutritional-Metabolic

The patient's appetite is usually excellent. He reports periods of increased hunger when he is receiving steroid therapy. He prepares his own food and follows a balanced diet. Over the past week, the patient has experienced a decreased appetite and has been unable to prepare meals because of shortness of breath (SOB) and fatigue.

Elimination

The patient denies burning upon urination or increased frequency and urgency to urinate. He has no difficulty starting a stream, and voids in large amounts. His usual pattern for BM is every other day without the use of laxatives. He reports one week of constipation.

Sleep-Rest

Kevin takes Serax (BID, PRN) for anxiety; he reports that he also takes it at bedtime (HS). He goes to bed at 12 AM and sleeps off and on throughout the night. He awakens every morning at 5 AM with increased coughing and shortness of breath.

Values-Beliefs

The patient is a practicing Roman Catholic who values relationships with his friends and family. Kevin views himself as a strong, honest person. He feels that faith in God helps him cope with stress.

Sexuality-Reproductive

Kevin has never married. He denies having had any children and prefers to "keep the topic private."

Anticipated Discharge Status

It is clear that Kevin's discharge needs have changed from those he had on prior admissions. His goal upon discharge is to return home with the home supports of the VNA, chest physical therapy (CPT), and a homemaker.

The patient's respiration status has declined over the past year, requiring frequent hospitalizations. Moreover, he has been experiencing increased shortness of breath and fatigue, which have resulted in decreased activity tolerance, sleep pattern disturbance, and nutritional alterations. The patient has many stressors, and he continues to smoke, despite being aware of the contraindications. Although he is compliant and demonstrates an understanding of his disease and the medications, he is not using the nebulizer properly. Consequently, he would benefit from home supervision to maximize respiratory function.

Assessment and Plan

The patient's continuing care assessment can be summarized under eight needs:

1. The patient's impaired gas exchange or ineffective airway clearance, which is related to the asthma
2. The patient's activity intolerance, which is related to DOE and fatigue
3. The patient's sleep-pattern disturbance, which is related to the increased shortness of breath every morning
4. The patient's anxiety, which is related to his declining health status, his fear of losing independence, and his changing occupational and financial status
5. The patient's potential for ineffective coping, which is secondary to these anxieties and his fear of drinking

6. The patient's ignorance about proper use of the nebulizer and the signs and symptoms that warrant hospitalization
7. The patient's altered bowel status—constipation (2°)—which is secondary to decreased activity, decreased fluid intake, and the use of Amphojel
8. Discharge planning

The eight assessed needs can be dealt with as follows:

1. Administer oxygen as ordered; administer bronchodilators and steroids intravenously as ordered; and assess the patient for any side effects of the medications. Check the pulse q 4h, and auscultate the lungs q 4h to assess the effectiveness of treatments. Perform CPT q 2 to 4h, and encourage the patient to cough and breathe deeply q 2h. Give Alupent treatment by nebulizer, 4 L/O₂—especially upon the patient's awakening. Elevate the head of the bed. Maintain adequate fluid intake to over 2 L/d.
2. Encourage the patient to pace his activities and to rest frequently. Collaborate with the patient in setting realistic exercise goals. For example, encourage him to walk for at least 15 to 20 min/d and devise a progressive exercise program. Teach energy conservation techniques—eg, bedside commode or urinal for home use.
3. Establish a consistent bedtime. Reinforce the use of the radio as a means of relaxation, and offer Serax and warm milk at bedtime. Also elevate the head of the bed to ease breathing.
4. Administer oxazepan (Serax) PRN as ordered, and encourage the patent to ventilate his feelings. Continue the involvement of social service to assist in the process for seeking medical disability. Explore the option of volunteer work with the patient.
5. Do not *pressure* the patient to quit smoking, but give gentle repetitious reminders that quitting may be important to his well-being. Give pamphlets on stop-smoking programs and hypnosis centers. Notify J.H., the AA counselor, of the patient's admission. Help the patient to explore alternative coping mechanisms.
6. Give the patient written and verbal information on asthma and its treatment. Moreover, encourage him to see a physician before symptoms become so severe. Instruct the patient in the proper use of a nebulizer. Give him a medication card and teach him about drug actions and side effects.
7. Administer milk of magnesia 30 ml, QHS and docusate sodium (Colace) 100 mg, TID. Provide prune juice and bran with breakfast, and maintain a liberal fluid intake to prevent constipation.
8. Discharge the patient to home with assistance from the VNA, CPT, and a homemaker. He will need home oxygen, a bedside commode, and possibly a hospital bed.

FHPA

Pattern Areas

Health Perception–Health Management

K.D., (or Kevin, as the patient prefers) feels that his respiratory status has progressively deteriorated over the past year; three exacerbations have required hospitalization. He has always viewed himself as an active, independent man and verbalizes his frustration and anxiety over his declining health status, which is due to asthma. The patient reports that he tries to pace his activities, to get adequate rest, and to take all medications in order to minimize the symptoms of asthma; however, he finds this hard to do. He reports also that he was hesitant to come to the hospital, but now that he is here, he is more relaxed.

The patient's past medical history includes asthma since 1978 (but no history of intubation); cigarette smoking (three packs per day for many years; presently 1/2 pack per day); ETOH abuse (abstinent for 10 years); hepatitis; S/P left herniorrhaphy (1968); and S/P vein-stripping for varicose veins (1980).

Medications include the following:

- anhydrous theophylline (Theo-Dur), 400 mg, p.o., TID
- prednisone, 60 mg, p.o., QD (Patient has been steroid dependent for one year; prior attempts to taper use led to exacerbations.)
- oxazepam (Serax), 30 mg, p.o., BID, for anxiety
- Alupent by nebulizer, q4h while awake
- Mylanta, alternating with Amphojel, QID

Dr. M. of the Boston Community Health Center is the health care provider. The patient has monthly appointments and drives himself to the appointments. He has Blue Cross and Blue Shield insurance.

Nutritional-Metabolic

The patient reports that he usually has an excellent appetite. A typical daily menu includes:

- Breakfast: 1 egg, a piece of toast with jelly, and a glass of orange juice.
- Lunch: a tunafish or cheese sandwich, a salad, and a glass of milk.
- Supper: Meat, a potato and other vegetables.

He tries to limit eggs and red meat to three times each week and eats two pieces of fruit daily.

The patient reports periods of increased hunger when he is on steroids; then he snacks between meals. He also states that he has a "sweet tooth" and eats three to four candy bars daily. He tries to maintain a liberal fluid intake to "keep secretions loose."

The patient does his own shopping and meal preparation. He views nutrition as important and looks forward to "pleasurable meal times." Over the past week, he has experienced decreased food and fluid intake because of his shortness of breath and fatigue. The patient's sister brought him his meals, but he was unable to eat anything substantial.

Elimination

The patient denies any burning when urinating or increased frequency or urgency to urinate. He has no difficulty in starting a stream and voids in large amounts. His usual pattern for BM is every other day without the use of laxatives. Kevin reports a week of constipation, moving only small hard stools. Usually the stools are brown, formed, and soft. Constipating factors over the past week include decreased fluid intake, decreased activity, and Amphojel. He reports that he ran out of Mylanta and was unable to get to a store because of the DOE.

Activity-Exercise

The patient is independent in his ADLs. However, he reports increased DOE and fatigue over the past year because of the asthma. He states that he paces his activities and takes frequent rest periods. Over the past week, the patient has been unable to care for himself properly. Even minimal activity causes severe DOE and fatigue—"Even brushing my teeth was too hard." The patient's bedroom is located on the third floor and the bathroom is on the first. He states, "I could hardly make it down the stairs to the bathroom at night." The patient did not want to sleep in the living room (to conserve energy) because he viewed this as a loss of independence. He reports that future plans include moving into a one-room apartment in order to conserve his energy and to maintain his independence. The patient feels that owning his own home is too much responsibility because he has experienced decreased ability to do home repairs. He feels that the move would also be financially beneficial.

Sleep-Rest

Kevin takes Serax (BID, PRN) for anxiety. He also takes one at bedtime to aid sleep and listens to the radio for relaxation. He sleeps with 2 pillows. Kevin goes to bed at 12 AM and sleeps off and on throughout the night. He awakens every morning at 5 AM with increased coughing and shortness of breath; then he sits on the side of the bed for relief. On his last discharge, Kevin was given a

nebulizer to be used q 4h when awake. He has attempted to use the nebulizer at 5 AM to relieve his shortness of breath, but he feels that he is not doing it properly. Kevin states that he has not felt rested over the past few weeks; yet, he dozes for only short periods during the day. He is more comfortable resting in a chair, with his legs elevated.

Cognitive-Perceptual

The patient (A+O×3) wears glasses for reading. He has good hearing and can hear a normal conversational tone. He is English-speaking and high-school educated. He denies any memory loss.

Roles-Relationship

Kevin has been living alone since the death of his mother in February 1985. He verbalizes feelings of grief over the loss of his mother, but reports that he has a strong, supportive relationship with his sister and brother-in-law, who reside nearby. He has never married because he "never found the right girl." However, he does report several strong friendships established over the past ten years while attending AA meetings.

The patient owns a one-family house with three flights of stairs. The bedrooms are on the third floor, and the bathroom is located on the first. He does his own shopping and cooking.

The patient has worked for many years as a machinist. During admission to the hospital in February 1985, the patient decided to apply for medical disability because of his declining health status. A social worker is involved in the case and has followed the patient since his last discharge.

Sexuality-Reproductive

The patient has never married. He denies having any children and prefers to "keep the topic private."

Coping-Stress

Kevin reports that he is anxious about and frustrated with his declining health status and the increased hospitalizations over the past year. Stressors include worsening asthma, his mother's recent death, the responsibility of caring for the house, concerns about his financial status and the "idle" time he will experience while he is in the process of being classified as medically disabled.

The patient understands the contraindications of smoking while having asthma, but he states that he smokes to prevent himself from drinking. He says, "I'm not going to lose my life to a bottle." He continues to attend AA meetings three to four times each week and states that this activity is effective in allaying his anxiety. He is willing to look into stop-smoking programs or hypnosis. The patient states that he is willing to verbalize feelings openly to the family and friends.

Values-Beliefs

The patient is a practicing Roman Catholic and values his relationship with his friends and family. He views himself as a strong, honest man. He also reports that, through AA attendance, he has established a strong faith in God and feels that his faith helps him cope with "what life sends his way." The patient states, "I try to utilize the 'One-day-at-a-time' approach in all aspects of my life." He needs to be around people and to be socially active.

Life-Patterns and Life-styles

A usual day for Kevin begins at 5 AM. After dealing with his shortness of breath, he prepares breakfast. Then he showers and goes to a local coffee shop, where he meets friends. He returns home for lunch and watches television. The patient attends AA meetings three to four times each week and socializes with friends at "Las Vegas" nights and church socials. His sister calls him daily, and they often "get together." He enjoys listening to the radio and reading.

Kevin views early retirement as the biggest change in life-style. It will be a hard adjustment for him, but feels that he can no longer adequately handle a demanding work situation. He approached the decision with ambivalence but was relieved after he made the decision. He fears that the "idle" time may lead to drinking, but he states that friends and the family try to keep him busy. Social service is helping the patient with his application for medical disability and the exploration of financial options.

NURSING CARE PLAN

NURSING HISTORY   FORMULATED BY Nancy O'Rourke, R.N.   DATE 4/28/85

49-year-old A&Ox3 w.m. w/long standing h/o asthma admitted on 4/28/85 with exacerbation of asthma. Reported usual precipitants of exacerbations include URI, stress, and dust. Presented with c.c. of increased SOB, fatigue, and productive cough (white sputum) for one week PTA. Symptoms persisted despite frequent rest periods and the use of an Alupent inhaler. On day of admission, pt noted increased wheezing, tightness, and breathlessness. Related present exacerbation to having apartment painted 2 weeks PTA and continued habit of smoking ½ pack of cigarettes per day. PMH includes asthma since 1978 (no h/o intubation), cigarette smoking 3 ppd for many years (presently smokes ½ ppd); h/o ETOH abuse (abstinent x 10 years), hepatitis, S/P, L herniorrhaphy, S/P vein stripping for varicose veins 1980. Needs PTA include Theodur 400 mg po tid, Prednisone 60 mg po qd (has been steroid dependent for 1 year; attempts to taper steroids prior to this led to exacerbations). Alupent inhaler q4° WA, Serax 30 mg po*

NURSING DIAGNOSIS	EXPECTED OUTCOME	NURSING CARE PLAN WITH NURSING ORDERS

1. Impaired gas exchange ineffective airway clearance related to asthma.	– To maintain adequate tissue oxygenation.
	– To decrease bronchial secretions and effectively drain secretions from airways.
		1. Administer O_2 2L nasal prong & room air heated nebulizer.
		2. Administer aminophylline and steroids intravenously as ordered.
		  A. Assess for side effects of meds.
		  B. Check heart rate q4°.
		  C. S/A urine.
		3. Encourage pt to cough and deep breathe q2°.
		4. Perform CPT q4° as ordered.
		5. Alupent treatments q4° as ordered, especially upon awakening.
		6. Maintain adequate fluid intake to 72L per day.
		7. Auscultate lungs to assess effectiveness of treatment.

2. Activity intolerance related to DOE and fatigue.	– To increase activity tolerance. – To enhance pt's self-esteem and combat fear of losing independence in ADL's.	1. Encourage pt to pace activities and to take frequent rest periods. 2. Set realistic exercise goals with pt. 3. Encourage walking at least 15–20" qd. 4. Devise a progressive activity program. 5. Teach energy conservation technique. A. Bedside commode or urinal for home use.
3. Sleep pattern disturbance related to increased SOB every morning.	– To promote restful sleep.	1. Encourage pt to establish a consistent bedtime. 2. Reinforce the use of the radio as a means for relaxation. 3. Offer Serax as ordered and warm milk at bedtime. 4. Elevate HOB to ease breathing. 5. Alupent treatment every morning upon awakening, as ordered.

*bid prn, and Mylanta alternating with Amphojel qid.
Resides alone in a one-family house (3 flights of stairs) in Boston. Presently in process of becoming medically disabled.

NURSING DIAGNOSIS	EXPECTED OUTCOME	NURSING CARE PLAN WITH NURSING ORDERS
4. Anxiety related to declining health status, fear of losing independence and changing occupational and financial status.	– To decrease anxiety.	1. Administer Serax prn as ordered. 2. Encourage pt to ventilate feelings. 3. Continued social service involvement to assist with medical disability. 4. Explore option of volunteer work with pt.
5. Potential ineffective coping secondary to problem #4 and fear of drinking.	– To help pt cope effectively, sobriety will be maintained.	1. Do not pressure pt to quit smoking. Give gentle, repetitious reminders that quitting may be important to him. 2. Give pamphlets on stop smoking programs and hypnosis centers. 3. Notify hospital's A.A. counselor of pt's admission. 4. Help pt explore alternative coping mechanisms.
6. Knowledge deficit R/T proper use of nebulizer and S/S that warrant hospitalization.	– Pt will demonstrate proper use of nebulizer.	1. Give written and verbal information about asthma and its treatment. 2. Encourage pt to see a doctor at onset of worsening symptoms or change in status. 3. Instruct pt on proper use of nebulizer with return demonstrations. 4. Give med card to pt and teach actions with drug administration.
7. Altered bowel status: constipation 2° to decreased activity, decreased fluid intake, and Amphojel.	– To establish regular bowel pattern.	1. Administer MOM qhs and Colace tid as ordered. 2. Provide prune juice and bran with breakfast. 3. Maintain liberal fluid intake. 4. Alternate Amphojel with Mylanta, as ordered.
8. D/C planning.	– Home with maximum supports.	1. VNA & chest physical therapy 3-4 x/week. 2. Home O₂. 3. Bedside commode. 4. ? hospital bed. 5. Medication teaching card. 6. Follow-up with private M.D. 7. Write and call in VNA referral.

Patient Care Referral Form

FROM: Dr. M.	Patient's Hospital Record # 03-25-58

FROM: Dr. M.

Unit/Clinic Beth Israel Hospital

ADDRESS 330 Brookline Ave.

Boston, MA   TEL. 735-2000

ADM. DATE 4/28/85   DISCH. DATE 5/8/85

TO: VNA

ADDRESS: 2 Main St.

Ringe, MA   TEL. 521-0011

MEDICARE NO. & LETTER 111-22-3121D   PLAN A B   BLUE CROSS NO.

CLINIC APPOINTMENTS   DATE   TIME

BCHC   5/15/85   3 pm

PATIENT NAME Kevin

ADDRESS: 1234 Pine Street

Ringe, MA   TEL. 123-4567

FLOOR 1   APT. #   BIRTHDATE 1/1/36

AGE 49   SEX M F   MARITAL STATUS M W D SEP.   RELIGION Catholic

RELATIVE OR GUARDIAN: J. Kin

ADDRESS: 2135 Maple Road

Ringe, MA   TEL. 765-4321

SOC. SEC. NO. 111-22-3333   OTHER

Agency Worker Office Address Telephone

DIAGNOSIS (S) Surgery Performed and Date, Allergies or Infections

Exacerbation of asthma

Is Patient   Family   aware of diagnosis? yes

Date of last physical

PHYSICIAN'S ORDERS: (Include specific orders for Diet, Lab Tests, Speech, and O.T.)

TRANSPORT BY: ☐ Ambulance ☒ Car

MEDICATION	STRENGTH AND FREQUENCY	DATE & TIME OF LAST DOSE
Theodur 400 mg po tid		
Prednisone 60 mg po qd		
Mylanta/Amphojel qid		
Serax 30 mg po bid prn		
Colace 100 mg po tid		
Alupent via nebulizer q4° while awake		

TREATMENTS & FREQUENCY: Assess lungs, arrange home O$_2$
CPT 3-4x/wk.

DIET: as tolerated

PHYSICAL THERAPY: Restrict Activity ☐Yes ☒No   Sensation Impaired ☐Yes ☐No

Precautions   Weight Bearing Status - Non-Weight ☐   Partial-Weight ☐   Full-Weight ☐

SPECIFIC TREATMENT & FREQUENCY: Chest p/t 3-4 x/wk. Respiratory rehabilitation.

ANTICIPATED GOALS: Pt to obtain optimal respiratory function.

REHABILITATION POTENTIAL IS: good

HOME HEALTH SERVICES: ☒NURSING ☐OCC. THERAPY ☐SPEECH THERAPY ☐SOCIAL WORK ☒H.H. AIDE ☐OTHER - SPECIFY

The above services require Level of Care: ☐I ☐II ☐III ☐IV

If Chronic Hospital, why?

CERTIFICATION: ✱(when applicable)
Services above needed to treat condition for which patient was hospitalized ☐Yes ☐No
I certify that the above named patient is: (check one)
☐Under my care (or has been referred to another physician having professional knowledge of patient's condition); is home bound except when receiving outpatient services; requires skilled nursing care on an intermittent basis or physical or speech therapy as specified in the orders.
☐Requires skilled nursing care on a continuing basis for any of the conditions for which he/she received care during this hospitalization.

Signature ___ M.D.

Dr. M. ___ M.D.
Print Name

Tel. 229-9222   Date 5/85   Will follow ☒Yes ☐No - If no, who?
___ M.D.

ADDRESS: 330 Brookline Ave.   TEL.

282-956   9/85

APPROVED BY THE MASSACHUSETTS DEPARTMENT OF PUBLIC HEALTH

DISTRIBUTION — **WHITE** — RECEIVING   **PINK** — MEDICAL RECORDS   **YELLOW** — C.C. SERVICE

Page 2
Patient Care Referral Form

Name _____ Kevin _____

Record # _____ 11-22-33 _____

Transfer to: _____

NURSING: Self Care Status Check Functional Level		Inde-pendent	Needs Assist-ance	Unable
Ambulation	Bed–Chair	X		
	Walking	X		
	Stairs	X		
	Wheelchair			
	Crutches			
	Walker			
	Cane			
Activities	Bathe self	X		
	Dress self	X		
	Feed self	X		
	Brushing teeth	X		
	Shaving			
	Toilet	X		
	Commode			
	Bedpan/Urinal			

Bowel & Bladder Program ☐ Yes ☐ No

Incontinence: Bladder☐ Bowel☐
Date of Last Enema

Catheter: Type
Date last changed:

Weight 154 Height 5'9" Date

Anointed Yes☐ No☐ Date

Check if Pertinent: (describe at right) ◊

DISABILITIES
- ☐ Amputation
- ☐ Paralysis
- ☐ Contractures
- ☐ Decubitus
- ☐ Other

IMPAIRMENTS
- ☐ Speech
- ☐ Hearing
- ☐ Vision
- ☐ Sensation
- ☑ Other reading glasses

COMMUNICATION
- ☐ Can Write
- ☐ Talks
- ☐ Understands Speaking
- ☐ Understands English
- ☐ If no, Other Language?
- ☐ Reads
- ☐ Non-Verbal

BEHAVIOR
- ☑ Alert
- ☐ Forgetful
- ☐ Noisy
- ☐ Confused
- ☐ Withdrawn
- ☐ Wanders
- ☐ Other

REQUIRES
Mark "S" if sent; "N" if needed
- ☐ Colostomy Care
- ☐ Cane
- ☐ Crutches
- ☐ Walker
- ☐ Wheelchair
- ☒ Other home oxygen, bedside commode, hospital bed
- ☐ Dentures
- ☐ Eye Glasses
- ☐ Hearing Aid
- ☐ Prosthesis
- ☐ Side Rails

PATIENT CARE PLAN
(Explain details of care, medications, treatments, teaching, habits, preferences, and goals.)

Medications: Note time last dose given on day of discharge.

49-year-old A + Ox3 w.m. admitted with acerbation of asthma. Patient presented with c.c. of increased SOB, fatigue, and productive cough (white sputum) 1 week PTA. Symptoms persisted despite frequent rest periods and use of Alupent inhaler. Relates precipitant of attack to apartment being painted 2 weeks PTA and continual smoking habit of ½ ppd. Usual precipitants of exacerbations are URI, stress, and dust. PMH asthma since 1978, no H/O intubation. ETOH abuse, cigarettes 3 ppd x many years (presently ½ ppd), hepatitis, S/P herniorrhaphy 1968, S/P vein stripping for varicose veins 1980.

Hospital Course

Resp On admission pt in mod resp distress. Initially treated with O$_2$2LNP, IV Aminophylline, IV steroids, CPT, and Alupent medications on 5/4/85. Tolerated this well. Continued to experience increased cough and SOB upon awakening, alleviated with O$_2$2LNP and Alupent via nebulizer on Prednisone 60 mg qd (steroid dependent for 1 year). FBS140 S/A Neg/Neg Theophylline level 5/7 14.2. Pt states his respiratory status is at baseline with minimal SOB upon exertion.

Lungs Clear with decreased breath sounds at bases; no rales, no pedal edema. Cough productive of clear-white sputum, benefits from CPT. VS T = 98, P = 88, R = 24, BP = 108/60.

Activity PTA pt unable to care properly for himself due to minimal activity causing severe fatigue and SOB. During early admission, pt required assist with ADL's; as resp status improved, pt returned to baseline of independence in conservation techniques.

Signature of Nurse _____
Telephone _____ Date _____

NUTRITION: (discuss food preferences, understanding of diet, teaching needs and goals) Diet enclosed ☐Yes ☐No

620-22M - 821-640 9/85

APPROVED BY THE MASSACHUSETTS DEPARTMENT OF PUBLIC HEALTH

Nutritionist Signature _____ Telephone _____ Date _____

White - Receiving Facility   Canary - Medical Records   Pink - C.C. Services

Page 2
Patient Care Referral Form

Name __Kevin__

Record # __11-22-33__

Transfer to: _____

NURSING: Self Care Status Check Functional Level		Independent	Needs Assistance	Unable
Ambulation	Bed--Chair			
	Walking			
	Stairs			
	Wheelchair			
	Crutches			
	Walker			
	Cane			
Activities	Bathe self			
	Dress self			
	Feed self			
	Brushing teeth			
	Shaving			
	Toilet			
	Commode			
	Bedpan/Urinal			

Bowel & Bladder Program ☐Yes ☐No

Incontinence: Bladder☐ Bowel☐
Date of Last Enema

Catheter: Type
Date last changed:

Weight	Height	Date
Anointed Yes☐ No☐		Date

Check if Pertinent: (describe at right) ▷

DISABILITIES
☐ Amputation
☐ Paralysis
☐ Contractures
☐ Decubitus
☐ Other

IMPAIRMENTS
☐ Speech
☐ Hearing
☐ Vision
☐ Sensation
☐ Other

COMMUNICATION
☐ Can Write
☐ Talks
☐ Understands Speaking
☐ Understands English
☐ If no, Other Language?
☐ Reads
☐ Non-Verbal

BEHAVIOR
☐ Alert
☐ Forgetful
☐ Noisy
☐ Confused
☐ Withdrawn
☐ Wanders
☐ Other

REQUIRES
Mark "S" if sent; "N" if needed
☐ Colostomy Care ☐ Dentures
☐ Cane ☐ Eye Glasses
☐ Crutches ☐ Hearing Aid
☐ Walker ☐ Prosthesis
☐ Wheelchair ☐ Side Rails
☐ Other

PATIENT CARE PLAN
(Explain details of care, medications, treatments, teaching, habits, preferences, and goals.)

Medications: Note time last dose given on day of discharge.

Presently living in a 1-family house with 3 flights of stairs. Bedroom is on the 3rd floor, and the bathroom is on the first floor. Reports DOE when going to the bathroom during the night. Bedside commode may be helpful.

Future plans include moving into a one-room apartment with goal to conserve energy and maintain independence. Feels owning home is too much responsibility financially and physically.

Anxiety Pt is an anxious man; he is well known to me from previous admissions. He openly verbalizes concerns re present declining health status and the probability of resp deterioration. Continues to smoke ½ ppd as a means of coping. ETOH abuse while hospitalized. Is willing to attend hypnosis or stop smoking programs. Will need FLU.

Other stresses include recent death of mother and being in the process of becoming medically disabled (Social Service following). Serax po bid 30 mg helped allay anxiety. Pt has supportive sister and friends.

Sleep Experiences difficulty sleeping; Serax 30 mg po with qhs. Warm milk at bedtime helped. Sleeps with HOB elevated. Awakes at 5 am with SOB and increased coughing. Alupent treatment and O_2 helped. Pt instructed on proper use of nebulizer, still feels "unsure" of himself with nebulizer. Will need supervision and home O_2.

Elimination Constipated upon admission, resolved with MOM. On antacids Mylanta/Amphojel qid for indigestion.

Signature of Nurse
Telephone _____ Date _____

NUTRITION: (discuss food preferences, understanding of diet, teaching needs and goals) Diet enclosed ☐Yes ☐No

620-22M - 821-640 9/85

APPROVED BY THE MASSACHUSETTS DEPARTMENT OF PUBLIC HEALTH

Nutritionist Signature
Telephone Date
White - Receiving Facility | Canary - Medical Records | Pink - C.C. Services

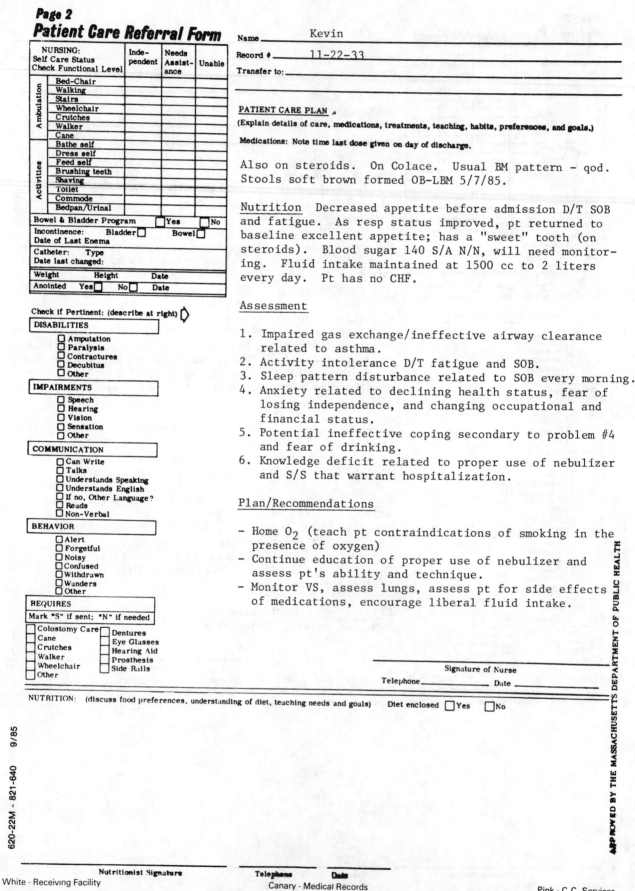

Page 2
Patient Care Referral Form

Name _____ Kevin

Record # _____ 11-22-33

Transfer to: _____

NURSING: Self Care Status Check Functional Level		Inde-pendent	Needs Assist-ance	Unable
Ambulation	Bed-Chair			
	Walking			
	Stairs			
	Wheelchair			
	Crutches			
	Walker			
	Cane			
Activities	Bathe self			
	Dress self			
	Feed self			
	Brushing teeth			
	Shaving			
	Toilet			
	Commode			
	Bedpan/Urinal			

Bowel & Bladder Program ☐ Yes ☐ No

Incontinence: Bladder ☐ Bowel ☐
Date of Last Enema

Catheter: Type
Date last changed:

Weight	Height	Date
Anointed Yes ☐ No ☐		Date

Check if Pertinent: (describe at right) ▷

DISABILITIES
- ☐ Amputation
- ☐ Paralysis
- ☐ Contractures
- ☐ Decubitus
- ☐ Other

IMPAIRMENTS
- ☐ Speech
- ☐ Hearing
- ☐ Vision
- ☐ Sensation
- ☐ Other

COMMUNICATION
- ☐ Can Write
- ☐ Talks
- ☐ Understands Speaking
- ☐ Understands English
- ☐ If no, Other Language?
- ☐ Reads
- ☐ Non-Verbal

BEHAVIOR
- ☐ Alert
- ☐ Forgetful
- ☐ Noisy
- ☐ Confused
- ☐ Withdrawn
- ☐ Wanders
- ☐ Other

REQUIRES
Mark "S" if sent; "N" if needed
- ☐ Colostomy Care
- ☐ Cane
- ☐ Crutches
- ☐ Walker
- ☐ Wheelchair
- ☐ Other
- ☐ Dentures
- ☐ Eye Glasses
- ☐ Hearing Aid
- ☐ Prosthesis
- ☐ Side Rails

PATIENT CARE PLAN ⌄
(Explain details of care, medications, treatments, teaching, habits, preferences, and goals.)

Medications: Note time last dose given on day of discharge.

Also on steroids. On Colace. Usual BM pattern – qod. Stools soft brown formed OB-LBM 5/7/85.

Nutrition Decreased appetite before admission D/T SOB and fatigue. As resp status improved, pt returned to baseline excellent appetite; has a "sweet" tooth (on steroids). Blood sugar 140 S/A N/N, will need monitoring. Fluid intake maintained at 1500 cc to 2 liters every day. Pt has no CHF.

Assessment

1. Impaired gas exchange/ineffective airway clearance related to asthma.
2. Activity intolerance D/T fatigue and SOB.
3. Sleep pattern disturbance related to SOB every morning.
4. Anxiety related to declining health status, fear of losing independence, and changing occupational and financial status.
5. Potential ineffective coping secondary to problem #4 and fear of drinking.
6. Knowledge deficit related to proper use of nebulizer and S/S that warrant hospitalization.

Plan/Recommendations

- Home O_2 (teach pt contraindications of smoking in the presence of oxygen)
- Continue education of proper use of nebulizer and assess pt's ability and technique.
- Monitor VS, assess lungs, assess pt for side effects of medications, encourage liberal fluid intake.

_____
Signature of Nurse
Telephone _____ Date _____

NUTRITION: (discuss food preferences, understanding of diet, teaching needs and goals)   Diet enclosed ☐ Yes ☐ No

_____
Nutritionist Signature
White - Receiving Facility

Telephone   Date
Canary - Medical Records

Pink - C.C. Services

620-22M - 821-640   9/85

APPROVED BY THE MASSACHUSETTS DEPARTMENT OF PUBLIC HEALTH

Page 2
Patient Care Referral Form

Name ___Kevin___

Record # ___11-22-33___

Transfer to: _____

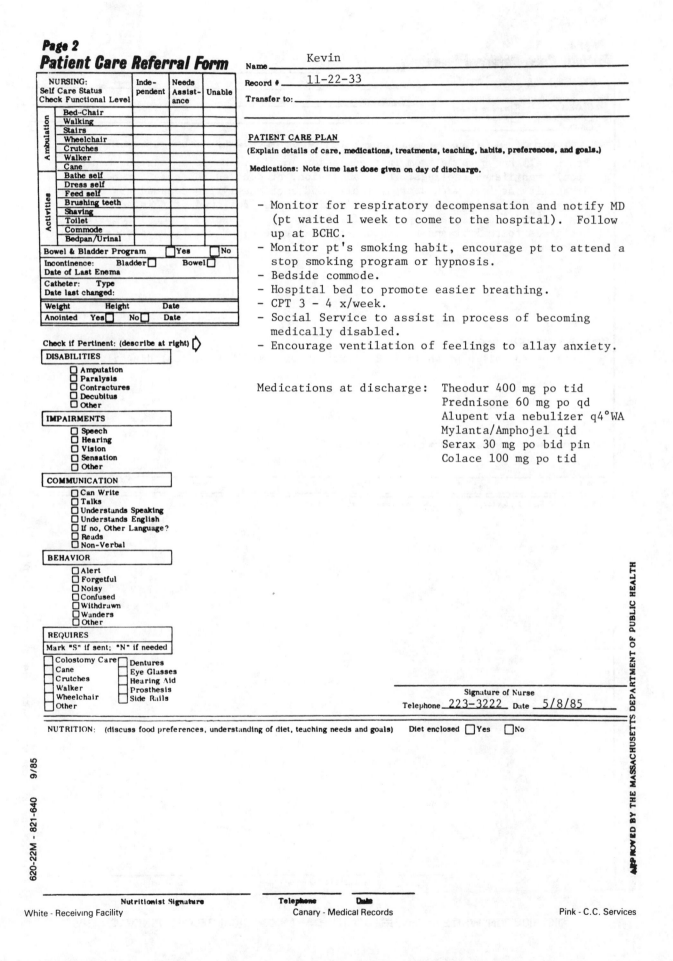

NURSING: Self Care Status Check Functional Level		Inde-pendent	Needs Assist-ance	Unable
Ambulation	Bed-Chair			
	Walking			
	Stairs			
	Wheelchair			
	Crutches			
	Walker			
	Cane			
Activities	Bathe self			
	Dress self			
	Feed self			
	Brushing teeth			
	Shaving			
	Toilet			
	Commode			
	Bedpan/Urinal			

Bowel & Bladder Program ☐ Yes ☐ No

Incontinence: Bladder ☐ Bowel ☐
Date of Last Enema

Catheter: Type
Date last changed:

Weight	Height	Date
Anointed Yes ☐ No ☐	Date	

Check if Pertinent: (describe at right) ▷

DISABILITIES
- ☐ Amputation
- ☐ Paralysis
- ☐ Contractures
- ☐ Decubitus
- ☐ Other

IMPAIRMENTS
- ☐ Speech
- ☐ Hearing
- ☐ Vision
- ☐ Sensation
- ☐ Other

COMMUNICATION
- ☐ Can Write
- ☐ Talks
- ☐ Understands Speaking
- ☐ Understands English
- ☐ If no, Other Language?
- ☐ Reads
- ☐ Non-Verbal

BEHAVIOR
- ☐ Alert
- ☐ Forgetful
- ☐ Noisy
- ☐ Confused
- ☐ Withdrawn
- ☐ Wanders
- ☐ Other

REQUIRES
Mark "S" if sent; "N" if needed
- ☐ Colostomy Care
- ☐ Cane
- ☐ Crutches
- ☐ Walker
- ☐ Wheelchair
- ☐ Other
- ☐ Dentures
- ☐ Eye Glasses
- ☐ Hearing Aid
- ☐ Prosthesis
- ☐ Side Rails

PATIENT CARE PLAN
(Explain details of care, medications, treatments, teaching, habits, preferences, and goals.)

Medications: Note time last dose given on day of discharge.

- Monitor for respiratory decompensation and notify MD (pt waited 1 week to come to the hospital). Follow up at BCHC.
- Monitor pt's smoking habit, encourage pt to attend a stop smoking program or hypnosis.
- Bedside commode.
- Hospital bed to promote easier breathing.
- CPT 3 - 4 x/week.
- Social Service to assist in process of becoming medically disabled.
- Encourage ventilation of feelings to allay anxiety.

Medications at discharge: Theodur 400 mg po tid
Prednisone 60 mg po qd
Alupent via nebulizer q4°WA
Mylanta/Amphojel qid
Serax 30 mg po bid pin
Colace 100 mg po tid

Signature of Nurse
Telephone ___223-3222___ Date ___5/8/85___

NUTRITION: (discuss food preferences, understanding of diet, teaching needs and goals) Diet enclosed ☐ Yes ☐ No

620-22M - 821-640   9/85

APPROVED BY THE MASSACHUSETTS DEPARTMENT OF PUBLIC HEALTH

Nutritionist Signature   Telephone   Date

White - Receiving Facility   Canary - Medical Records   Pink - C.C. Services

Page 3
Patient Care Referral Form

Name: _____Kevin_____

Record # ___11-22-33_____

Transfer to: _____

SOCIAL SERVICE:

Prior to hospitalization, patient lived:
- [X] Alone
- [ ] With Family
- [ ] Other _____
- [ ] Nursing Home
- [ ] With Friends

SOCIAL INFORMATION (including patient's personality, attitude toward illness and family constellation and inter-relationships)

Pt is well known to me from last admission in 2/85. He is an anxious man and openly ventilates feelings. Last admission, pt decided to apply for medical disability as felt work was physically and emotionally too demanding. Process was initiated; presently awaiting finalizations. Followed pt this admission, his work will continue to pay him for 26 weeks. Presently lives in one-family but plans to sell it and rent a one-room apartment. Has a close sister and many

Identified Problems: friends.

Plan (include short and long range plans)

Continue to follow pt while in the process of obtaining medical disability.

Will referring unit social worker plan to follow patient: Yes [X]   No [ ]

Jane Kane   735-2000   5/8/85

| Name | Signature & Title | Phone | Date |

THERAPIES (P.T., O.T., Speech)   Instructions enclosed: Yes [ ] No [ ]

Signature of Therapist   Phone   Date

620-17M - 681-262 - 9/85

APPROVED BY THE MASSACHUSETTS DEPARTMENT OF PUBLIC HEALTH

RECEIVING FACILITY
DISTRIBUTION: **WHITE**-RECEIVING FACILITY; **CANARY**-MEDICAL RECORD; **PINK**-C.C. SERVICE

BURNS

FHPAA

General Summary

The patient, a 31-year-old white woman, was admitted to the emergency unit on June 22, 1985, with a 2° burn on her right thigh. She was accompanied by a neighbor. The patient was boiling water on the stove. When removing it, she lost her grip on the handle so that water spilled and splashed on her leg. An active, healthy housewife and mother of two preschool-aged children, she had no health problems and took no medications. She indicated that she was allergic to penicillin. She had no valuables in her possession. Her husband was notified; he came to the hospital. The children were cared for by a neighbor.

The patient was alert, oriented ×3, and without pain in the right thigh. The wound was approximately 7 × 12 cm, with irregularly shaped edges. The tissue was pink, had several intact blisters, and blanched to the touch. There was no surrounding inflammation. The limb distal to the wound was without edema; warm to the touch; and had good color, sensation, and movement. The patient's vital signs were recorded as follows: Temp, 36.9°C, p.o.; pulse rate, 88 beats per minute; respirations, 28/min; BP, 140/92. She received tetanus toxoid in the emergency unit.

Pattern Areas

Health Perception–Health Management

The patient has no other medical problems—no past surgeries. She takes no medications. She smokes one pack of cigarettes each day, and ETOH is minimal.

Self-Perception–Self-Concept

The patient is upset about this admission on account of the uncertainty about child care. She is visibly restless and speaks very quickly. Her muscles are tense.

Roles-Relationship

The patient lives with her husband and two preschool-aged children. The husband, when notified of her admission, indicated that he would come to the hospital. The children are presently with a neighbor. The patient is anxious about the care of the children while she is hospitalized.

Coping-Stress

The patient has the usual coping pattern. She uses talking with her husband and friends to resolve conflict.

Cognitive-Perceptual

Alert and oriented ×3, the patient has no problems with her vision, her hearing, her speech, or her sensation. She has no prostheses.

Activity-Exercise

The patient is presently unable to ambulate because of 2° pain. However, she has full range of movement in all extremities.

Nutritional-Metabolic

The patient has no special diet and no food dislikes or allergies. She does not wear dentures. Her skin is dry; her hair and nails are in good condition.

Elimination

The patient moves bowels every day without laxatives.

Sleep-Rest

She has no difficulty sleeping at night and uses no sleeping aids.

Values-Beliefs

The patient deferred response.

Sexuality-Reproductive

The patient deferred response.

Anticipated Discharge Status

The patient can return to her home. VNA will provide assistance for dressing changes.

Assessment and Plan

The patient's continuing care assessment is as follows:

- impaired skin integrity from 2° burn
- alteration in comfort from 2° burn
- potential for infection from 2° burn
- impaired physical mobility from 2° pain and burn
- moderate anxiety related to child care

The continuing care plan calls for wound care, pain relief, protection from infection, and increase of patient's mobility.

FHPA

Pattern Areas

Health Perception–Health Management

This is the patient's first hospital admission. She perceives herself as healthy; she eats well; and she gets plenty of exercise. She has a yearly physical examination by the family physician. The last examination was received eight months ago. She takes no medications. Although she is allergic to penicillin, she does not wear an allergy bracelet. The burn has not changed the patient's feelings about her perceived health; she feels that being healthy means being free of any long-term disease.

Nutritional-Metabolic

The patient describes a daily intake of three well-balanced meals. Although she follows no special diet, she does avoid foods high in calories and cholesterol and does not snack. She drinks one glass of wine each day with dinner. She is 5 ft 5 in tall and weighs 120 lb. There has been no change in weight over the past year. She is pleased with her present weight. The patient is responsible for grocery shopping and meal preparation. She does not wear dentures. She has her teeth cleaned every six months by a hygienist and sees her dentist once each year. Her teeth are in good condition; there is no gum disease; the mucosa is pink and moist. Her nails and hair are clean and well groomed. She reports that because she has chronic dry skin, she uses baby oil during her shower. Her right-thigh wound is pink with granulation tissue present; there is one intact blister and much serous fluid.

Elimination

The patient has a daily BM. She has no history of constipation or diarrhea and does not use laxatives. There is no history of frequency or urgency of urination, and no nocturia. She drinks plenty of fluids.

Activity-Exercise

The patient is very active with the children and housework. Although she enjoys walking, skiing in winter, and feels that exercise is important to both health and physical appearance, the patient has no formal exercise regime. Nevertheless, she feels physically fit. She ambulates very slowly and needs much encouragement because of the 2° pain.

Sleep-Rest

The patient, who sleeps 7 to 8 h/night, is well rested upon awakening. She does not use sleeping pills and has no difficulty falling asleep. Usually, she does not awaken during the night. She does not nap during the day, but she does relax with her husband after dinner.

Cognitive-Perceptual

The patient has no problems with vision, so she does not wear glasses. Observations of her speech and hearing are normal. She hears normal speech or sensation and uses no assistive devices. She learns best by reading and verbal instruction. The patient admits to having a low tolerance for pain. She complains of pain in her right thigh and grimaces and cries. Her BP increases during dressing changes. Oxycodone hydrochloride with acetaminophen (Percocet) provides the patient with partial relief.

Self-Perception–Self-Concept

The patient is satisfied in her role as wife and mother. She takes pride in her appearance and is meticulous. Anxious about "What the leg will look like after the burn heals," she verbalizes her reluctance to have the leg exposed (ie, in shorts or a bathing suit). The patient will not allow her husband to see the wound. She will not watch dressing changes; moreover, she is unwilling to learn dressing-change procedure. The patient's children are staying with a neighbor during her hospitalization. This arrangement is satisfactory to her.

Roles-Relationship

The patient lives with her husband and two preschool-aged children. She is a housewife who assumes responsibility for the care of her home and her children. She does not have post-discharge arrangements for day care. Her husband works full time; his income is adequate to support the family.

Sexuality-Reproductive

She reports satisfaction with her sexual relationship with her husband. Because the patient does not wish to have any more children, she uses the diaphragm for birth control. She does not perform breast self-examination on a regular basis.

Coping-Stress

The patient has had no major stressors in the past. Her husband is her main support. She depicts a stable family life. (See admission assessment for her usual coping pattern.)

Values-Beliefs

The patient is a Roman Catholic but does not practice her religion. She does not wish to see a religious leader. She values most her health and the health of her family. The patient also values the relationship she shares with her family and close friends.

NURSING CARE PLAN

NURSING HISTORY   FORMULATED BY   Heidi B. Picard, RN   DATE 6/22/85

31-year-old female admitted via Emergency Unit with a 2° burn on right thigh due to spillage of boiling water. Received tetanus toxoid. Wound is 7 x 12 cm with one intact blister. Patient has a husband and 2 preschool children. No significant past medical history and does not take any medications. Allergic to Penicillin.

NURSING DIAGNOSIS	EXPECTED OUTCOME	NURSING CARE PLAN WITH NURSING ORDERS
1. Impaired skin integrity 2° burn.	Pt will state the reasons for wound care and its importance.	A. Dressing Change T.I.D.: 1. Wash off old Silvadene cream – debride any loose eschar prn. 2. Assess progress of granulation and epithelialization of wound. 3. Leave blister intact until opens on its own. 4. Culture wound Q.O.D. 5. Dressing: – contact layer: apply thin layer of Silvadene (1/8") – absorbent layer: apply 4x4 gauze. – protective layer: wrap with Kerlix gauze. * Use Xeroform once granulation begins. B. Precautions if needed – consult infectious disease nurse. C. Monitor circulatory status of extremity: monitor pulses, color, sensation, and movement of right thigh. D. Explain all steps of wound care to pt and its importance.
2. Alteration in comfort 2° burn.	Pt will verbalize the presence of pain and degree of relief after medication is given. Pt will state the degree of pain on a scale of 1 (mild) to 10 (severe) before and after pain medication.	A. Premedicate pt with narcotic analgesic (i.e. Percocet) ½ hour prior to dressing change and ambulation. B. Teach relaxation techniques (distraction, guided imagery). C. Elevate thigh on pillow to decrease swelling. D. Allow pt some flexibility in scheduling of dressing changes, but adhere to prearranged schedule except in extraordinary circumstances. E. Encourage pt to verbalize presence of pain and degree of relief after medication.

NURSING DIAGNOSIS	EXPECTED OUTCOME	NURSING CARE PLAN WITH NURSING ORDERS
		F. Assess and document degree, severity, and duration of pain - use pain scale (1-10) before and after medication to assess relief.
3. Body image disturbance 2° body disfigurement.	Pt will verbalize her feelings regarding the impact of the burn on her appearance.	A. Provide an outlet for pt to express her concerns, feelings and fears. B. Use pt's coping mechanism of talking to elicit feelings and to allay fears. C. Encourage verbalization of fears. D. Teach pt relaxation techniques and use diversion during dressing changes (i.e. television and conversation). E. Support pt through the grieving process. F. Involve husband in her care and support. G. Social Service referral, psychiatric referral prn. H. Arrange visit from a successfully recovered burn patient. I. Be open and honest with pt, provide realistic reassurance, explain all procedures and the healing process. Emphasize the temporary aspect of the disfigurement.
4. Impaired physical mobility 2° pain and burn.	Pt will ambulate outside her room three times per day for 10 minute periods.	A. Physical therapy consult, occupational therapy if needed. B. Ensure proper alignment while in bed or chair. C. Elevate affected area above level of heart. D. Assist pt through active assisted ROM exercises during dressing change. E. Encourage frequent and brief ambulation as tolerated to preserve function of unaffected extremity. F. Premedicate ½ hour prior to ambulation.
5. Potential for infection 2° burn.	Pt will state the signs and symptoms of infection.	A. Assess for signs and symptoms of infection (increased temperature, erythema, edema, pain, purulent drainage, and foul odor). B. Antibiotics as per physician. C. Restrict visitors/personnel with infections from entering the room. D. Teach pt signs and symptoms of infection and the importance of informing her physician if such signs occur after discharge.

NURSING DIAGNOSIS	EXPECTED OUTCOME	NURSING CARE PLAN WITH NURSING ORDERS
6. Health management deficit related to discharge planning 2° in ability to perform wound care.	Pt will return to her home upon discharge with support services. Pt will perform dressing change and skin care independently.	A. Wound Care 1. Involve pt in dressing change once she is able to look at her wound. 2. Teach pt continued skin care: normal bathing, moisturizing cream daily (cocoa butter, vitamin E, lanolin); prevent exposure to direct sunlight for 1 year - use sunscreen; prevent exposure to cold - protect thigh with layers of clothing in winter months. 3. VNA referral for dressing changes. B. Nutrition 1. Instruct pt to maintain a balanced diet. 2. Instruct pt to add one extra serving containing protein and vitamin C. C. Safety 1. Review safety issues with pt as her burn resulted from spillage of boiling water. D. Support Services 1. VNA for wound care. 2. Social Service to arrange day care services for children. 3. Outpatient social worker or therapy to support pt and family and to assist pt to resolve her feelings regarding self-concept.

Patient Care Referral Form

Patient's Hospital Record # _____

FROM: _____ Beth Israel Hospital

Unit/Clinic _____ Burn Unit

ADDRESS _____ 330 Brookline Ave.

_____ Boston, MA _____ TEL. 735-0000

| ADM. DATE | 6/20/85 | DISCH. DATE | 6/30/85 |

TO: _____

ADDRESS: _____

_____ TEL. _____

PATIENT NAME _____

ADDRESS: 22 Red Road

Jason Village, MA _____ TEL. 999-6666

| FLOOR | | APT. # | BIRTHDATE |
| AGE 31 | SEX M X | MARITAL STATUS S M W D SEP. | RELIGION Roman Catholic |

RELATIVE OR GUARDIAN: Husband - John

ADDRESS: Same as above

_____ TEL. _____

| MEDICARE NO. & LETTER | PLAN A B | BLUE CROSS NO. 543210 | SOC. SEC. NO. 111-999-0000 | OTHER |

| CLINIC APPOINTMENTS | DATE | TIME | Agency Worker Office Address Telephone |
| Vascular Clinic | 7/3/85 | 10 am | |

DIAGNOSIS (S) Surgery Performed and Date, Allergies or Infections

2° burn on right thigh
Allergic to Penicillin

Is Patient Family aware of diagnosis? Yes

Date of last physical 10/84

PHYSICIAN'S ORDERS: (Include specific orders for Diet, Lab Tests, Speech, and O.T.)

TRANSPORT BY: ☐ Ambulance ☒ Car

| MEDICATION | STRENGTH AND FREQUENCY | DATE & TIME OF LAST DOSE |
| Percocet T | tabs q 4-6° prn pain | 6/30/85 |

TREATMENTS & FREQUENCY: Dressing changes B.I.D.

DIET: regular with increased protein and vitamin C

PHYSICAL THERAPY: Restrict Activity ☐ Yes ☐ No Sensation Impaired ☐ Yes ☐ No

Precautions Weight Bearing Status - Non-Weight ☐ Partial-Weight ☐ Full-Weight ☐

SPECIFIC TREATMENT & FREQUENCY: Not needed at this time.

ANTICIPATED GOALS: _____

REHABILITATION POTENTIAL IS: _____

HOME HEALTH SERVICES: ☒ NURSING ☐ OCC. THERAPY ☐ SPEECH THERAPY ☐ SOCIAL WORK ☐ H.H. AIDE ☒ OTHER - SPECIFY Child day care

The above services require Level of Care: ☐ I ☐ II ☐ III ☐ IV

If Chronic Hospital, why? _____

9/85

282-956

CERTIFICATION: ✱(when applicable)
Services above needed to treat condition for which patient was hospitalized ☐ Yes ☐ No
I certify that the above named patient is: (check one)
☐ Under my care (or has been referred to another physician having professional knowledge of patient's condition); is home bound except when receiving out-patient services; requires skilled nursing care on an intermittent basis or physical or speech therapy as specified in the orders.
☐ Requires skilled nursing care on a continuing basis for any of the conditions for which he/she received care during this hospitalization.

_____ M.D.
Signature
Dr. East
_____ M.D.
Print Name
Tel. 222-2112 Date 6/26/85 Will follow ☒ Yes ☐ No - If no, who?
_____ M.D.
ADDRESS: _____ TEL. _____

APPROVED BY THE MASSACHUSETTS DEPARTMENT OF PUBLIC HEALTH

DISTRIBUTION — WHITE — RECEIVING   PINK — MEDICAL RECORDS   YELLOW — C.C. SERVICE

Page 2
Patient Care Referral Form

Name _____

Record # _____

Transfer to: _____ Home _____

NURSING: Self Care Status Check Functional Level		Inde- pendent	Needs Assist- ance	Unable
Ambulation	Bed-Chair	X		
	Walking	X		
	Stairs	X		
	Wheelchair			
	Crutches			
	Walker			
	Cane			
Activities	Bathe self	X		
	Dress self	X		
	Feed self	X		
	Brushing teeth	X		
	Shaving			
	Toilet	X		
	Commode	X		
	Bedpan/Urinal	X		

Bowel & Bladder Program ☐ Yes ☒ No

Incontinence: Bladder ☐ Bowel ☐

Date of Last Enema

Catheter: Type
Date last changed:

Weight 120 Height 5'5" Date

Anointed Yes ☐ No ☐ Date

Check if Pertinent: (describe at right) ▷

DISABILITIES
- ☐ Amputation
- ☐ Paralysis
- ☐ Contractures
- ☐ Decubitus
- ☐ Other

IMPAIRMENTS
- ☐ Speech
- ☐ Hearing
- ☐ Vision
- ☐ Sensation
- ☐ Other

COMMUNICATION
- ☐ Can Write
- ☐ Talks
- ☐ Understands Speaking
- ☐ Understands English
- ☐ If no, Other Language?
- ☐ Reads
- ☐ Non-Verbal

BEHAVIOR
- ☐ Alert
- ☐ Forgetful
- ☐ Noisy
- ☐ Confused
- ☐ Withdrawn
- ☐ Wanders
- ☐ Other

REQUIRES
Mark "S" if sent; "N" if needed
- ☐ Colostomy Care
- ☐ Cane
- ☐ Crutches
- ☐ Walker
- ☐ Wheelchair
- ☐ Other
- ☐ Dentures
- ☐ Eye Glasses
- ☐ Hearing Aid
- ☐ Prosthesis
- ☐ Side Rails

PATIENT CARE PLAN
(Explain details of care, medications, treatments, teaching, habits, preferences, and goals.)

Medications: Note time last dose given on day of discharge.

Pt is a 31-year-old female who was admitted to Beth Israel Hospital on 6/20/85 due to a 2° burn incurred after spilling boiling water on her right thigh. She is married with 2 children. She has been hospitalized for one week for dressing changes, mobilization, and pain control. She has an allergy to Penicillin but has no other significant past medical history. Her care plan for discharge is as follows:

Nursing Diagnosis	Nursing Care Plan
1. Impaired skin integrity 2° burn.	1. Dressing change: Xeroform to areas of granulation, 4x4 and Kerlix wrap. Assess for infection.
2. Alteration in comfort 2° pain.	2. Percocet T - q4-6° for pain, premedicate prior to dressing change. Continue to reinforce use of relaxation techniques. Assess pain relief after medication.
3. Body image disturbance.	3. Encourage verbalization of fears, use pt coping mechanism of talking to allay fears. Encourage pt to observe wound. Social worker/therapist to follow pt. Continue to emphasize the temporary aspect of the disfigurement. Support pt and husband.

_____
Signature of Nurse

Telephone _____ Date _____

NUTRITION: (discuss food preferences, understanding of diet, teaching needs and goals) Diet enclosed ☐ Yes ☒ No

Increase protein   – likes milkshakes, yogurt, and fish.
Increase Vitamin C – likes fruit juices.

Pt has been taught reasons for importance of increased protein and Vitamin C.

9/85

620-22M - 821-640

APPROVED BY THE MASSACHUSETTS DEPARTMENT OF PUBLIC HEALTH

_____
Nutritionist Signature

Telephone **Date**

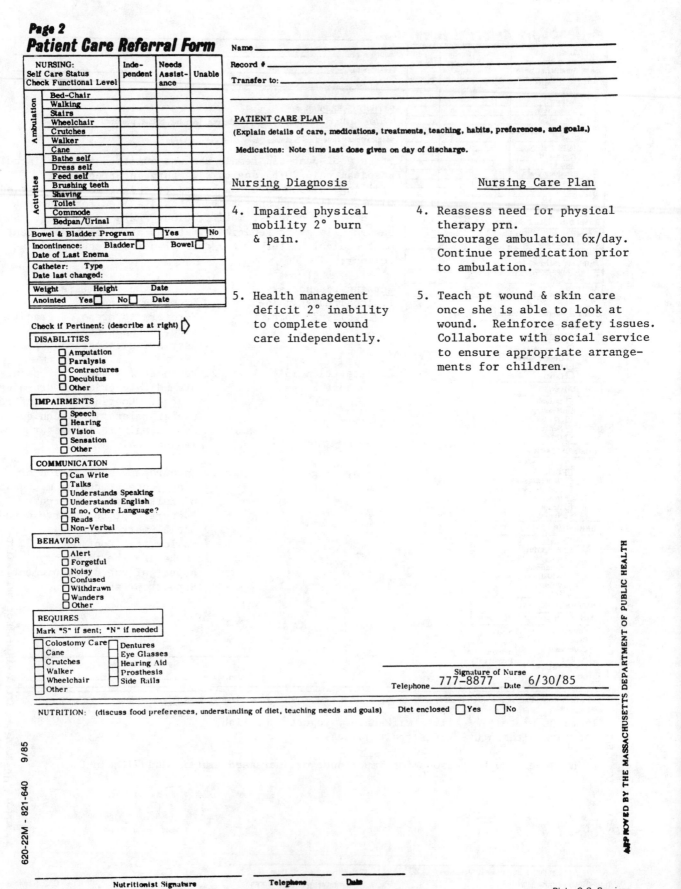

Page 2
Patient Care Referral Form

Name _____

Record # _____

Transfer to: _____

NURSING: Self Care Status Check Functional Level	Inde-pendent	Needs Assist-ance	Unable
Ambulation — Bed–Chair			
Walking			
Stairs			
Wheelchair			
Crutches			
Walker			
Cane			
Activities — Bathe self			
Dress self			
Feed self			
Brushing teeth			
Shaving			
Toilet			
Commode			
Bedpan/Urinal			

Bowel & Bladder Program ☐ Yes   ☐ No

Incontinence: Bladder ☐   Bowel ☐
Date of Last Enema

Catheter: Type
Date last changed:

Weight	Height	Date
Anointed Yes ☐ No ☐		Date

Check if Pertinent: (describe at right) ▷

DISABILITIES
☐ Amputation
☐ Paralysis
☐ Contractures
☐ Decubitus
☐ Other

IMPAIRMENTS
☐ Speech
☐ Hearing
☐ Vision
☐ Sensation
☐ Other

COMMUNICATION
☐ Can Write
☐ Talks
☐ Understands Speaking
☐ Understands English
☐ If no, Other Language?
☐ Reads
☐ Non-Verbal

BEHAVIOR
☐ Alert
☐ Forgetful
☐ Noisy
☐ Confused
☐ Withdrawn
☐ Wanders
☐ Other

REQUIRES
Mark "S" if sent; "N" if needed
☐ Colostomy Care   ☐ Dentures
☐ Cane   ☐ Eye Glasses
☐ Crutches   ☐ Hearing Aid
☐ Walker   ☐ Prosthesis
☐ Wheelchair   ☐ Side Rails
☐ Other

PATIENT CARE PLAN
(Explain details of care, medications, treatments, teaching, habits, preferences, and goals.)

Medications: Note time last dose given on day of discharge.

Nursing Diagnosis	Nursing Care Plan
4. Impaired physical mobility 2° burn & pain.	4. Reassess need for physical therapy prn. Encourage ambulation 6x/day. Continue premedication prior to ambulation.
5. Health management deficit 2° inability to complete wound care independently.	5. Teach pt wound & skin care once she is able to look at wound. Reinforce safety issues. Collaborate with social service to ensure appropriate arrangements for children.

Signature of Nurse
Telephone 777-8877   Date 6/30/85

NUTRITION: (discuss food preferences, understanding of diet, teaching needs and goals)   Diet enclosed ☐ Yes ☐ No

Nutritionist Signature
Telephone   Date
White - Receiving Facility   Canary - Medical Records   Pink - C.C. Services

APPROVED BY THE MASSACHUSETTS DEPARTMENT OF PUBLIC HEALTH

Page 3
Patient Care Referral Form

Name: _____

Record # _____

Transfer to: _____

_____

<u>SOCIAL SERVICE:</u>

Prior to hospitalization, patient lived:
- ☐ Alone
- ☐ Nursing Home
- ☒ With Family
- ☐ With Friends
- ☐ Other _____

SOCIAL INFORMATION (including patient's personality, attitude toward illness and family constellation and inter-relationships)

Pt is being discharged to home with her husband and 2 preschool aged children. She is at this time unable to accept the disfigurement caused by her burn.

Identified Problems:

Body image disturbance 2° burn/disfigurement.
Child care services.

Plan (include short and long range plans)

Day care for children.
Support for pt to work through issues regarding disfigurement.

Will referring unit social worker plan to follow patient: Yes ☒ No ☐

Joan Williams _____   777-3333   6/30/85

| Name | Signature & Title | Phone | Date |

THERAPIES (P.T., O.T., Speech)   Instructions enclosed: Yes ☐ No ☐

Physical therapy and occupational therapy are not needed at this time.

Signature of Therapist   Phone   Date

620-17M - 681-282   9/85

APPROVED BY THE MASSACHUSETTS DEPARTMENT OF PUBLIC HEALTH

RECEIVING FACILITY
DISTRIBUTION: WHITE-RECEIVING FACILITY; CANARY-MEDICAL RECORD; PINK-C.C. SERVICE

CHRONIC OBSTRUCTIVE PULMONARY DISEASE (COPD)

FHPAA

General Summary

Mrs. F., an 84-year-old, widowed woman, was admitted from Star Bright Nursing Home (SBNH) on May 25, 1985, with severe shortness of breath and DOE. Upon admission to the emergency ward, she was diagnosed with hypoxemia and hypercapnea exacerbated by a long-standing history of chronic obstructive pulmonary disease. The patient's daughter states that, two weeks before admission, her mother began experiencing increased weakness and shortness of breath. She also showed transient mild confusion. Three days before admission, she was seen by her private physician, who found her to be baseline.

In the early morning of the day she was admitted, the patient developed an abrupt increase in dyspnea, with Cheyne-Stokes respirations of 34/min. Her BP was recorded as 92/60; pulse rate, 100 beats per minute (regular); and temp 37°C. The patient was cyanotic and disoriented.

Examination of the lungs showed rales halfway up, bilaterally. The patient received an IV push of furosemide (Lasix), 80 mg; IV methylprednisolone sodium succinate with lactose, sodium biphosphate, sodium phosphate, and benzyl alcohol (Solu-Medrol), 40 mg; and was begun on an aminophylline drip, 30 mg/h. The patient also received 1g Cefamandole (IV) for gram-positive cocci in the sputum. CPT was instituted. When the patient arrived on the unit at 2 PM, she was alert and oriented to person and place but not to time. She was wearing upper and lower dentures and was carrying bifocal glasses. Valuables were left at SBNH. She reported being allergic to penicillin. Her vital signs were recorded as follows: BP, 120/80; pulse rate, 96 beats per minute (regular); respirations, 36/min (slightly labored and shallow); temp, 36.9°C, p.o. Her height was recorded as 5 ft 7 in; her weight, 67 lb. Urine and blood were sent from the emergency ward for laboratory studies.

Pattern Areas

Health Perception–Health Management

The patient's general health has been "gradually failing" since her husband's death in 1982. She reports that over the past 5 years she has had increased weakness and DOE, accompanied by cachexia and anorexia. The patient smoked 1½ packs of cigarettes each day for 50 years and claims she stopped 20 years ago. However, her record indicates that she stopped smoking 4 to 5 years ago. She drinks an occasional glass of red wine (one or two times each month). The patient has been admitted for hypoxemia and hypercapnea, secondary to long-standing COPD.

The patient's past medical history includes the following:

- 1980, colon cancer; high sigmoid, well-differentiated; negative nodes at resection; colostomy closed; no known recurrence
- 1978, a bilateral goiter, which was treated with thyroid globulin (Proloid)
- Chronic depression
- 1970, subarachnoid bleeding that caused a coma, right hemiparesis, and aphasia (The only residual is a slight decrease in memory.)
- 1965, a right renal cyst; surgically removed
- 1964, arthritis; diagnosed as Reiters syndrome
- 1961, myocardial infarction; arterial sclerotic coronary vascular disease
- 1932, salpingo-oophorectomy

Medications include the following:

- furosemide (Lasix), 20 mg, p.o. QD
- thyroid globulin (Proloid), 50 mg, p.o., q6h
- Terbutaline, 50 mg, p.o., q6h
- trimethobenzamide hydrochloride (Tigan), 250 mg, p.o., TID
- trimethoprim with sulfamethoxazole (Septra DS), one tablet p.o., BID
- nitroglycerin, 1/150 grain, 1–2 tablets, SL, PRN
- milk of magnesia, 30 cc, p.o., QH, PRN
- prochlorperazine (Compazine), 10 mg, p.o., PRN
- docusate sodium (Colace), 100 mg, p.o., TID, PRN

Dr. Katherine Martein is the primary provider of health care.

Self-Perception–Self-Concept

The patient understands that she has been hospitalized for shortness of breath; it is unclear whether she realizes the prognosis and the progression of the disease. She is frustrated with her increased dependence and her loss of functional ability. She has always tried to function independently and to remain active.

Roles-Relationship

The patient's primary support is her only daughter, Jane S., who is married, has two grown sons, and teaches the sixth grade. Her telephone number is 333-3333.

The patient has lived at SBNH for three years. She has shared a room with one other woman since arriving there and considers her to be a friend. The patient belongs to reading and craft groups and also enjoys music and current events. Meals, recreation, and medical and nursing supervision are supplied around-the-clock at SBNH.

Coping-Stress

The patient has experienced many stressors in life— especially her husband's death. She now relies on her daughter, other family members, and several close friends for support.

Cognitive-Perceptual

The patient uses bifocals for reading. She speaks both Russian and English. Her mental status waxes and wanes with hypoxia; however, when she is not hypoxic, she is alert and oriented ($\times 3$).

Activity-Exercise

Weather permitting, the patient enjoys a 30-minute daily walk at SBNH. She walks to the bathroom and the dining room alone. She further enjoys reading large-print books, attending craft and storytelling classes, and listening to music.

Nutritional-Metabolic

The patient eats a no-salt-added diet. Her height is 5 ft 7 in; her weight is 67 lb, which reflects an approximate 40-lb weight loss over the past five years. She wears full upper dentures (intact) and partial lower dentures, which are broken and in need of repair. Her pale skin shows poor turgor and is dry. A quarter-sized stage I decubitus ulcer has been noted on her coccyx.

Elimination

In the emergency ward, the patient has been incontinent of both urine and feces. There is no report, however, of incontinence while at SBNH. She usually has one BM every other day, and takes medicines as needed for constipation. The patient is taking Septra DS (one tab BID) for urinary tract infection (UTI). She is now in the fifth day of medication.

Sleep-Rest

The patient's sleep pattern is nocturnal. She sleeps 7 to 8 hours each night. Occasionally she naps in the afternoon. She experiences occasional orthopnea.

Values-Beliefs

The patient actively practices the Jewish religion. She would like to see the Rabbi.

Sexuality-Reproductive

The patient had an ectopic pregnancy in 1932, the uterine tube and ovary were excised at that time. Gravida 3 and para 3, she had normal vaginal deliveries. One child died when 4 years old; another died when 19 years old.

Anticipated Discharge Status

The patient will return to SBNH when she is stable.

Assessment

The nursing diagnosis can be summarized as follows:

- hypoxia, secondary to exacerbation of long-standing COPD
- acute confusional state, secondary to hypoxia
- urinary incontinence and UTI
- inadequate nutrition
- stage I pressure sore on coccyx
- fecal incontinence
- decreased functional status
- mild memory loss, secondary to subarachnoid bleeding in 1970
- Knowledge deficit about COPD pathophysiology and prognosis

FHPA

Pattern Areas

Health Perception–Health Management

To Mrs. F., being healthy means having the ability to "do what I want without assistance from anyone or anything." Being frequently bedridden in the hospital and dependent on oxygen has made her feel helpless and depressed. At the SBNH she is ambulatory and occasionally requires oxygen. She is also able to bathe, feed, toilet, and dress herself there.

Mrs. F. describes her present health as "fair." Since her admission to SBNH, after her husband's death in 1982, her ability to function independently has declined. The only activity she does to preserve her present state of health is to walk for approximately 30 minutes each day; one person accompanies her. She requires 3 to 4 short rests during this period. The patient drinks an occasional glass of red wine—one or two times each month.

The patient is followed on a regular basis by Dr. K. Martein at SBNH. The dates and types of immunizations are unknown. She is allergic to penicillin. Her blood type is AB positive.

The patient's past medical history can be summarized as follows:

- colon cancer; high sigmoid, well-differentiated; negatives notes at resection; colostomy closed; no known recurrence (1980)
- a bilateral goiter, which was treated with thyroid globulin (Proloid) (1978)
- chronic depression
- subarachnoid bleeding that caused a coma, right hemiparesis, and aphasia; the only residual is a slight decrease in memory (1970)
- a right renal cyst; surgically removed (1965)
- arthritis; diagnosed as Reiters syndrome (1964)
- myocardial infarction; arterial sclerotic coronary vascular disease (1961)
- salpingo-oophorectomy (1932)

Current medications include the following:

- furosemide (Lasix) 20 mg, p.o. QD
- KC1, 40 mEq, p.o., QD
- Terbutaline, 0.25 mg, SQ, q4h
- cefamandole, 1 g, IV, q6h
- aminophylline, 10 mg/h, IV
- Solu-Medrol, 125 mg, IV, q6h
- isoetharine hydrochloride (Bronkosol), 0.25 ml, q4h, alternating with Terbutaline injections
- Mylanta, 30 ml p.o., q4h
- thyroid globulin (Proloid), 2 g, p.o., daily
- docusate sodium (Colace), 100 mg, p.o., TID
- trimethoprim with sulfamethoxazole (Septra DS) one tab, p.o. BID

As a part of her health management program, the patient is receiving Bronkosol treatments q4h by respiratory therapists. The department is also administering oxygen therapy at 4 L by nasal prong; 40 per cent by Ventimask.

Examination of the patient's respiratory system shows protruding ribs, secondary to cachexia and use of accessory muscles. The diaphgram is flat; tympanic decreases inspiration/expiration. Examination of the lungs shows diffuse rales and occasional rhonchi. Decreased breath sounds bilaterally (with wheezes) could be noted over the entire right lobe. Respirations are 34/min and slightly shallow when the patient is wearing the Ventimask (40%) or nasal prong (4 L). The patient shows no pain on respirations, but has occasional dyspnea at night. There is productive coughing of a green, watery sputum, which the patient occasionally swallows. Gram-positive cocci in the sputum are being treated with Cefamandole, 1g, IV, q6h. Although the patient experiences respiratory distress when the bed is flat, she is comfortable at 35 to 45-degree angles (Fowler's position). ABGs on O_2, 4 L by nasal prong: 53/68/7.40.

Examination of the patient's cardiovascular system reveals the following values: strong apical heart rate, 80 beats per minute; BP 105/65. The patient's extremities are warm and pink and non-edematous. Although the patient does not complain of palpitations or chest pains, she does occasionally experience exertional chest pain, which is always relieved by sublingual administration of one or two tablets of nitroglycerin, 1/150 grain. She reports occasional nocturnal dyspnea.

Musculoskeletal examination reveals muscle atrophy over the patient's entire body. Range of motion active/passive in exercises. No contractions, deformities, weakness, pain, tenderness, or cramps are present. The patient requires minimal assistance when bathing or setting up her tray. Her gait has not been assessed, secondary to her bedrest status.

Neurological examination of the patient shows a person who is generally alert and oriented, when not hypoxic. She is occasionally unpleasant, usually because of poor positioning on the tender coccyx area or poor positioning for maximal breathing. She is friendly and talkative, but she tires easily. The patient is slightly depressed; she expresses concern about her hospitalization and her general inability to function independently. There is no complaint, however, of insomnia, amnesia, hallucinations or phobias.

The patient's motor status is best characterized by the phrase, bedrest-to-chair. She must be lifted out of the bed and placed in the chair. Fine motor movements are performed with some difficulty because of tremulousness. The patient has no paresthesia. Her extremities are warm, and she does not complain of pain. The patient discriminates between warm and cool when bathing or applying Keri lotion.

Examination of the hematopoietic system discloses the following results: blood type, AB positive; Fe, 32 μg/dl (anemic); hematocrit, 39%; hemoglobin, 12.4g/dl. Lymph nodes are normal.

Nutritional-Metabolic

Mrs. F. is a cachectic, anorexic, tired-looking woman with muscular atrophy. Her bones are visible at the joint and prominence. The tissue breakdown over the coccyx is apparently due to little flesh. The patient is on a no-added-salt diet. She states that she is not a "fussy eater"; but she claims that the food would be more palatable if she could use a salt substitute. Her height is 5 ft 7 in; her weight, 67 lb. Her ideal weight is 110 lbs; however, she has lost 40 lb over the past five years.

The following list is a typical 24-hour recall of the patient's food intake from three meals.

1. Breakfast
   - 1 slice of white bread
   - 1 tsp of grape jam
   - 1½ pats of margarine
   - 3 small bites of scrambled eggs

- 2 fl oz of black coffee
- 2 tsp of whole milk
- 4 fl oz of orange juice
2. Lunch
  - ½ oz of macaroni & cheese
  - 4 fl oz of coffee
  - 2 tsp of whole milk
  - 1 tbsp of chicken-noodle soup
3. Dinner
  - 4 small bites of baked scrod
  - 2 bites of mashed potatoes
  - 6 pieces of sliced carrots
  - 4 fl oz of tea
  - 2 tsp of whole milk
  - 2 oz of vanilla ice cream

Breakfast is the patient's "favorite meal." Sputum production and the weakness associated with COPD do not seem to affect her appetite.

Assessment of the patient's integumentary reveals a light brown skin, poor tone with muscle atrophy, drooping musculature, poor turgor, and dry texture. It is warm to the touch. There is no pruritus. A quarter-sized stage I pressure sore on the coccyx is responding well to applications of vitamin A and vitamin D 4 QID. No other lesions have been noted. The patient's fingernails have pink nail beds; however, they need cleaning, trimming, and polish removal. Slight clubbing can be noted in both hands. Her toenails, which are long, hard, and yellow, are beginning to curl.

Examination of the patient's oral cavity and its vestibulum discloses dry and irritated lips, mouth, and throat. A few pustules on the tongue are aggravated by KCl replacement. The patient's teeth are in very poor condition. She wears upper full-plate dentures; her lower dentures, which are cracked, are a partial plate. The remaining teeth are ground down due to the buildup of caries. Her gums are tender and dark pink. She denies dysphagia, altered taste, and changes in the voice. No hoarseness can be noted.

Examination of the patient's nose and sinuses shows an occasional clear discharge from the nose, especially when she eats or when she changes her position. There is no tenderness or pain in the sinuses. The olfactory senses are intact.

An assessment of the patient's endocrine system is reflected in the following observations and test results:

- hair: normally distributed, gray, and thin
- skin: dry, but not flaky or scaly
- weight: 40 lb loss since 1980
- GU/GI: no complaint of polyuria, polydipsia, or polyphagia; the throat and mouth are frequently dry
- blood glucose, 154 mg/dl; creatinine, 2.8 mg/dl

- history of goiter—treated with thyroid globulin (Proloid)

Elimination

The patient usually has a BM every other day; it is small and soft. If she has no BM every other day, the patient takes milk of magnesia, 30 ml, at bedtime and docusate sodium (Colace), 100 mg, p.o., TID, PRN. At SBNH, she walked to the bathroom and was continent; here, she is incontinent. She asks for the bedpan only if the nurse is in the room. Examination of the patient's GI tract reveals occult blood (stool); positive bowel sounds; and an abdomen that is soft, concave, nontender, and has well-healed surgical scars. There are no palpable masses. A S/P colon cancer (1980) has not recurred.

Mrs.F. urinates approximately 150 ml every one to two hours. She denies any burning sensation, dysuria, increased urgency to urinate, or polyuria. The patient usually urinated once nightly at SBNH. She was continent at SBNH; she is incontinent here. Urinalysis showed concentration > 100,000 of gram-negative rods in the patient's urine. After treatment with Septra DS, the urine is clean and clear and has no odor. A S/P right renal cyst was surgically removed; there has been no recurrence.

Activity-Exercise

Mrs. F. enjoys a daily walk for approximately 30 minutes with an aide or a family member. Before her declining health, she enjoyed vigorous walks and dancing. She states that walking, especially, improved her endurance and increased her energy level. During the winter, she avoids walks because she has poor circulation and occasional chest pain. Nevertheless, she currently continues to enjoy walking and experiences a small "surge of energy" after her daily walks, although she requires two to three short rest periods to "catch her breath." She is able to climb stairs without assistance but must take frequent rests. She does use an elevator, when one is available.

At SBNH, she belongs to a craft class, enjoys listening to music, regularly reads large-print books, and attends weekly story-telling seminars. She occasionally watches television in the evening. The patient's daughter visits her each week and has dinner with her twice each month.

Sleep-Rest

The patient's sleep pattern at the hospital is nocturnal. She sleeps seven to eight hours each night. However, when she is hypoxic at night, her sleeping pattern is irregular. Then she takes several long naps 1/2- to 1-hour long during the day (she also did this at SBNH). Mrs. F. generally claims to feel rested in the morning and has no complaint of inability to fall asleep. However, the patient's tired appearance—sunken eyes and the drooping bags beneath them—seems to belie this claim. (She is extremely cachectic and anorexic.) Although she reports an occasional nightmare, her dreams are generally pleasant. She needs to have the bed linens changed three to four times at night, but she falls asleep after the changes. The patient likes to read before bedtime because it makes her drowsy.

Cognitive-Perceptual

The patient has no complaint of change in her hearing. She does not wear a hearing aid. Although she has a yearly physical examination, she does not recall when her hearing was last tested formally. She has noted no change in balance; no tinnitus. Physical examination reveals normally shaped auricles (the canals were not assessed). She responds to whispered sounds at two feet.

Mrs. F. wears bifocals for reading; however, she reads large print only. In 1978, she had bilateral cataract removal, but there is no report of recent visual changes. Her pupils are equal, round, and respond to light. There is no edema, itching, pain, or lacrimation. The conjunctiva is pink.

The patient has no complaint of any change in her ability to discriminate odors. Physical examination shows a midline septum and no epistaxis, sneezing, tenderness, or pain. Occasionally, she has a clear nasal discharge when eating or when changing her position. Her claim that the food is bland and unpalatable (because of sodium restriction) probably indicates that her sense of taste—like her sense of smell—is unchanged. However, she does report increased sensitivity to cold, although she makes no complaint of an inability to discriminate between hot or cold (eg, she discriminates warm when bathing and cool when applying lotion). She also shows good tolerance of pain.

Mrs. F., who describes her memory as good, is in tune with current events. (Her educational level includes one semester of college in Vermont.) The patient is alert and oriented ($\times 3$) except when she is hypoxic. She exhibits occasional irritability, which is due to her immobility and oxygen dependence. Although she understands the reason for her hospitalization, she has fair-to-poor understanding of the pathophysiology and prognosis of COPD.

Self-Perception–Self-Concept

One of Mrs. F's primary concerns is her weight loss. Over the past five years, she has lost 40 lb. She has "always been thin" but not "emaciated."

The patient describes herself as friendly, outgoing, and in touch with the world. She feels that she has had a satisfying, long life and has attained most of her goals. Even so, she would like her health to improve.

Roles-Relationship

The patient has been a resident at SBNH for three years. Her primary support is her 51-year-old (and only) daughter, Jane S., who visits weekly and calls daily. Mrs. F. has two grandchildren and four great-grandchildren, who call weekly also and try to visit monthly. The family lives in the New England area.

The patient has befriended her roommate and has made several good companions through the groups she belongs to at SBNH. Most of her old friends have died. She maintains telephone communication with two of those who are still alive. She misses her husband's love, companionship, and support.

The patient assumes responsibility for paying her bills; she has done this throughout her adult life.

Mrs. F. reports that she worked with her husband in the clothing business they opened in the 1920s; and often brought her children with her to work. She describes her life style as "comfortable" after World War II; she owned a home before her admission at SBNH.

The patient is unaware of the progressive disability she faces as a result of the COPD.

Sexuality-Reproductive

The patient's secondary sexual characteristics are appropriate for her age. She does not complain of burning, pain, discharge, or lesions in the vaginal area. She does not recall the date of her last pap test. Her menopause was uneventful; it began when she was 48 years old and lasted approximately five years. The patient is a gravida 3 and para 3. In 1932, her uterine tube and ovary were excised as the result of an ectopic pregnancy. She does not examine her breasts for masses.

Coping-Stress

The patient has described her feelings of isolation, loneliness, and depression after her husband's death. She was admitted to SBNH shortly after his death. His death and her being uprooted from her home have been very stressful. Yet she reports that she handles stress "well." She generally feels that she has had a "good happy life" and does not appear to be bitter or withdrawn. Numerous stressors in her life have enabled her to cope with multiple losses.

She has confided in her family that she feels she has adjusted to SBNH and has made new friends there. The basic change in life that she would like to make is to increase her independence and mobility.

Mrs. F. appears to have led a healthy and satisfying life. Her friendly attitude and willingness to share past experiences indicate this outlook. Although she is uncooperative with the staff at times, she usually interacts well and complies with the therapeutic and medical regimens.

Values-Beliefs

The patient is an active practitioner of the Jewish religion. She visits the synagogue weekly and is often visited by the Rabbi weekly. She reports that religion has always helped her to cope with life stressors; therefore, she derives comfort in practicing it. She values her family, friends, and health above all else.

Life Patterns and Life-style

Mrs. F. describes a typical day in her life as "full." She likes to get up around 8 AM, attend breakfast, listen to the news, and then read for a short time until lunch. After lunch, the weather permitting, she likes to walk with an aide or family member. Two afternoons each week are spent in craft class and one afternoon in story-telling seminars. In the evening, she enjoys listening to music and reading until bedtime. She occasionally watches television.

The patient enjoys socializing at SBNH. She looks forward to her family visits and outings. Her loss of eyesight has had an impact upon some of her interests, especially needlework and sewing.

NURSING CARE PLAN

NURSING HISTORY   FORMULATED BY   Ellen Kitchen, R.N.   DATE 5/26/85

Mrs. F. is an 84-year-old woman who was admitted from Bright Star Nursing Home 5/25/85 with severe shortness of breath and dyspnea on exertion. Diagnosis: hypoxemia and hypercapnea exacerbated by a long standing history of chronic obstructive pulmonary disease. Over past several weeks Mrs. F. has experienced increased weakness, shortness of breath, and mild transient confusion. Upon admission to the emergency ward VS: 130/80; 100 regular; 36, regular; 98.8 po ABGs on 4 liters nasal prong: 43/79/7.26/37. Patient was cyanotic and disoriented times 3. Lungs: rales half way up bilaterally. Received 80 mg IV push lasix, 40 mg IV solumedrol, 1gm IV cetamandole secondary to gm + cocci in sputum, and was started on aminophylline drip 30 mg/hr.

NURSING DIAGNOSIS	EXPECTED OUTCOME	NURSING CARE PLAN WITH NURSING ORDERS
1. Hypoxia secondary to exacerbation of long standing chronic obstructive pulmonary disease.	Short Term Goal #1: Pt will have improved ventilation and respirations, as evidenced by less shortness of breath, productive coughing, proper breathing, decreased inhalations, improved lab and arterial blood gas values, and improved mental status.	1. Administer 40% venti mask or 4 liters nasal prongs continuously as ordered. 2. Perform deep breathing exercises 4 times daily for ten minutes each time. 3. Teach pt to purse-lip breathe while performing deep breathing exercises. 4. Position pt for maximal postural drainage. 5. Teach pt effective coughing. 6. Assess vital signs every 4 hours. 7. Auscultate lungs before and after treatments, assess respirations, rate, rhythm. 8. Administer bronchodilators and anti-inflammatory medications as ordered. 9. Check results of hematocrit and RBC count daily. 10. Assess ABGs when performed. 11. Medicate with subcutaneous heparin bid as ordered. 12. Assess pt's mental status ongoing. 13. Record I+O, weight daily. 14. Encourage pt to drink 2 liters of water daily. 15. Follow prescribed NAS diet, request physician to order salt substitute. 16. Perform active and passive range of motion 3 times daily. 17. Perform chest percussion, clapping, tapping, and vibrating when performing chest physical and respiratory therapy. 18. Assist pt with meticulous oral care. Rinse mouth and swab with toothette with solution of half hydrogen peroxide and half mouthwash in morning, after KCl administration, after meals, and at bedtime.

NURSING DIAGNOSIS	EXPECTED OUTCOME	NURSING CARE PLAN WITH NURSING ORDERS
	Long Term Goal: Pt will maintain existing lung function as evidenced by decreased dependence on oxygen, effective coughing and breathing, return to baseline mental status, and normalization of lab and ABG values.	1. Continue to teach pt methods which promote deep breathing and coughing; have pt demonstrate. 2. Teach pt how to position herself for maximal postural drainage; have pt demonstrate. 3. Teach and assist pt with active and passive range of motion; have pt demonstrate. 4. Abulate pt, as tolerated. 5. Teach pt importance of adequate fluid intake. 6. Teach pt to report any pain or dyspnea immediately to her nurse. 7. Teach pt to report any tenderness felt in her calves. 8. Teach pt to report increased sputum production and/or changes in sputum color. 9. Review and teach pt about medications she is being discharged with; send her home with medication teaching card. 10. Teach pt the necessity of good oral hygiene.
	Short Term Goal #2: Pulmonary irritant and sources of infection to the pt will be reduced, as evidenced by decreased incidence in respiratory infections, productive coughing, and meticulous oral hygiene.	1. Remove or reduce all chemical irritants, dust, smoke, etc. from pt's environment. 2. Observe hand washing techniques. 3. Encourage nasal breathing. 4. Encourage productive coughing, diaphragmatic breathing, pursed lip breathing. 5. Encourage postural drainage; perform chest physical therapy. 6. Maintain relatively high environmental humidity. 7. Encourage high fluid intake – at least 2 liters water daily. 8. Provide a nutritionally well balanced diet, high in vitamin C. 9. Assist pt with meticulous oral care. 10. Assist pt with active/passive range of motion. 11. Assess VS every 4 hours. 12. Assess lab values and ABGs when drawn.

NURSING DIAGNOSIS	EXPECTED OUTCOME	NURSING CARE PLAN WITH NURSING ORDERS
	Long Term Goal #2: Environment will be free of irritants and sources of infection, as evidenced by diminished or no recurrence of respiratory infections at Bright Star Nursing Home.	1. Incorporate teaching interventions into discharge plan; send them home with pt. 2. Teach pt nasal breathing, have her return demonstration. 3. Continue to have pt demonstrate coughing, deep breathing, pursed lipped breathing, postural drainage, and range of motion. 4. Teach pt to avoid irritants and to alert staff when they are present. 5. Teach pt to avoid large crowds during flu season. 6. Teach pt to avoid very cold air and very humid environments. 7. Teach pt the role of sound nutrition in preventing infection. 8. Teach pt importance of adequate rest. 9. Teach pt importance of meticulous oral hygiene.
	Short Term Goal #3: Pt will have decreased bronchospasms as evidenced by increased vital capacity.	1. Administer bronchodilator medications as ordered. 2. Auscultate lungs – assess rate, rhythm, respirations. 3. Remove or avoid environmental irritants. 4. Avoid temperature extremes. 5. Continue to teach pt methods which promote deep breathing, coughing, and postural drainage. 6. Assess results of vital capacity via pulmonary function tests. 7. Praise pt for efforts to relieve bronchospasm and for any increase in vital capacity.
	Long Term Goal #3: Pt will participate in measures which reduce bronchospasm, as evidenced by verbal and psychomotor demonstration.	1. Review and teach pt about the medications she is taking; send her home with medication teaching card. 2. Teach pt to alert staff to any wheezing she notes. 3. Teach pt to avoid environments which can irritate her respiratory function. 4. Teach pt to avoid temperature extremes. 5. Continue to teach pt methods which promote maximal respiratory function. 6. Assess pulmonary function test results.

NURSING DIAGNOSIS	EXPECTED OUTCOME	NURSING CARE PLAN WITH NURSING ORDERS

2. Acute confusional state secondary to hypoxia.	Short Term Goal #1:
	Pt will demonstrate improved mental status, as evidenced by improving ABG levels and improved orientation to person, place and time.
		1. Call BSNH to determine prior level of cognitive function.
		2. Assess mental status.
		3. Identify factors which influence cognitive function:
		  a. physiological-metabolic status
		  b. drug effects
		  c. sensory deficits/overload
		  d. environment
		  e. psychosocial stressors
		4. Assess pt's ability to adapt to physiological and psychological stressors.
		5. Adjust pt's routine and environment to enhance adaptation and orientation (milieu therapy).
		6. Notify physician of changes or fluctuations in mental status.
		7. Educate daughter concerning factors which influence cognitive functioning.
		8. Educate family and staff to plan of care which fosters the pt's
		  a. orientation
		  b. reduced anxiety
		  c. familiarity with the environment
		  d. prevention of injury
		9. Follow care plan above which promotes improved oxygenation of cells.
		10. Closely monitor ABG values.

	Long Term Goal #1: Pt will return to baseline mental status, as evidenced by her ability to maintain attentive thought and behavior; state person, place, and time; name and recall objects and events; and make judgments consistent with safe behaviors.	1. Assess pt's ability to maintain attentive thought and behavior. 2. Assess pt's ability to name and recall objects. 3. Assess pt's orientation to person, place, and time. 4. Assess pt's ability to make critical judgments.

NURSING DIAGNOSIS	EXPECTED OUTCOME	NURSING CARE PLAN WITH NURSING ORDERS
3. Urinary incontinence/ urinary tract infection	Short Term Goal #1: Pt's urinary tract infection will resolve.	1. Weigh pt daily, follow I+Os carefully. 2. Assess 24-hour fluid status. 3. Assess for signs and symptoms of dehydration or fluid overload. 4. Use principles of milieu therapy to reorient pt. 5. Check mental status frequently. 6. Orient pt to call light and location of bedpan. 7. Obtain bedside commode. 8. Check for incontinent episodes and place pt on bedpan or commode every 2 hours. Document on sheet on door. 9. Check repeat urine analysis and urine culture and sensitivity. 10. Monitor pt for frequency, burning, hesitancy, and urgency. 11. Ambulate pt as tolerated. 12. Assure adequate hydration - at least 2 liters water daily. 13. Encourage independence in ADL's. 14. Medicate with Septra DS one tablet twice daily as ordered. 15. Provide frequent perianal care.
	Long Term Goal #1: Pt will return to prior normal voiding pattern.	1. Encourage increased activity; ambulate as tolerated. 2. Assess mental status ongoing. 3. Assess pt for signs and symptoms of urinary tract infection. 4. Teach pt perianal hygiene. 5. Praise pt for her efforts. 6. Continue to assure adequate hydration.
4. Inadequate nutrition	Short Term Goal #1: Pt will not lose weight, as evidenced by increase or stabilization of weight.	1. Provide small, frequent meals high in carbohydrates, fats, proteins, minerals, and vitamins. 2. Provide high nutrient milkshakes and snack 2 times daily. 3. Cut food into small pieces for chewing and swallowing. 4. Encourage intake of 2 liters of water daily. 5. Weigh pt every morning; tell pt her weight. 6. Record I+O.

NURSING DIAGNOSIS	EXPECTED OUTCOME	NURSING CARE PLAN WITH NURSING ORDERS
		7. Medicate with prescribed antacids.
		8. Assess pt for any abdominal pain or increased indigestion.
		9. Plan daily meals with pt to ascertain likes and dislikes.
		10. Have dietary nutritionist assess pt.
		11. Request physician to order salt substitute.
		12. Assess bony prominences for tissue breakdown.
		13. Massage coccyx area with vitamin A + D ointment every shift.
		14. Assess lab values: BUN, creatinine, Hematocrit, Hemoglobin, and iron.
	Intermediate Term Goal #1: Pt's weight will increase by one pound weekly.	1. Continue ongoing assessment of nutritional problems and needs.
		2. Utilize nutritionist to promote teaching.
		3. Teach pt the necessity of maintaining a balanced diet (i.e. to maintain tissue integrity and maximize immunological response).
		4. Provide small frequent meals high in carbohydrates, fats, minerals, proteins, and vitamins.
		5. Provide high nutrient milkshakes for snack.
		6. Gradually increase caloric intake to 2500 calories, as tolerated.
		7. Continue to encourage increased fluid consumption.
		8. Weigh pt on same scale every morning.
		9. Medicate pt with Colace as ordered.
		10. Medicate pt with antacids as ordered.
		11. Plan discharge menu with nutritionist.
	Long Term Goal #1: Pt will return to prior ideal weight of 110 pounds within 9 months.	1. Assist pt in planning a daily menu consisting of 2500 calories.
		2. Teach pt to record her weight weekly.
		3. Note in discharge plans to BSNH the pt's current weight and teaching interventions.
		4. Request dietary to write referral.
		5. Repair dentures at BSNH.

NURSING DIAGNOSIS	EXPECTED OUTCOME	NURSING CARE PLAN WITH NURSING ORDERS
5. Stage I pressure sore on coccyx.	Short Term Goal #1: Tender coccyx area will heal. Long Term Goal #1: Pt will not develop pressure sores.	1. Keep linens dry; change sheets when soiled; clean perianal area, pat dry. 2. Apply A + D ointment after each episode of incontinence. 3. Change pt's position every 2 hours while on bedrest. 4. Place air mattress on bed. 5. Perform active/passive range of motion every shift. 6. Provide nutritious diet, high in protein. 7. Provide a smoothe, wrinkle-free bed. 8. Ensure adequate hydration. 1. Massage bony prominences every shift. 2. Lubricate dry skin with Keri lotion. 3. Ambulate pt, as tolerated. 4. Instruct pt to reposition self frequently when in bed. 5. Continue to instruct pt to drink 2 liters of water daily. 6. Continue to teach pt necessity of highly nutritional diet. 7. Teach pt to alert nurse to any tenderness or inflammation noted on skin.
6. Fecal incontinence.	Short Term Goal: Pt will notify nurse if she needs to defecate.	1. Determine pt's bowel pattern prior to admission. 2. Assess 24-hour fluid status. 3. Assess pt for symptoms of dehydration. 4. Use principles of milieu therapy to orient patient. 5. Check mental status frequently. 6. Orient pt to call light and location of bedpan. 7. Obtain bedside commode. 8. Ambulate pt, as tolerated. 9. Assure adequate hydration, at least 2 liters of water daily. 10. Medicate with 100 mg Colace three times daily as ordered. 11. Ensure high fiber diet. 12. Assess need to defecate when placing pt on bedpan to urinate.

NURSING DIAGNOSIS	EXPECTED OUTCOME	NURSING CARE PLAN WITH NURSING ORDERS
	Long Term Goal: Pt will return to prior bowel function.	1. Orient pt to call light and location of bedpan. 2. Ambulate pt, as tolerated. 3. Assure adequate hydration, at least 2 liters of water daily. 4. Ensure high fiber diet. 5. Medicate with 100 mg Colace 3 times daily as ordered. 6. Encourage pt to try to defecate after meals.
7. Decreased functional status	Short Term Goal #1: Pt's physical health will improve as evidenced by her ability to promote and maintain muscle strength, body flexibility and body balance skills.	1. Determine pt's functional status prior to hospitalization. 2. Explain your goal to pt. 3. Have pt perform deep breathing and pursed lip exercises prior to all physical activity. 4. Perform active and passive range of motion 3 times daily. 5. Begin increasing activity by having pt transfer from bed to chair by pivoting with 2 person assist. Pt should be wearing oxygen at 4 liters nasal prong as ordered. 6. As tolerated, increase her activity by having her walk approximately 10 feet to the bathroom with assistance. She should continue wearing oxygen at 4 liters nasal prong if needed. 7. Gradually increase duration of walks, as tolerated. Utilize portable oxygen, as needed. 8. Ensure adequate rest periods. 9. Gradually increase pt's areas of former independence in personal toilet; bathing; sitting self up for meals; ambulating short distances unassisted; and controlling continence. 10. Have pt attend unit based exercise program 3 times weekly for 30 minutes as tolerated. 11. Praise pt for increasingly independent status. 12. Assess vital signs and lungs before and after activity. 13. Call Social Worker for consult.

NURSING DIAGNOSIS	EXPECTED OUTCOME	NURSING CARE PLAN WITH NURSING ORDERS
	Long Term Goal #1: Pt will return to baseline functional level, as evidenced by her ability to ambulate to bathroom unassisted, bathe self, sit self up for meals, perform personal toilet, and control continence.	1. Teach pt to perform range of motion exercises independently. 2. Remind pt to perform deep breathing and pursed lip exercises prior to all activity. 3. Remind and teach pt importance of well balanced diet to improve strength and stamina. 4. Praise pt for return to independent functional status. 5. Teach pt to report any wheezing, chest pain, or shortness of breath with activity.
8. Mild memory loss secondary to sub-arachnoid bleed in 1970.	Goal: Pt will be able to maintain an optimal level of cognitive function.	1. Determine level of cognitive function at BSNH. 2. Perform ongoing mental status assessments with pt. 3. Assess pt's ability to adapt to physiological and psychological stressors. 4. Make adjustments in the pt's routines and environment which foster adaptation and orientation (milieu therapy). 5. Encourage daily exercise routine. 6. Maintain a daily routine for the pt. 7. Provide adequate nutrition and hydration. 8. Continue promotive respiratory function practices. 9. Reinforce strengths and maintain positive input which will boost self esteem. 10. Reinforce and praise pt for independence in ADL's. 11. Educate family and staff, as needed.
9. Knowledge deficit re chronic obstructive pulmonary disease pathophysiology and prognosis.	Short Term Goal #1: Pt will understand basic pathophysiology of chronic obstructive pulmonary disease and its prognosis, as evidenced by her ability to articulate basic pathophysiology and measures which promote maximal breathing capacity and endurance.	1. Determine pt's knowledge of the pathophysiology and prognosis of chronic obstructive pulmonary disease. 2. Assess pt's willingness to learn about the disease and its prognosis. 3. Describe the normal function of the lungs, including bronchi, mucous secretion, cilia, alveoli, and alveolar capillary bed.

NURSING DIAGNOSIS	EXPECTED OUTCOME	NURSING CARE PLAN WITH NURSING ORDERS
		4. Utilize pt teaching diagrams of anatomy of the respiratory system when teaching; label important landmarks.
		5. After pt can demonstrate basic understanding of normal lung function (through verbalization), explain patho-physiology of chronic obstructive pulmonary disease and its causes.
		6. Utilize pt teaching diagrams which allow visualization of pathophysiological changes.
		7. Encourage pt to ask questions; clarify teaching needs.
		8. Review measures which promote maximal breathing capacity and endurance, such as breathing exercises; adequate hydration; nutritious meals; avoiding infection; exercise, as tolerated; and adequate rest periods.
		9. Praise pt for efforts to learn above materials.
	Long Term Goal #1: Pt will demonstrate behaviors which are consistent. in promoting effective management of chronic obstructive pul-monary disease, as evidenced by her ability to perform behaviors consistent with promoting maximal ventilation, identify environmental factors impacting on respiratory function, and perform ADL's independently.	1. Review measures which promote maximal breathing capacity and endurance, such as breathing exercises; adequate hydration, nutritious meals; avoiding infection; exercise, as tolerated; and adequate rest periods.
		2. Assess pt's performance of above intellectual and physical activities.
		3. Continue to assess need for review.
		4. Continue to praise pt for taking active interest in learning about disease prognosis, pathophysiology, and treatment.

Patient Care Referral Form

Patient's Hospital Record # _____

FROM: Beth Israel Hospital	PATIENT NAME: Mrs. F.
Unit/Clinic: 6 North - Medicine	ADDRESS: BSNH, Jamaica Plain, MA
ADDRESS: 330 Brookline Ave.	
Boston, MA TEL. 999-0000	TEL. 555-5555

ADM. DATE 5/25/85	DISCH. DATE 5/31/85

FLOOR	APT. #	BIRTHDATE 11/15/1901
AGE 84	SEX M F̶	MARITAL STATUS S M̶ W D SEP.	RELIGION Jewish

TO: BSNH

RELATIVE OR GUARDIAN: Mrs. Jane Relative

ADDRESS: Jamaica Way, Jamaica Plain, MA   TEL. 222-2222

ADDRESS: Hummingbird Lane, Nahant, MA   TEL. 999-0099

MEDICARE NO. & LETTER 000-11-2222A	PLAN A B	BLUE CROSS NO.	SOC. SEC. NO. 000-111-2222	OTHER

CLINIC APPOINTMENTS	DATE	TIME	Agency Worker Office Address Telephone

DIAGNOSIS (S) Surgery Performed and Date, Allergies or Infections

1. End stage COPD
2. ASCVD
3. S/P Colon Ca 1980
4. S/P subarachnoid hemmorrhage 1970
5. Depression
6. Goiter

Is Patient X Family X aware of diagnosis?   yes

Date of last physical _____

PHYSICIAN'S ORDERS: (Include specific orders for Diet, Lab Tests, Speech, and O.T.)

TRANSPORT BY: ☒ Ambulance ☐ Car

MEDICATION	STRENGTH AND FREQUENCY	DATE & TIME OF LAST DOSE
1. Slo-Phyllin	125 mg po q 8 hrs	12A-8A-4P
2. KCl	40 mq po daily	8A
3. Lasix	40 mg po daily	8A
4. Terbutaline	2.5 mg po q 6°	12A-6A-12P-6P
alternate with:		
Bronkometer	2 puffs q 6 hrs	2A-8A-2P-8P
5. Proloid	5 mg po qd to taper @ HRCA	8A
6. Colace	100 mg po tid	

TREATMENTS & FREQUENCY: O_2 at 4L np prn or 40% ventimask prn

DIET: NAS with salt substitute

PHYSICAL THERAPY: X   Restrict Activity ☒ Yes ☐ No   Sensation Impaired ☐ Yes ☒ No

Precautions   Weight Bearing Status - Non-Weight ☒   Partial-Weight ☐   Full-Weight ☐

SPECIFIC TREATMENT & FREQUENCY: decreased functional status 2° immobility during hospitalization. Requires minimal support of one to ambulate.

ANTICIPATED GOALS: Will return to prior functional level

REHABILITATION POTENTIAL IS: good

HOME HEALTH SERVICES: ☐ NURSING ☐ OCC. THERAPY ☐ SPEECH THERAPY ☐ SOCIAL WORK ☐ H.H. AIDE ☐ OTHER - SPECIFY

The above services require Level of Care: ☐ I ☐ II ☒ III ☐ IV

If Chronic Hospital, why? _____

CERTIFICATION: ✱(when applicable)
Services above needed to treat condition for which patient was hospitalized ☒ Yes ☐ No
I certify that the above named patient is: (check one)
☐ Under my care (or has been referred to another physician having professional knowledge of patient's condition); is home bound except when receiving out-patient services; requires skilled nursing care on an intermittent basis or physical or speech therapy as specified in the orders.
☐ Requires skilled nursing care on a continuing basis for any of the conditions for which he/she received care during this hospitalization.

_____ M.D.
Signature

Mary Doe _____ M.D.
Print Name

Tel. 000-1000 Date 5/31/85 Will follow ☐ Yes ☒ No - If no, who?

Katherine Jones _____ M.D.

ADDRESS: BSNH _____ TEL. 999-9999

9/85   282-956

APPROVED BY THE MASSACHUSETTS DEPARTMENT OF PUBLIC HEALTH

DISTRIBUTION — WHITE — RECEIVING   PINK — MEDICAL RECORDS   YELLOW — C.C. SERVICE

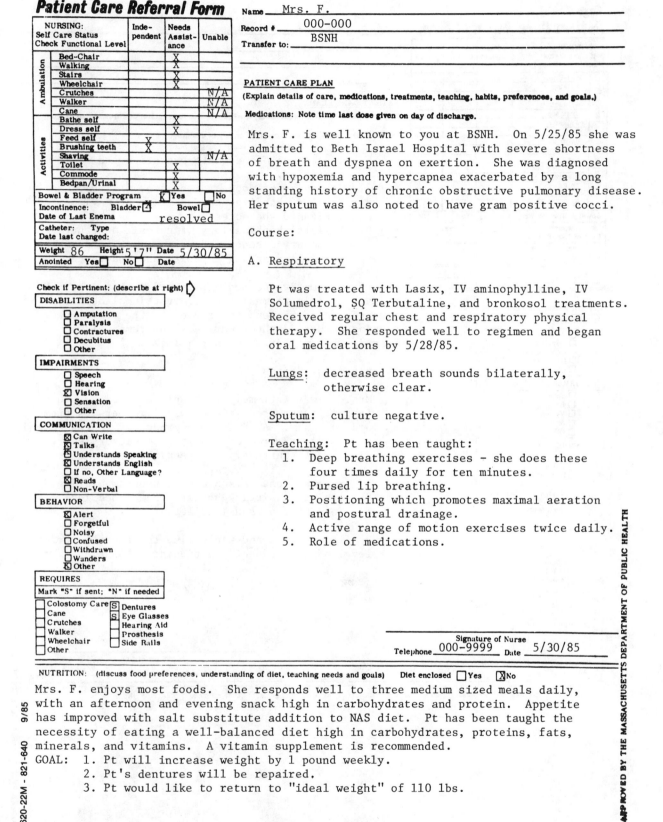

Page 2
Patient Care Referral Form

Name __Mrs. F.__

Record # ___000-000___

Transfer to: ___BSNH___

NURSING: Self Care Status Check Functional Level		Independent	Needs Assistance	Unable
Ambulation	Bed-Chair		X	
	Walking		X	
	Stairs		X	
	Wheelchair		X	
	Crutches			N/A
	Walker			N/A
	Cane			N/A
Activities	Bathe self		X	
	Dress self		X	
	Feed self	X		
	Brushing teeth	X		
	Shaving			N/A
	Toilet		X	
	Commode		X	
	Bedpan/Urinal		X	

Bowel & Bladder Program	X Yes	No
Incontinence: Bladder X	Bowel	
Date of Last Enema	resolved	
Catheter: Type		
Date last changed:		

Weight 86	Height 5'7"	Date 5/30/85
Anointed Yes☐	No☐	Date

Check if Pertinent: (describe at right) ▷

DISABILITIES
- ☐ Amputation
- ☐ Paralysis
- ☐ Contractures
- ☐ Decubitus
- ☐ Other

IMPAIRMENTS
- ☐ Speech
- ☐ Hearing
- ☒ Vision
- ☐ Sensation
- ☐ Other

COMMUNICATION
- ☒ Can Write
- ☒ Talks
- ☒ Understands Speaking
- ☒ Understands English
- ☐ If no, Other Language?
- ☒ Reads
- ☐ Non-Verbal

BEHAVIOR
- ☒ Alert
- ☐ Forgetful
- ☐ Noisy
- ☐ Confused
- ☐ Withdrawn
- ☐ Wanders
- ☒ Other

REQUIRES
Mark "S" if sent; "N" if needed

☐ Colostomy Care	S Dentures
☐ Cane	S Eye Glasses
☐ Crutches	☐ Hearing Aid
☐ Walker	☐ Prosthesis
☐ Wheelchair	☐ Side Rails
☐ Other	

PATIENT CARE PLAN
(Explain details of care, medications, treatments, teaching, habits, preferences, and goals.)

Medications: Note time last dose given on day of discharge.

Mrs. F. is well known to you at BSNH. On 5/25/85 she was admitted to Beth Israel Hospital with severe shortness of breath and dyspnea on exertion. She was diagnosed with hypoxemia and hypercapnea exacerbated by a long standing history of chronic obstructive pulmonary disease. Her sputum was also noted to have gram positive cocci.

Course:

A. Respiratory

Pt was treated with Lasix, IV aminophylline, IV Solumedrol, SQ Terbutaline, and bronkosol treatments. Received regular chest and respiratory physical therapy. She responded well to regimen and began oral medications by 5/28/85.

Lungs: decreased breath sounds bilaterally, otherwise clear.

Sputum: culture negative.

Teaching: Pt has been taught:
1. Deep breathing exercises - she does these four times daily for ten minutes.
2. Pursed lip breathing.
3. Positioning which promotes maximal aeration and postural drainage.
4. Active range of motion exercises twice daily.
5. Role of medications.

Telephone ___000-9999___   Signature of Nurse   Date ___5/30/85___

NUTRITION: (discuss food preferences, understanding of diet, teaching needs and goals)   Diet enclosed ☐ Yes ☒ No

Mrs. F. enjoys most foods. She responds well to three medium sized meals daily, with an afternoon and evening snack high in carbohydrates and protein. Appetite has improved with salt substitute addition to NAS diet. Pt has been taught the necessity of eating a well-balanced diet high in carbohydrates, proteins, fats, minerals, and vitamins. A vitamin supplement is recommended.

GOAL: 1. Pt will increase weight by 1 pound weekly.
2. Pt's dentures will be repaired.
3. Pt would like to return to "ideal weight" of 110 lbs.

Nutritionist Signature   Telephone ___000-9999___   Date ___5/30/85___

9/85

620-22M - 821-640

APPROVED BY THE MASSACHUSETTS DEPARTMENT OF PUBLIC HEALTH

White - Receiving Facility   Canary - Medical Records   Pink - C.C. Services

Page 2
Patient Care Referral Form

Name ___ Mrs. F. ___

Record # ___ 000-000 ___

Transfer to: ___ BSNH ___

NURSING: Self Care Status Check Functional Level		Inde-pendent	Needs Assist-ance	Unable
Ambulation	Bed-Chair			
	Walking			
	Stairs			
	Wheelchair			
	Crutches			
	Walker			
	Cane			
Activities	Bathe self			
	Dress self			
	Feed self			
	Brushing teeth			
	Shaving			
	Toilet			
	Commode			
	Bedpan/Urinal			

Bowel & Bladder Program ☐ Yes ☐ No

Incontinence: Bladder ☐ Bowel ☐
Date of Last Enema

Catheter: Type
Date last changed:

Weight	Height	Date
Anointed Yes ☐ No ☐	Date	

Check if Pertinent: (describe at right) ⟩

DISABILITIES
- ☐ Amputation
- ☐ Paralysis
- ☐ Contractures
- ☐ Decubitus
- ☐ Other

IMPAIRMENTS
- ☐ Speech
- ☐ Hearing
- ☐ Vision
- ☐ Sensation
- ☐ Other

COMMUNICATION
- ☐ Can Write
- ☐ Talks
- ☐ Understands Speaking
- ☐ Understands English
- ☐ If no, Other Language?
- ☐ Reads
- ☐ Non-Verbal

BEHAVIOR
- ☐ Alert
- ☐ Forgetful
- ☐ Noisy
- ☐ Confused
- ☐ Withdrawn
- ☐ Wanders
- ☐ Other

REQUIRES
Mark "S" if sent; "N" if needed
- ☐ Colostomy Care
- ☐ Cane
- ☐ Crutches
- ☐ Walker
- ☐ Wheelchair
- ☐ Other
- ☐ Dentures
- ☐ Eye Glasses
- ☐ Hearing Aid
- ☐ Prosthesis
- ☐ Side Rails

PATIENT CARE PLAN
(Explain details of care, medications, treatments, teaching, habits, preferences, and goals.)

Medications: Note time last dose given on day of discharge.

6. Importance of adequate hydration and sound nutrition.
7. Necessity of good oral hygiene.
8. To alert staff to any wheezing or environmental irritants she notes.
9. Basic pathophysiology of chronic obstructive pulmonary disease and measures which promote maximal breathing capacity and endurance.

Mrs. F. was motivated and interested in her care. Her primary goal is to maximize her functional ability. She requires reinforcement and review of the above interventions. Her daughter was very instrumental when teaching her mother about her illness.

B. Functional Status

Mrs. F. was extremely weak upon admission. She initially required lifting with two persons from bed to chair. Activity was gradually increased and pt was weaned from oxygen when ambulatory short distances. Currently she requires:

1. Moderate one person assist when ambulating.
2. Assist in sitting up (if done at bedside).
3. Setup for personal toilet.

Pt is motivated and would like to return to prior level of independent functioning at BSNH.

Signature of Nurse
Telephone _____ Date _____

NUTRITION: (discuss food preferences, understanding of diet, teaching needs and goals) Diet enclosed ☐ Yes ☐ No

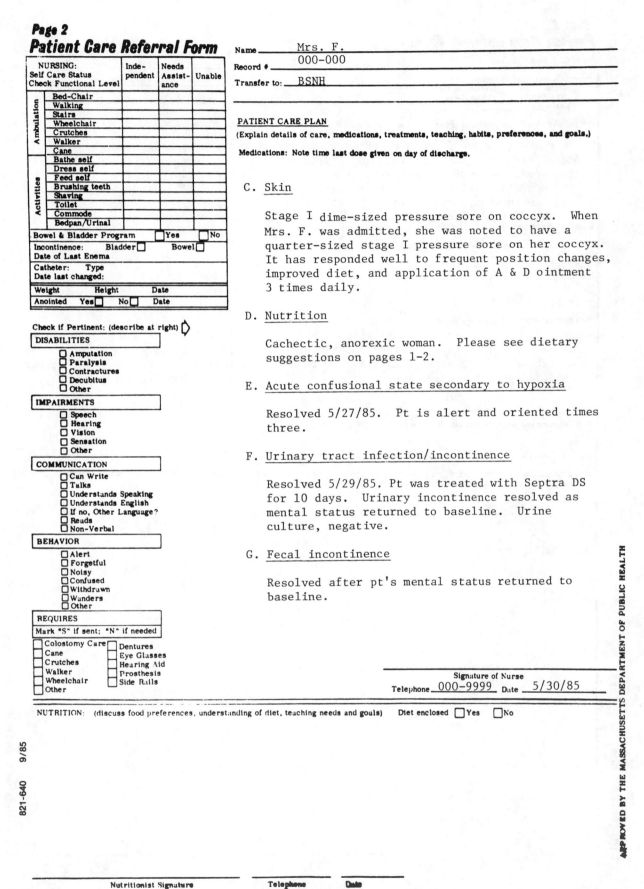

Page 2
Patient Care Referral Form

Name ___Mrs. F.___

Record # ___000-000___

Transfer to: ___BSNH___

NURSING: Self Care Status Check Functional Level		Inde-pendent	Needs Assist-ance	Unable
Ambulation	Bed-Chair			
	Walking			
	Stairs			
	Wheelchair			
	Crutches			
	Walker			
	Cane			
Activities	Bathe self			
	Dress self			
	Feed self			
	Brushing teeth			
	Shaving			
	Toilet			
	Commode			
	Bedpan/Urinal			

Bowel & Bladder Program ☐ Yes ☐ No
Incontinence: Bladder☐ Bowel☐
Date of Last Enema
Catheter: Type
Date last changed:

Weight	Height	Date
Anointed Yes☐ No☐	Date	

Check if Pertinent: (describe at right) ▷

DISABILITIES
☐ Amputation
☐ Paralysis
☐ Contractures
☐ Decubitus
☐ Other

IMPAIRMENTS
☐ Speech
☐ Hearing
☐ Vision
☐ Sensation
☐ Other

COMMUNICATION
☐ Can Write
☐ Talks
☐ Understands Speaking
☐ Understands English
☐ If no, Other Language?
☐ Reads
☐ Non-Verbal

BEHAVIOR
☐ Alert
☐ Forgetful
☐ Noisy
☐ Confused
☐ Withdrawn
☐ Wanders
☐ Other

REQUIRES
Mark "S" if sent; "N" if needed
☐ Colostomy Care ☐ Dentures
☐ Cane ☐ Eye Glasses
☐ Crutches ☐ Hearing Aid
☐ Walker ☐ Prosthesis
☐ Wheelchair ☐ Side Rails
☐ Other

PATIENT CARE PLAN
(Explain details of care, medications, treatments, teaching, habits, preferences, and goals.)
Medications: Note time last dose given on day of discharge.

C. Skin

Stage I dime-sized pressure sore on coccyx. When Mrs. F. was admitted, she was noted to have a quarter-sized stage I pressure sore on her coccyx. It has responded well to frequent position changes, improved diet, and application of A & D ointment 3 times daily.

D. Nutrition

Cachectic, anorexic woman. Please see dietary suggestions on pages 1-2.

E. Acute confusional state secondary to hypoxia

Resolved 5/27/85. Pt is alert and oriented times three.

F. Urinary tract infection/incontinence

Resolved 5/29/85. Pt was treated with Septra DS for 10 days. Urinary incontinence resolved as mental status returned to baseline. Urine culture, negative.

G. Fecal incontinence

Resolved after pt's mental status returned to baseline.

Signature of Nurse
Telephone ___000-9999___ Date ___5/30/85___

NUTRITION: (discuss food preferences, understanding of diet, teaching needs and goals) Diet enclosed ☐ Yes ☐ No

Nutritionist Signature   Telephone   Date

White - Receiving Facility   Canary - Medical Records   Pink - C.C. Services

APPROVED BY THE MASSACHUSETTS DEPARTMENT OF PUBLIC HEALTH

821-640 9/85

Page 3
Patient Care Referral Form

Name: _____Mrs. F._____

Record # _____000-000_____

Transfer to: _____BSNH_____

_____

SOCIAL SERVICE:

Prior to hospitalization, patient lived:
- ☐ Alone
- ☐ Nursing Home
- ☐ With Family
- ☐ With Friends
- ☐ Other _____

SOCIAL INFORMATION (including patient's personality, attitude toward illness and family constellation and inter-relationships)

84-year-old widowed woman referred to social service for past medical history of depression and questionable inability to cope with her chronic illness. Mrs. F. is a resident a BSNH since 1982 and has become increasingly debilitated due to chronic obstructive pulmonary disease. Significant others include her daughter and numerous supportive grandsons and great-grandchildren. Despite her chronic illness she has been independent with occasional need of assist while in the nursing

Identified Problems: home. While in the hospital she has exhibited increased dependence and depression.

Plan (include short and long range plans)

Mrs. F. articulates her frustration about declining health over the past 5 years or so. She strives for former independence and improved respiratory status. She understands her current limitations with her illness and will need ongoing support, especially as the disease progresses. If there are any questions, please call.

Will referring unit social worker plan to follow patient: Yes ☐   No ☒

Carol Smith		000-9999	5/30/85
Name	Signature & Title	Phone	Date

THERAPIES (P.T., O.T., Speech)   Instructions enclosed: Yes ☐   No ☒

_____ | _____ | _____
Signature of Therapist | Phone | Date

620-17M - 681-282   9/85

APPROVED BY THE MASSACHUSETTS DEPARTMENT OF PUBLIC HEALTH

RECEIVING FACILITY
DISTRIBUTION: **WHITE**-RECEIVING FACILITY; **CANARY**-MEDICAL RECORD; **PINK**-C.C. SERVICE

DIABETES

FHPAA

General Summary

Mrs. Collins, a 50-year-old woman, was first admitted to the Beth Israel Hospital emergency unit on October 7, 1984, with diabetic ketoacidosis and a new onset of diabetes mellitus. She was in her usual health until about one month ago when she noted increasing malaise, sickness, lethargy, and new blurred vision. She also complained of polydipsia, polyuria, decreased appetite, and weight loss. On the day of admission, she developed nausea and vomiting and abdominal pain. When Mrs. C. was admitted her blood glucose level was 474 mg/dl; potassium, 3.2 mEq/l; PCO_2, 15 mmHg. Her vital signs were recorded as follows: temp, 36.6°C; pulse rate, 100 beats per minute; respirations, 16/min; BP, 140/80. Urinalysis studies showed 4+ glucose, 4+ ketones, 4+ protein, and moderate to large serum acetone. The patient was transferred to MICU; there she was stabilized and treated with vigorous IV hydration and insulin drip. When the insulin drip was completed, medication was changed to NPH insulin q AM and the patient was transferred to 8N CRC on October 9 for teaching about diabetes and for further control. When she arrived at 2 PM in a wheelchair, she was alert and appeared to be comfortable and in no acute distress. Her vital signs were recorded as follows: temp, 36.7° C; pulse rate, 84 beats per minute; respirations 20/min; BP, 130/74; height, 5 ft 4 in; weight, 150 lb. The patient has no known allergies. She has no valuables with her. She has eyeglasses.

Pattern Areas

Health Perception–Health Management

The patient's past medical history includes hypertension (on HCTZ, 50 mg, QD); arthritis—naproxen (Naprosyn), 250 mg BID—and chronic low back pain. An S/P appendectomy was performed 20 years ago. The patient sees her private physician about once a year for a checkup. She does not smoke, but uses alcohol—a few drinks a week socially. Mrs. C. was admitted with diabetic ketoacidosis and a new onset of diabetes mellitus after about one month of increasing weakness, polyuria, polydipsia, and blurred vision. She was stabilized in MICU with hydration and insulin drip, then transferred to 8N for further control of diabetes mellitus and teaching.

Self-Perception–Self-Concept

The patient perceives diabetes mellitus as requiring a great change in her life style and diet that will be difficult to adapt to and accept. She is fearful that it will be limiting and will interfere with normal activities. She is "shocked" about her illness; she is "so used to being healthy." Moreover, she does not know much about diabetes mellitus, which makes her "nervous." She is also fearful of insulin injections and the complications of diabetes mellitus. During hopitalization, she wants to learn as much as possible about diabetes mellitus and how to take care of herself. Her husband and family are as shocked and upset as she is.

Roles-Relationship

Mrs. C's husband, Bill (telephone no. 663-4245), is to be notified in the event of an emergency. The patient lives with her husband; they have three children who live nearby. There are also grandchildren. She describes the family as "very close" and "supportive" of each other. A housewife and a retired music teacher, she teaches piano part time.

Coping-Stress

The patient feels that she usually handles stress or problems fairly well. Talking about her worries and how she feels helps. She states that her husband is her greatest support. Nevertheless, she feels that the diagnosis of diabetes mellitus is a major stress for her and is afraid that it will be "too much to handle. But I guess I just have to accept it; I don't have much choice."

Cognitive-Perceptual

Alert and oriented $\times 3$, Mrs. C. speaks English. She prefers to be called Julia. She wears glasses for reading, and has them with her. She complained of blurry vision before admission; now it is resolving. She appears comfortable and is without pain at present.

Activity-Exercise

The patient walks every day in the neighborhood and goes dancing every weekend. She keeps very active with hobbies and has many interests. Occasionally, she is restricted in some activities (eg, gardening and craftwork) by arthritis and back pain, but she states that she "tries not to let it stop her."

Nutritional-Metabolic

Mrs. C. follows a no-added-salt diet. She is concerned about the diabetes mellitus diet restrictions because she enjoys cooking, eating, and sweets. Her recent weight loss of about 15 lb took place over about one month. The patient is usually slightly overweight. Her skin is dry and intact, without lesions. She has her own dentition.

Elimination

The patient has a normal BM each day. Recent polyuria and nocturia (two to three times each night) are now resolving.

Sleep-Rest

The patient usually gets about six to seven hours of sleep each night. Although she has frequent insomnia, she does not use any sleep aids. She reads to help her fall asleep.

Values-Beliefs

Because religion (Congregationalist) is important in her life, the patient feels that her faith will help her handle this problem. No needs have been identified at present.

Sexuality-Reproductive

The patient has experienced S/P four normal pregnancies and deliveries and S/P menopause.

Anticipated Discharge Status

The patient can return to her home. Diabetic clinic appointments will be used to provide follow up.

Assessment and Plan

Assessment of the patient's needs can be summarized as follows:

- Problem No. 1 is the patient's knowledge deficit about diabetes mellitus.
- Problem No. 2 is the patient's anxiety (2°) resulting from the diagnosis.
- Problem No. 3 is discharge planning.

The patient will be enabled to understand the diagnosis and treatment and will be able to perform self-care safely and accurately. Follow-up care will be arranged to monitor her after discharge.

FHPA

Pattern Areas

Health Perception–Health Management

Mrs. C. describes her general health as "fairly good." To her, being "healthy" means feeling well and being without illness. "Eating right" and getting enough exercise and rest are all important to her. Although she knows how to "eat right," she does not give it much thought or effort; she

"could do better." The patient, who walks every day for exercise, states that she is always very active. She also tries to get enough rest but is not always able to rest. Because the patient has been healthy all of her life, without major health problems, she now finds it difficult to accept this new problem and life style. She sees a private physician for regular checkups; the last examination was about six months ago. Before admission, the patient's medicine included HCTZ, 50 mg, p.o., QD and naproxen (Naprosyn), 250 mg, p.o., BID. She has no known allergies. The family history reveals that the patient's father had an adult onset of diabetes mellitus, and her mother had a myocardial infarction. She does not smoke; she drinks alcohol socially—a few drinks each week.

The patient feels shocked and scared about her diabetes, in spite of the family history. (She is "so used to being healthy.") Her other health problems are considered to be minor (arthritis, hypertension) compared with this one. Being hospitalized is a stress for her; the only previous admissions have been for childbirth and for an appendectomy several years ago. Her lack of information about diabetes makes her "nervous." Moreover, she is frightened about the insulin injections, and the complications of the disease (she is aware of potential blindness and amputations). She is also concerned about diet and change in life style, because she feels it will be difficult to get used to the changes and that they will interfere with her normal activities.

Nutritional-Metabolic

A typical daily food intake includes the following:

- Breakfast: egg, toast, and butter
- Lunch: a sandwich, soup, or salad
- Dinner: meat, chicken, or fish; vegetable and potato.

The patient eats sweets frequently (she "really enjoys them"); she also regularly enjoys dessert after dinner. She feels that she will have a difficult time restricting her intake of sweets. The patient also enjoys fatty, creamy foods. She does all the cooking at home and "loves cooking for the family and entertaining." The patient considers herself to be slightly overweight. She feels that she should lose weight. Occasionally, she has tried, but has never been very successful. She states that diet restrictions will be a major and difficult change in her life-style. Nevertheless, she is willing to try because it can be a good opportunity to lose some weight.

Normally, the patient has had minimal fluid intake; recently, however, her thirst and fluid intake have increased markedly—"I couldn't get enough to drink, which is unusual for me." Her appetite, which is usually excellent, has been very poor in last few weeks. She has also had a weight loss of about 15 lb in this time; normally, her weight remains steady. The patient experiences occasional indigestion, which she attributes to "not eating what's good for me at times." She uses antacids PRN. Mrs. C. does not follow any diet restrictions, although she is aware that she should limit salt intake for a 2° hypertension (she does not use much, but she does not actively avoid it). She has not noted any problem with healing, but she has noted very dry skin. She also has dental problems. Her height is 5 ft 4 in; her weight, 150 lb. The oral mucous membranes are pink and moist with no lesions. She has her own dentition; there are multiple cavities. Her skin is warm; dry, with normal turgor; intact; and without lesions, rashes, or ulcerations.

Elimination

The patient describes her usual elimination pattern as a normal BM every day, without need for laxatives. She denies constipation or diarrhea. A few weeks before admission, she noted an increase in urination—frequent and large amounts. She has also developed recent nocturia, two to three times each night. She denies having any problem with control and denies excess perspiration.

Activity-Exercise

Mrs. C. states that she has always had sufficient energy for all activities, until recently. For about one month, she has been fatigued and unable to tolerate the usual activities. Her exercise normally includes daily walks in the neighborhood with her husband, dancing each weekend with her husband and friends, and gardening. She frequently babysits with her young grandchildren. She also teaches piano part-time and does all the cooking, cleaning, and shopping for the family. Her leisure activities include family activities and gatherings, entertaining friends, social groups, dancing, gardening, music, cooking, and crafts. Normally, she is able to perform all ADLs. Her perceived ability to carry out activities is as follows (0 = full self-care): feeding, 0; dressing, 0; general mobility, 0; bathing, 0; grooming, 0; home maintenance, 0; bed mobility, 0; toileting, 0; shopping, 0; cooking, 0. Her only prior restriction has been the result of arthritis and back pain, which occasionally limited gardening activity and craftwork. These, however, were not a major problem; she "does what (she) can, which is usually a lot." Since the recent onset of fatigue, her major problem has been decreased energy and the inability to perform all of the usual activities. She denies chest pain or shortness of breath, and her lungs are clear. Her handgrip is strong; her muscles, firm. Range of motion is normal at present; however, it is sometimes restricted in the hands and the wrists because of arthritis. Her gait and posture are normal. The patient's vital signs are as follows: temp, 36.4°C; pulse rate, 80 beats per minute; respirations, 20/min; BP, 128/70.

Sleep-Rest

The patient attempts to get six to seven hours of sleep each night. Often, however, she has difficulty getting to sleep and occasionally wakes up during the night. When this occurs, she does not feel rested in morning. Nevertheless, she does not take drugs to induce sleep; she prefers to avoid them. Instead, the patient usually reads when she is unable to sleep. It occasionally helps. She does not know why she has occasional insomnia, but she does know that she must avoid caffeine at night. Mrs. C. feels that the insomnia is most of the time due to "nerves" and her "overactive mind." She denies problems with dreams. Until recently, she never took naps. Now, she has been taking naps because she is "exhausted" during the day, which was very unusual.

Cognitive-Perceptual

The patient denies difficulty with hearing. Aids are not needed; she is able to hear a whisper. She wears glasses for reading; her last eye examination was about one year ago. Recently, she has noted increasingly blurred vision and thought she needed to have her prescription changed. Although the blurred vision has decreased since the patient's hospitalization, her vision still is "not quite normal" at times. She is able to read newsprint with glasses. Mrs. C. denies recent, noticeable memory change. She states, however, that she tends to be "on the forgetful side," which is not new for her. The patient finds that she learns more easily when she is interested in the subject and when it is something that involves her personally. She needs concrete learning experiences along with conceptual ones. She also needs to verbalize and perform activities while learning. College-educated, the patient was a music teacher; now she teaches piano part-time.

Occasionally Mrs. C. experiences mild to moderate pain from arthritis and back pain. She tries "not to give in to it" and attempts her usual daily activities despite any pain. She is being treated with naproxen (Naprosyn), which (she states) usually "helps." The patient appears comfortable and relaxed at present. She expresses herself well and easily and appears to be comfortable talking about herself. Maintaining eye contact and exhibiting good attention span, she appears to have no problem concentrating.

Self-Perception–Self-Concept

Mrs. C. describes herself as "talkative, usually energetic, strong, capable, fun, busy, sociable." Most of the time, she feels good about herself. She normally does not allow anything to limit her and is determined to "do what she wants—and usually does." However, the patient is afraid that the diabetes will be too limiting for her. She feels that to adapt to and accept the enormous change will mean a major change in life style and diet. Content and happy with life as it was, she is resistant to change. Nevertheless, she denies feeling frequently angry, annoyed, or depressed and states that she is usually calm and even-tempered—"easy going."

Roles-Relationship

The patient lives with her husband. She has three children who no longer live at home but live nearby. Two are married and have children. Denying the existence of family problems, she asserts that everyone generally "gets along well." She enjoys her children and her grandchildren—they "mean the world" to her. They visit frequently, and she babysits often. She feels that her children depend a lot on her for support, advice, and guidance. She also feels that she and her husband depend a lot on each other for support, and feels that they have a "wonderful relationship with great communication, which is the most important thing." If there ever is a problem, she and her husband "talk things out" as needed. She states that her husband depends on her for all the cooking and housework, but she also states that "he's managing fine without me, surprisingly!" The husband and the family are as shocked and upset about the diagnosis and the hospitalization as the patient is. They are "not used to mother being sick." The patient and her husband have many friends and are very sociable. She belongs to a church group and a craftwork group.

Sexual-Reproductive

The patient has had S/P four normal pregnancies and deliveries and S/P menopause. She denies having any problems with sexual relations.

Coping-Stress

The patient feels that she normally handles stress fairly well, though she describes herself as a "worrier" and as being frequently "nervous." Her problem, she feels, is that she tries to do too much; she keeps very busy—"sometimes too busy"—and is a perfectionist. Talking about her worries and how she feels helps; in this, her husband especially is her greatest support. "It's best to let it all out," she declares. She has always been able to handle any major problems in her past, she feels, because she was usually emotionally strong and had her husband's support. Unsure of how to handle this new diagnosis, she feels overwhelmed and afraid that it may be too much to handle. "But I guess I just have to accept it," she says; "I don't have any choice." She states that she feels resistant to "the whole idea" at present. She does not want to accept the consequences of her illness; yet she knows she must.

Values-Beliefs

The patient generally gets what she wants out of life, she feels, because she is "determined" and "sets her mind" to it. Religion is important in her life, and she has faith that it will help her through this stressful period. She is a Congregationalist. Hospitalization will not interfere with her religious practices. The patient states that she has valued most in life her family, her friends, and her religion; now she would add her "health."

NURSING CARE PLAN

NURSING HISTORY   FORMULATED BY Nancy Brown, R.N.   DATE 10/10/84

Mrs. Collins is a 50-year-old woman admitted to BI Emergency Ward on 10/7/84 with DKA, new onset DM. PMH includes HTN, arthritis, chronic low back pain, S/P appendectomy. In usual health until 1/mo PTA noted increasing malaise, weakness, lethargy, new blurred vision. Also c/o polydipsia, polyuria, decreased appetite, and weight loss. Adm. to EW with BS 474, K 3.2, CO_2 15. RA ABG's: 100/19/7.23. Mod. to lge. serum aletone. To MICU was stabilized and Rx'd with vigorous IV hydration and insulin gtt. Transferred to 8N CRC 10/9 for teaching and further control of DM.

NURSING DIAGNOSIS	EXPECTED OUTCOME	NURSING CARE PLAN WITH NURSING ORDERS
1. Knowledge deficit re DM	Pt will understand patho-physiology of diabetes.	1. Explain and provide written information re normal insulin and blood glucose relationship and how altered in DM. 2. Teach symptoms of DM and their causes. 3. Encourage questions; validate understanding with questioning. 4. Avoid too much information at once; provide gradually. 5. Include family (husband) in teaching whenever possible.
	Pt will understand how insulin works and action of different types of insulin.	1. Teach what different types of insulin are and how they work; provide written information. 2. Go over this each time insulin given; explain when insulin is working and wearing off according to pt's BS's during day. 3. Validate understanding by questioning pt. 4. Have pt view film (Trainex): "Insulin Management and Use".
	Pt will be able to draw up and mix insulins accurately and safely.	1. Demonstrate procedure of drawing up insulin; also provide written instructions. 2. Have pt return demonstration using practice vials. 3. Demonstrate mixing insulins; provide written instructions to use at first as guideline. 4. Have pt return demonstration using practice vials. 5. Have pt draw up and mix insulins each time given, starting as soon as possible. Assist prn at first, monitor each time to assess accuracy.

158 CONTINUING CARE

NURSING DIAGNOSIS	EXPECTED OUTCOME	NURSING CARE PLAN WITH NURSING ORDERS
	Pt will be able to administer insulin to self accurately and safely.	6. Teach husband if possible. 7. Have pt view film (Trainex): "Insulin Management and Use". 1. Demonstrate procedure of administering insulin; explain while giving pt insulin. 2. Have pt return demonstration, practicing with an orange first then with normal saline to self when ready. 3. Have pt administer own insulin each time needed, starting as soon as possible; monitor to assess technique and accuracy and to provide support and encouragement. 4. Teach husband if possible.
	Pt will understand rotating sites and will know sites for injection.	1. Teach where sites are and importance of rotating. 2. Provide rotation chart for pt to mark area injected each time; keep at bedside, to continue at home.

	Pt will be able to perform home blood glucose monitoring (HBGM).	1. Teach importance of following BS.
		2. Explain what times to check fingersticks.
		3. Demonstrate procedure of testing fingersticks:
		  – use of autolet.
		  – visually reading chem-strips.
		  – accucheck if plans to purchase.
		4. Have pt practice fingersticks each time needed during hospitalization, starting as soon as possible; practice more often as needed.
		5. Monitor and stay with pt each time to assess accuracy and provide support.
		6. Provide written instructions and booklets to use as guide at first if needed.
		7. Have pt view Trainex film: "Home Blood Glucose Monitoring".
		8. Teach pt to record fingerstick values each time in a chart of insulin dose and time, BS's, and sugar and acetones (S & A) to follow control. Keep at bedside, to continue at home.
		9. Provide information about equipment available to purchase for HGBM.
		10. Teach husband if possible.

NURSING DIAGNOSIS	EXPECTED OUTCOME	NURSING CARE PLAN WITH NURSING ORDERS
	Pt will be able to test for ketones in urine accurately.	1. Explain what ketones are, why they would be in urine, and importance of checking for them. 2. Explain "2nd void specimen" procedure and rationale; teach times to check S & A. 3. Demonstrate procedure for testing S & A; have pt return demonstration. 4. Have pt check S & A each time in hospital; monitor at first to check accuracy. 5. Have pt record result each time in bedside chart, to continue at home. 6. Have pt view Trainex film: "Home Monitoring, Urine and Ketones".
	Pt will understand and be able to identify and properly treat hypo- and hyperglycemic episodes.	1. Explain causes of and symptoms of hypo- and hyperglycemia; provide written info. 2. Teach appropriate actions for treatment. 3. Verify pt's understanding by discussion and questioning ("What would you do if you felt _____ ?") 4. Include husband in teaching. 5. Have pt view Trainex film: "Hypoglycemia and Hyperglycemia".
	Pt will understand diet restrictions and modifications; will understand her calorie counts and exchanges and be able to follow.	1. Explain relationship of diet and BS. 2. Obtain dietary consult to explain exchanges and diet; weight reduction per dietary and M.D. 3. Verify understanding by discussion; have pt go over exchanges at each meal. 4. Provide written information re diet and exchanges. 5. Include husband in teaching. 6. Teach and stress importance of maintaining proper diet, keeping to meal and snack times, and eating after taking insulin. 7. Have pt view Trainex film: "Diet and Exercise for Type I DM".

NURSING DIAGNOSIS	EXPECTED OUTCOME	NURSING CARE PLAN WITH NURSING ORDERS
	Pt will understand how to begin or continue an exercise program properly and safely with DM.	1. Explain relationship of exercise and BS. 2. Teach and stress importance and benefit of exercise with DM. 3. Provide verbal and written information re guidelines for starting or continuing an exercise program. 4. Teach precautions to take with exercise. 5. Have pt view Trainex film: "Diet and Exercise for Type I DM". 6. Encourage exercise in hospital, walking as much as possible.
	Pt will understand importance of and how to do diabetic foot care.	1. Teach and stress importance of regular foot care. 2. Provide verbal and written information about proper foot care and precautions. 3. Teach problems to watch for and when to consult MD. 4. Verify understanding with discussion and questioning.
	Pt will understand appropriate actions to take when ill.	1. Explain relationship of DM and illness. 2. Provide verbal and written information about "sick day" guidelines. 3. Verify understanding with discussion and questioning.
2. Anxiety 2° diagnosis of DM.	Pt will be able to perform all aspects of self care with as minimal anxiety as possible. Pt will be able to learn about dx of DM without being overwhelmed and overloaded with information. Pt will be discharged with as minimal anxiety as possible re performing self care at home.	1. Provide multiple practice sessions for pt to improve abilities and confidence. 2. Provide maximum assistance for pt with procedures and techniques at first, gradually increasing independence as pt is able and ready until pt is able to do independently (especially with injections). 3. Continuously assess pt's readiness to learn and practice and her anxiety level. 4. Attempt to space information to avoid overloading pt. 5. Encourage pt to do as much of own care as soon as possible and when emotionally ready; continually assess anxiety level. 6. Stay with pt when she is performing own DM care for emotional support and verbal coaching prn (especially with injections). 7. Involve family, husband in care and teaching. 8. Encourage pt to take as much control of care as possible to prepare for discharge and to decrease anxiety re discharge plans.

NURSING DIAGNOSIS	EXPECTED OUTCOME	NURSING CARE PLAN WITH NURSING ORDERS
		9. Provide as much information as possible and as pt wants or can accept. 10. Provide written information and referral information for discharge to decrease anxiety re discharge plans. 11. Encourage and allow pt to verbalize fears and anxieties. 12. Encourage questions; provide information as requested.
3. Discharge planning.	Pt will have adequate and safe knowledge level of DM and treatment, self-care and monitoring, diet and exercise, precautions, special problems, and treatment.	1. Teach and provide information as in above care plan; continually verify understanding. 2. Verify accurate techniques with observation. 3. Gradually work up to having pt perform all aspects of care by discharge as will do at home. 4. Have pt record progress in self-monitoring chart at bedside, to be continued at home. 5. Make medication card and discuss insulin doses and times, sliding scale (if necessary), and times to check fingersticks with pt. 6. Discuss with pt and make written list re equipment, supplies needed at home. Discuss where and how to obtain supplies. 7. Involve husband in all teaching and discharge plans.

	Pt will have follow-up care arranged at discharge to monitor control and compliance, assist with any problems, answer questions, and continue and/or complete teaching.	1. Ascertain that pt has follow-up care arranged at discharge:
		  a) M.D. appt
		  b) diabetic clinic appt
		  c) clinic appt. with dietician
		  d) eye exam if needed
		2. Provide information re how to and when should contact appropriate caretakers if any problems or questions.
		3. Provide information re community resources available for follow-up care/information as needed or desired; how to contact and where to get information.

Patient Care Referral Form

Patient's Hospital Record # _____

FROM: _____ Beth Israel Hospital _____

Unit/Clinic _____ 8 N CRC _____

ADDRESS _____ 330 Brookline Ave. _____

Boston, MA   TEL. 777-0090

| ADM. DATE 10/7/84 | DISCH. DATE 10/13/84 |

TO: _____ Beth Israel Diabetic Clinic _____

ADDRESS: _____ 330 Brookline Ave. _____

Boston, MA   TEL. 777-0990

PATIENT NAME   Mrs. Collins

ADDRESS: _____ 17 Broad Rd. _____

Newton, MA   TEL. 666-6666

| FLOOR | APT. # | BIRTHDATE 12/6/33 |
| AGE 50 | SEX M ⊠ | MARITAL STATUS S ⊠ W D SEP. | RELIGION Congregationalist |

RELATIVE OR GUARDIAN: Husband

ADDRESS: Same as above

TEL.   Same as above

| MEDICARE NO. & LETTER | PLAN A ⊠ B | BLUE CROSS NO. 543210 | SOC. SEC. NO. 000-111-4444 | OTHER |

| CLINIC APPOINTMENTS | DATE | TIME | Agency Worker Office Address Telephone |

DIAGNOSIS (S) Surgery Performed and Date, Allergies or Infections

Diabetic ketoacidosis, new onset diabetes mellitus

Is Patient yes Family yes aware of diagnosis?

PHYSICIAN'S ORDERS: (Include specific orders for Diet, Lab Tests, Speech, and O.T.)

Date of last physical

TRANSPORT BY: ☐ Ambulance   ☐ Car

MEDICATION	STRENGTH AND FREQUENCY	DATE & TIME OF LAST DOSE
HCTZ	50 mg po qd	10/13/84 8 am
Naprosyn	250 mg po BID	10/13/84 8 am
NPH Humulin insulin	20u sc q am	10/13/84 8 am
Regular Humulin insulin	8u sc q am	10/13/84 8 am
NPH Humulin insulin	10u sc q pm	10/12/84 5 pm
Regular Humulin insulin	6u sc q pm	10/12/84 5 pm

TREATMENTS & FREQUENCY: Monitor blood glucose and control of DM, appts. q week then re-evaluate. Assess home self-care management.

DIET: 1600 cal. ADA, NAS diet.

PHYSICAL THERAPY: Restrict Activity ☐ Yes ☐ No   Sensation Impaired ☐ Yes ☐ No

Precautions   Weight Bearing Status - Non-Weight ☐   Partial-Weight ☐   Full-Weight ☐

SPECIFIC TREATMENT & FREQUENCY: _____

ANTICIPATED GOALS: Stabilize control of DM for self-care management with health problem.

REHABILITATION POTENTIAL IS: _____

HOME HEALTH SERVICES: ⊠ NURSING   ☐ OCC. THERAPY   ☐ SPEECH THERAPY   ☐ SOCIAL WORK   ☐ H.H. AIDE   ☐ OTHER - SPECIFY

The above services require Level of Care: ☐ I   ☐ II   ☐ III   ☐ IV

If Chronic Hospital, why? _____

CERTIFICATION: ✱(when applicable)
Services above needed to treat condition for which patient was hospitalized ☒ Yes ☐ No
I certify that the above named patient is: (check one)
☒ Under my care (or has been referred to another physician having professional knowledge of patient's condition); is home bound except when receiving outpatient services; requires skilled nursing care on an intermittent basis or physical or speech therapy as specified in the orders.
☐ Requires skilled nursing care on a continuing basis for any of the conditions for which he/she received care during this hospitalization.

_____ M.D.
Signature

Mary Brown _____ M.D.
Print Name

Tel. 777-9999   Date 10/13/84 Will follow ☒ Yes ☐ No - If no, who?

_____ M.D.

ADDRESS: _____   TEL. _____

9/85   282-956

APPROVED BY THE MASSACHUSETTS DEPARTMENT OF PUBLIC HEALTH

DISTRIBUTION — WHITE — RECEIVING   PINK — MEDICAL RECORDS   YELLOW — C.C. SERVICE

Page 2
Patient Care Referral Form

Name: Mrs. Collins
Record #: _____
Transfer to: _____

NURSING: Self Care Status Check Functional Level	Independent	Needs Assistance	Unable
Bed-Chair	X		
Walking	X		
Stairs	X		
Wheelchair			
Crutches			
Walker			
Cane			
Bathe self	X		
Dress self	X		
Feed self	X		
Brushing teeth	X		
Shaving			
Toilet	X		
Commode			
Bedpan/Urinal			

Bowel & Bladder Program ☐Yes ☐No
Incontinence: Bladder☐ Bowel☐
Date of Last Enema
Catheter: Type
Date last changed:

Weight 147 Height 5'4" Date
Anointed Yes☐ No☐ Date

Check if Pertinent: (describe at right) ▷

DISABILITIES
☐ Amputation
☐ Paralysis
☐ Contractures
☐ Decubitus
☐ Other

IMPAIRMENTS
☐ Speech
☐ Hearing
☐ Vision
☐ Sensation
☐ Other

COMMUNICATION
☐ Can Write
☐ Talks
☐ Understands Speaking
☐ Understands English
☐ If no, Other Language?
☐ Reads
☐ Non-Verbal

BEHAVIOR
☐ Alert
☐ Forgetful
☐ Noisy
☐ Confused
☐ Withdrawn
☐ Wanders
☐ Other

REQUIRES
Mark "S" if sent; "N" if needed
☐ Colostomy Care ☐ Dentures
☐ Cane ☐ Eye Glasses
☐ Crutches ☐ Hearing Aid
☐ Walker ☐ Prosthesis
☐ Wheelchair ☐ Side Rails
☐ Other

PATIENT CARE PLAN
(Explain details of care, medications, treatments, teaching, habits, preferences, and goals.)

Medications: Note time last dose given on day of discharge.

Mrs. Collins is a 50-year-old woman, admitted to BIEW 10/7/84 with DKA, new onset DM. PMH: mild HTN, arthritis, chronic low back pain. S/P appendectomy 20 years ago.

About one month PTA, c/o weakness, blurred vision, polydipsia, polyuria, decreased appetite, and weight loss. On adm: BS 474, K 3.2, CO_2 15. ABG's RA: 100/19/7.23. Mod. to large serum acetone. Stabilized with IV hydration and insulin gtt. Changed to NPH Humulin insulin q am with regular coverage until BS in control with 20u NPH and 8u reg q am and 10u NPH and 6 regular q pm. FBS's decreased from 240 to 95 on day of D/C 10/13. On 10/12, BS's were as follows: 7^a 85 11^a 150 4^P 118 10^P 126. SA's before D/C were running N/N to 1+/N - serum acetone.

Pt instructed on how to draw up and mix insulins, how to inject insulin, and rotate sites. Began with fear of injecting self but able to overcome enough to learn and now able to perform all aspects of insulin administration accurately. States she is still slightly uncomfortable with injecting self but able to do with only slight hesitation. Needs glasses to draw up insulin to read lines. Eyesight still occasionally blurry, but able to draw up accurately with glasses. Had eye exam in hospital and to have FLU eye exam after D/C. Pt given written material re insulin and administration and written guidelines for all steps. No longer needs to use however. Also has site rotation chart which she has been using in hospital and is to use at home.

Signature of Nurse _____
Telephone _____ Date _____

NUTRITION: (discuss food preferences, understanding of diet, teaching needs and goals) Diet enclosed ☒Yes ☐No

Pt instructed in 1600 cal ADA, NAS diet and exchange system. Reviewed importance of 3 meals a day and qhs snack. Reviewed food purchasing and preparation. Pt verbalized understanding of instruction. Pt enjoys cooking and eating high concentrated sugars but states understands importance of diet restrictions and willing to attempt. Wt. 150 lb on admission, 147 lb at D/C. Has tried wt. reduction in past without success. Feels this is good opportunity to attempt again. From observation in hospital, appears will comply. Pt feels will likely have questions after D/C. Please evaluate compliance, knowledge, answer questions, work on any problems. Re-evaluate for any diet changes needed and for need of further follow up. If any questions, please call. Diet enclosed.

Nutritionist Signature _____
Telephone 777-9999 Date 10/12/84

9/85 620-22M - 821-640

APPROVED BY THE MASSACHUSETTS DEPARTMENT OF PUBLIC HEALTH

White - Receiving Facility   Canary - Medical Records   Pink - C.C. Services

Page 2
Patient Care Referral Form

Name _____ Mrs. Collins

Record # _____

Transfer to: _____

_____

NURSING: Self Care Status Check Functional Level		Inde-pendent	Needs Assist-ance	Unable
Ambulation	Bed-Chair			
	Walking			
	Stairs			
	Wheelchair			
	Crutches			
	Walker			
	Cane			
Activities	Bathe self			
	Dress self			
	Feed self			
	Brushing teeth			
	Shaving			
	Toilet			
	Commode			
	Bedpan/Urinal			

Bowel & Bladder Program ☐Yes ☐No

Incontinence: Bladder☐ Bowel☐
Date of Last Enema

Catheter: Type
Date last changed:

Weight	Height	Date
Anointed Yes☐ No☐		Date

Check if Pertinent: (describe at right) ▷

DISABILITIES
- ☐ Amputation
- ☐ Paralysis
- ☐ Contractures
- ☐ Decubitus
- ☐ Other

IMPAIRMENTS
- ☐ Speech
- ☐ Hearing
- ☐ Vision
- ☐ Sensation
- ☐ Other

COMMUNICATION
- ☒ Can Write
- ☒ Talks
- ☒ Understands Speaking
- ☒ Understands English
- ☐ If no, Other Language?
- ☒ Reads
- ☐ Non-Verbal

BEHAVIOR
- ☒ Alert
- ☐ Forgetful
- ☐ Noisy
- ☐ Confused
- ☐ Withdrawn
- ☐ Wanders
- ☐ Other

REQUIRES
Mark "S" if sent; "N" if needed

- ☐ Colostomy Care
- ☐ Cane
- ☐ Crutches
- ☐ Walker
- ☐ Wheelchair
- ☐ Other
- ☐ Dentures
- ☐ Eye Glasses
- ☐ Hearing Aid
- ☐ Prosthesis
- ☐ Side Rails

PATIENT CARE PLAN
(Explain details of care, medications, treatments, teaching, habits, preferences, and goals.)

Medications: Note time last dose given on day of discharge.

Pt was taught HBGM using chem-strips and also accuschedule machine, which she plans to purchase. Pt has excellent and accurate technique with accucheck, can also visually read chem-strips if necessary. Instructed to check FS's q am after breakfast, after lunch, after dinner, and at hs at first. Please re-evaluate and change prn. Given written info. about HBGM, guidelines for all steps (which no longer needs to use to do), and times to check FS's. Kept chart at BI to record insulin doses and BS's during hospitalization which she has been doing. Will continue at home and will bring chart to clinic appts. Has been r'ing S & A in hospital by self accurately, records in chart also, to continue at home. Understands what ketones are and to watch for them.

Pt was taught basics of normal insulin/BS relationship and the alteration in DM. Verbalizes understanding of basics. Given much written info. to take home and also given info. re resources to get further info. if desired. Verbalizes understanding of hypo- and hyperglycemia, S/S, and Rx. Has not experienced insulin Rx yet. Has been taught and given info. about insulin effects and peak of action but will need further teaching on this. Sick day rules gone over with pt; will need reinforcement. Diet instruction by RD (see below). Teaching re exercise begun but will need further instruction. Taught foot care but will need reinforcement. Complications of DM not gone over in detail to avoid unnecessary anxiety at this point and too much info. at once. Has fear of complications from what she already knows. Will need teaching in this area stressing prevention, precautions.

_____
Signature of Nurse

Telephone_____ Date _____

NUTRITION: (discuss food preferences, understanding of diet, teaching needs and goals)   Diet enclosed ☐Yes ☐No

821-640 9/85

APPROVED BY THE MASSACHUSETTS DEPARTMENT OF PUBLIC HEALTH

_____
Nutritionist Signature   Telephone   Date

Page 2
Patient Care Referral Form

Name _____ Mrs. Collins _____

Record # _____

Transfer to: _____

NURSING: Self Care Status Check Functional Level	Inde-pendent	Needs Assist-ance	Unable
Ambulation Bed-Chair			
Walking			
Stairs			
Wheelchair			
Crutches			
Walker			
Cane			
Activities Bathe self			
Dress self			
Feed self			
Brushing teeth			
Shaving			
Toilet			
Commode			
Bedpan/Urinal			

Bowel & Bladder Program ☐ Yes ☐ No
Incontinence: Bladder ☐ Bowel ☐
Date of Last Enema
Catheter: Type
Date last changed:

Weight	Height	Date
Anointed Yes ☐ No ☐	Date	

Check if Pertinent: (describe at right) ▷

DISABILITIES
☐ Amputation
☐ Paralysis
☐ Contractures
☐ Decubitus
☐ Other

IMPAIRMENTS
☐ Speech
☐ Hearing
☐ Vision
☐ Sensation
☐ Other

COMMUNICATION
☐ Can Write
☐ Talks
☐ Understands Speaking
☐ Understands English
☐ If no, Other Language?
☐ Reads
☐ Non-Verbal

BEHAVIOR
☐ Alert
☐ Forgetful
☐ Noisy
☐ Confused
☐ Withdrawn
☐ Wanders
☐ Other

REQUIRES
Mark "S" if sent; "N" if needed
☐ Colostomy Care ☐ Dentures
☐ Cane ☐ Eye Glasses
☐ Crutches ☐ Hearing Aid
☐ Walker ☐ Prosthesis
☐ Wheelchair ☐ Side Rails
☐ Other

PATIENT CARE PLAN
(Explain details of care, medications, treatments, teaching, habits, preferences, and goals.)

Medications: Note time last dose given on day of discharge.

Pt knows what equipment to get and where to obtain supplies. Plans to get supplies from pharmacy on way home from hospital. Will purchase accucheck, autolet, and chem-strips.

Pt is very intelligent, a quick learner, retains well, and is highly motivated to learn. Most anxiety was re injections, which she has handled well. Please continue to evaluate this. Husband has been included in all aspects of teaching and is also highly motivated. Verbalizes understanding of teaching but has not done any of care yet. Has seen pt perform all aspects of care. Further teaching with husband may be an area to work on.

Please continue to evaluate BS control, home self care management, compliance, knowledge, answer questions, work on problems prn. Re-evaluate for further F/U needed and frequency of appts. Will begin with weekly appts. with first appt. arranged for 10/19/84 at 11 am. Pt is aware. Any questions or problems, please call.

Signature of Nurse
Telephone 777-9999 Date 10/13/84

NUTRITION: (discuss food preferences, understanding of diet, teaching needs and goals) Diet enclosed ☐ Yes ☐ No

Nutritionist Signature   Telephone   Date

White - Receiving Facility   Canary - Medical Records   Pink - C.C. Services

620-22M - 821-640   9/85

APPROVED BY THE MASSACHUSETTS DEPARTMENT OF PUBLIC HEALTH

Page 3
Patient Care Referral Form

Name: _____ Mrs. Collins _____

Record # _____

Transfer to: _____

_____

SOCIAL SERVICE:

Prior to hospitalization, patient lived:
- ☐ Alone
- ☐ With Family
- ☐ Other _____
- ☐ Nursing Home
- ☐ With Friends

SOCIAL INFORMATION (including patient's personality, attitude toward illness and family constellation and inter-relationships)

Social Services not required.

Identified Problems:

Plan (include short and long range plans)

Will referring unit social worker plan to follow patient: Yes ☐   No ☐

Name	Signature & Title	Phone	Date

THERAPIES (P.T., O.T., Speech)   Instructions enclosed: Yes ☐   No ☐

Therapies not required.

Signature of Therapist	Phone	Date

RECEIVING FACILITY

DISTRIBUTION: **WHITE**-RECEIVING FACILITY; **CANARY**-MEDICAL RECORD; **PINK**-C.C. SERVICE

620-17M - 681-282   9/85

APPROVED BY THE MASSACHUSETTS DEPARTMENT OF PUBLIC HEALTH

HEAD TRAUMA

FHPAA

General Summary

Betsy H. is a 22-year-old, right-handed, single female, who was admitted to Beth Israel Hospital on May 13, 1985, with head trauma after being struck by a van. Onlookers reported that she was unresponsive but made agitated movements of all extremities. Brought to the hospital by ambulance, the patient required cervical spine immobilization and had to be ambu-bagged because of apnea en route. She had multiple scalp lacerations and multiple hand, extremity, and trunk abrasions.

When she was admitted, her blood pressure was 260/120; her pulse rate, 80 beats per minute. No eye opening or vocalization occurred; she was unresponsive. There was nonpurposeful movement of all extremities and questionable seizure activity. Bilateral reflexes were 4+. Her pupils were equal, sluggish, and dysconjugate. Clear fluid drained from the right ear. Battle's sign appeared behind the left ear. The patient was hyperventilated, intubated, and was given IV administration of dexamethasone (Decadron), furosemide (Lasix), and mannitol. An indwelling catheter was inserted. Peritoneal lavage produced a clear return. Results of radiographs of the chest, cervical spine, the pelvis, and hands were all normal. A computed tomography (CT) scan showed brain contusions and severe contusion and swelling of the right temporal lobe, herniating over the tentorial notch. The patient underwent emergency partial temporal lobectomy on the right side, acute subdural hematoma evacuation, and revision of occipital laceration on the left side. Postoperative diagnoses were temporal contusion and hemorrhage on the right side, diffuse cerebral edema, frontal contusion on the right side, acute subdural hematoma, basilar fracture of the left side of the skull, bilateral scalp lacerations, and multiple trunk and extremity abrasions.

Betsy was admitted at 5 PM to the surgical intensive care unit (ICU) directly from the operating room. She received peripheral intravenous D_5 (dextrose 5%) and NS (normal saline) with KC1, 60 mEq at 50 mL/h; peripheral heparin lock flush of left brachial arterial line; endotracheal tube; oral gastric tube; Foley catheter; and head dressing saturated with serosanguineous drainage (changed by the physician). The head of the bed was elevated to 45°. The patient's temp decreased from 38.9°C to 37.8°C after she received two acetaminophen (Tylenol) suppositories. Her blood pressure was 130–135/60s; her pulse rate, 80s and 90s (beats per minute), in normal sinus rhythm. She required various ventilator adjustments for hyperventilation. The patient's breath sounds were clear bilaterally. She received 1-phenethyl-4-(N-propionylanilino)-piperi-dine (Fentanyl) and pancuronium bromide (Pavulon). Her eyes were closed; she showed no response to stimuli. Decerebrate posturing was noted once; pupils were 3 mm and sluggish. The patient has been placed on phenytoin (Dilantin), phenobarbital, dexamethasone (Decadron), and mannitol. Her urine output was 50 to 60 mL/h. The nursing plan calls for the use of steroids, mannitol, dehydration, hyperventilation, and head-of-bed elevation (45°).

Because the patient is unable to participate, the medical record and the patient's mother, Mrs. H., are the sources of information.

Pattern Areas

Health Perception–Health Management

Mrs. H. states that Betsy has normally been in good health and physically very active. Her past medical history includes acne for 12 years and lower-back pain after prolonged sitting. Her past surgical history lists only tonsillectomy when the patient was three years old. The patient is a nonsmoker, and her use of alcohol (according to her mother) is limited to one to two social drinks each week. For the past four months preceding her admission, she was taking prednisone, 5 mg, p.o. QD for acne. She has no known allergies to drugs or food. Betsy uses the "Musician's Clinic" at Massachusetts General Hospital for low-back pain which is due to piano playing. For any other needs, she is referred to specialists by an obstetrician who is a friend of the family. Her insurance is through Aetna. All family members are aware of the reason for her admission.

Self-Perception–Self-Concept

No assessment of this area can be made at this time.

Roles-Relationship

Betsy's parents, siblings, and boyfriend—all live locally—awaited her arrival in ICU from surgery. Her mother and father wish to be notified in case of an emergency. Betsy lives in a Brookline apartment with one roommate. She works as a jazz pianist-composer at two local restaurants. Mrs. H. says that Betsy has a "large circle of friends" who may need to be restricted from visiting the patient, though they may speak with the family.

Coping-Stress

Mrs. H. states that Betsy has never had to deal with a crisis like the one she is now facing. She becomes "flustered" and tends to rely on others' opinions when making decisions. Mrs. H. wonders how Betsy will "handle being laid up"—especially if she has "handicaps." She began to cry and verbalize her fear that Betsy "may not make it." Social service has been consulted and will meet with the family tomorrow.

Cognitive-Perceptual

The patient likes to be called Betsy. She has no speech or learning problems and no hearing deficit. Nearsighted, she has worn glasses for five years. She is a recent college graduate. The mother states that the patient is a very talented musician, despite her age.

Activity-Exercise

Betsy ran five miles each day within a busy schedule. She enjoyed most sports and had no limitations. Presently on bedrest, the patient is without spontaneous motor movement—except intermittent abnormal posturing. She has full range of motion to all extremities.

Nutritional-Metabolic

The patient has no dietary restrictions; but her mother says that Betsy "never eats well-balanced meals because she's always on the go." Her weight is stable. Currently she is receiving nothing by mouth, only by IV. The oral mucous membranes are pink and moist; her dentition is good. Her skin is dry and has abrasions which have been cleaned with providone-iodine (Betadine). There is a 2-×-3-inch bruise on the left hip.

Elimination

Betsy's mother is not aware of problems with elimination. The patient now has decreased bowel sounds and a soft abdomen. Clear, pale urine is draining from the indwelling catheter.

Sleep-Rest

The patient sleeps from 11 PM to 7 AM. There is no history of difficulties related to sleep.

Values-Beliefs

The patient belongs to the Hebrew religion, but her mother is unsure of the role it plays in Betsy's life. Mrs. H. requests to see Rabbi.

Sexuality-Reproductive

Mrs. H. is unaware of any history of gynecological problems for Betsy. Further information in this area cannot be obtained at this time.

Anticipated Discharge Status

In view of the severity of Betsy's head trauma, she will most likely require various therapies to assist her in returning to the optimal level of function. Therefore, a rehabilitative facility will be the probable place of discharge when she is medically stable.

Assessment and Plan

The patient's continuing care assessment points up eight problems that must be dealt with:

1. Increased intracranial pressure secondary to severe head trauma and brain surgery; the peak swelling time is approaching
2. Ineffective breathing pattern: apnea secondary to the increased intracranial pressure
3. Fluid volume deficit *or* fluid and electrolyte imbalance secondary to the use of diuretics and the fluid restriction
4. Impaired physical mobility secondary to the comatose state, the need for activity restriction and the potential posttrauma motor deficits
5. Potential for ineffective family coping secondary to life-threatening crisis, and the potential to become a long-term situation
6. Impaired skin integrity secondary to the traumatic wounds and surgical incisions, which is compounded by inadequate nutrition, use of steroids, and immobility
7. Nutrition deficit secondary to baseline inadequate diet, nothing-by-mouth status, and catabolic state
8. Total self-care deficit secondary to a comatose state

The eight assessed problems must be dealt with as follows:

1. Reduce intracranial pressure to a normal range by the use of constant intracranial pressure monitoring, pharmacologic agents, hyperventilation, head-of-bed elevation and proper head-body alignment, and the modification of nursing interventions that tend to increase intracranial pressure.
2. Stabilize the patient's respiratory status by reducing intracranial pressure, by providing adequate oxygenation and ventilation, and by administering routine pulmonary care interventions from nursing and chest physical therapists.
3. Stabilize fluid and electrolyte balance by mildly dehydrating the patient through diuretic administration according to the physician's measurement; by close monitoring of serum chemistries, hematocrit, intake and output, ECG; and by observing the patient for signs of excess dehydration.

4. Maintain musculoskeletal function by proper positioning and extending range of motion and by consultation with physical and occupational therapists. Prevent complications related to immobility (eg, atelectasis and pneumonia, blood-clot formation, and pressure sores) by appropriate interventions.

5. Assist the family to cope with the crisis by providing them with appropriate information, by encouraging them to ask questions and ventilate concerns and feelings, by assessing their understanding of the patient's condition and treatment, and by consulting with social service for intervention.

6. Promote wound healing by routine wound care and assessment of cleanliness, healing, and nutritional support. Prevent further skin breakdown through good hygiene and lubrication, repositioning on air mattress, and the use of a pull-sheet.

7. Provide for adequate nutrition by establishing alternative routes and methods to feed the patient during team discussion—if she should remain unable to eat by mouth within two days—and by consulting with the nutritionist.

8. Perform all necessary ADLs for the patient.

FHPA

General Summary

Betsy H. is a 22-year-old, right-handed, single female admitted to Beth Israel Hospital with head trauma after being hit by a van. On May 14, a CT scan showed a new, moderate-large, acute parietal epidural hematoma of the left side which was immediately evacuated by craniectomy. This procedure was accompanied by complication of an upper lobe collapse (right side) due to a mucous plug.

The patient was treated with mannitol, dexamethasone (Decadron), phenytoin (Dilantin), fluid restriction, and head-of-bed elevation. Intracranial monitoring revealed high intracranial pressures (ICP). Betsy was still having decerebrate and decorticate posturing, sluggish and unequal pupils, agitation, and vital sign changes (high BP and low pulse). She responded temporarily to hyperventilation, pancuronium bromide (Pavulon), Fentanyl, and mannitol. The patient was then put on thiopental sodium (Pentothal drip) to reduce ICP, with good results. Her neurological status began to improve. Now awake for longer periods, she is without abnormal posturing and has begun to move her right upper extremity laterally (questionably to command). She withdraws the right leg in response to painful stimuli. There is no response to painful stimuli administered to the left side—except, perhaps, a slight muscle contraction. The pupils are unequal (the left is larger); both are reactive to light. Physical and occupational therapists have been working regularly with the patient. She wears hand and footdrop splints. She gets up

and into the chair only with total assistance. Her family and her boyfriend have been taught range-of-motion and some stimulation techniques (cassettes, pictures). They participate daily in her care.

The patient had a tracheostomy and a gastrostomy feeding tube placement on May 23 without problems. The pneumothorax has resolved; the chest tube has been discontinued. She was weaned from the ventilator on May 30, and antibiotics for tracheitis were discontinued. Her vital signs have returned to normal ranges: respirations, 18–24 min; pulse rates, 80–100 beats per minute; and BP 120–130/60s, afebrile.

Gastrostomy tube feedings are well tolerated. The patient is being followed by nutrition therapy. Social service has also been seeing the parents frequently—mostly the mother—since admission. The patient arrived on the floor at 1 PM.

Sources of information continue to be Mrs. H. and the medical record. The patient is still unable to participate in the interview.

Pattern Areas

Health Perception–Health Maintenance

Betsy's parents have requested to be kept informed of any changes in her condition. Mrs. H. verbally demonstrates an accurate understanding of the patient's injuries and condition. She perceives her daughter as "improved but still very serious."

Nutritional-Metabolic

Mrs. H. says that Betsy's diet before admission consisted mainly of salads, cottage cheese, and yogurt because these are "fast and easy." She does enjoy well-balanced meals and has a good appetite when the food is prepared for her. She is satisfied with her baseline weight of 125 lb. Her height is 5 ft 5 in.

The patient currently has no oral intake and has a 1800-mL fluid restriction. She receives Osmolyte-HN with vegetable oil and Propac at 80 mL/h by gastric tube. She has active bowel sounds. Her weight is 99.6 lb. The oral mucous membranes are pink and intact, but dry. Her skin is dry and without pressure areas. Abrasions are healing and clean.

Elimination

The patient is now incontinent of urine and stool. She shows no signs or symptoms of urinary tract infection. Urine output is sufficient. She has a BM every other day on the current regimen.

Activity-Exercise

Mrs. H. describes Betsy as normally very active and "peppy." Her motor status is unchanged. Occupational and physical therapies work together for a block of time each day; this activity tires her. She is not able to participate in ADLs. The patient has full range-of-motion in all extremities, but the left shoulder girdle is beginning to tighten. She moves her head from side to side, but with poor control. The patient wears pneumatic compression boots. Patient wears heated nebulizer tracheostomy mask, (O_2, 40%). Her breath sounds are clear and equal bilaterally. There are no signs or symptoms of dyspnea.

Sleep-Rest

The patient stays awake up to 4h and naps briefly (30 to 60 minutes) during the day. Her sleep pattern at night is still disturbed, especially by her need for care interventions.

Cognitive-Perceptual

Mrs. H. says that Betsy "has always been an excellent student." She graduated from college with honors in music. Her neurological status remains unchanged; however the patient does appear to follow her mother with her eyes for short periods. Because she is nonverbal, on account of the tracheostomy, language or speech cannot be assessed.

Self-Perception–Self-Concept

Information about this pattern is unavailable from the patient. Mrs. H. states that "being a pianist is a part of Betsy," so she "will not feel the same about herself without that ability." She also mentioned that her daughter will have difficulty adjusting to the shaven head.

Roles-Relationship

Mrs. H. describes Betsy as "a very friendly girl" who has always been socially popular. Friends have limited their visits only because of the family's request. The family has arranged for at least one member to be with the patient at all times during visiting hours; they have been able to pull together and to support each other. They feel that Betsy is "lucky to be alive." She was to become engaged this fall, but (her mother states) they will need to reconsider and postpone it if necessary, depending on her progress. Her boyfriend is aware of this possibility.

Sexuality-Reproductive

No new information is available.

Coping-Stress

Mrs. H. has identified areas with which Betsy will have to cope: ongoing therapy for an unspecified amount of time in another setting, uncertainty about the potential level of function, postponement of the engagement, and job security.

The patient's parents—especially her mother—have been meeting regularly with social service. They verbalize their appreciation for being kept fully informed, because it helps them to be more realistic and to cope. They report feeling very "sad," and frustrated that all they can do is "wait and watch." They want to continue to participate in Betsy's care as much as possible.

Values-Belief

Mrs. H. says that Betsy really values her relationship with her family members and close friends, which she describes as "mutually satisfying." She further says that her daughter's career as a pianist-composer is also important to her—especially when she puts so much work into it.

NURSING CARE PLAN

NURSING HISTORY

FORMULATED BY Patricia Cassaccio   DATE 5/14/85

Betsy H. is a 22-year-old right-handed single female admitted to Surg. ICU 5/13/85 with severe head trauma. 5/13-right partial temporal lobectomy for herniation, acute sub-basilar skull fracture, multiple trunk & extremity abrasions. 5/14-new left epidural hematoma evacuated via craniectomy and complicated by right pneumothorax. 5/16-19-entothal drip to reduce intracranial pressure with good effect. 5/23-tracheostomy and gastrostomy tube placement. 5/30-off ventilator. 6/3-transferred to floor. Initially post-op, was comatose, no spontaneous movement except abnormal posturing, agitation, sluggish & unequal pupils, vital signs changes. Good progress over last few weeks. Now awake 4° at a time, beginning to move right arm laterally. Right leg withdraws to pain. Left side without spontaneous movement. Pupils remain unequal, left larapies. No significant past medical or surgical history. No known allergies. Admission vital signs 99.4 r - 76-20 128/62. Family very supportive and involved in daily care.

NURSING DIAGNOSIS	EXPECTED OUTCOME	NURSING CARE PLAN WITH NURSING ORDERS
1. Ineffective airway clearance, 2° impaired level of consciousness, and inability to mobilize own secretions.	Pt will regain ability to maintain patient airway with increasingly less dependence on staff assistance as level of consciousness and mobility improve, beginning immediately.	- Assist pt to deep breathe and cough q2°, using ambubag. - Reposition pt side to side q2°, maintaining aspiration precautions with HOB 45° or more. - Maintain oxygen at 40% heated nebulizer via trach mask as ordered. - Provide with fluids up to 1800 cc fluid restriction as ordered. - Monitor intake and output. - Observe character of respirations q2° & prn. - Auscultate breath sounds q2°, monitoring for adventitious or decreased breath sounds. - Administer chest physical therapy q4°, assessing before and after treatment for effectiveness and pt's tolerance as ordered. - Assess need for tracheal suction with chest physical therapy treatments. - Observe color, consistency, amount, odor of sputum obtained. - Observe for symptoms and signs of hypoxemia (restlessness, confusion, lethargy, headache, dyspnea, diaphoresis, vital sign changes).

NURSING DIAGNOSIS	EXPECTED OUTCOME	NURSING CARE PLAN WITH NURSING ORDERS
2. Potential for increased cranial pressure 2° recent multiple head traumas, Decadron taper, and increased activity.	Pt will not develop signs and symptoms of increased intra-cranial pressure with Decadron taper and activity increase.	– Assess mental status and neuro and vital signs q4° for changes from baseline and/or signs of increasing intra-cranial pressure. – Administer Decadron taper as ordered, carefully observing pt's response. – Maintain head and body in proper alignment at all times. – Prevent valsalva – remind pt to exhale to help straining with moving about, and administer bowel meds to avoid constipation. – Maintain HOB 45° or higher at all times.
3. Impaired physical mobility: no spontaneous, voluntary motor movement (except right arm laterally), 2° damage S/P head trauma.	Pt will regain optimal level of mobility through participation in physical and occupational therapies over long term.	– Reposition pt side to side q2°, maintaining proper body alignment. – Perform passive range of motion to all joints q4°, encouraging pt's participation. – Apply hand splints 2° on and 2° off, increasing time on as tolerated. – When pneumatic compression boots are off, apply footdrop splints. – Monitor pt's progress with physical and occupational therapies; follow through on treatment plans. – Assess readiness for assistive devices.
	Complications related to immobility will be prevented.	Additional preventing interventions: – Apply pneumatic compression boots 3° on/1° off, and increase time on as tolerated. – Observe extremities for signs thrombophlebitis qs. – See #1 for respiratory care interventions. – Observe pt and urine for signs and symptoms of urinary tract infection. – Provide pt with up to 1800 cc fluid/day. – Chem-stick all urine. – Administer MOM every two nights if no bowel movement and follow with Dulcolax suppository in morning as ordered.

NURSING DIAGNOSIS	EXPECTED OUTCOME	NURSING CARE PLAN WITH NURSING ORDERS
4. Potential for in-effective family coping related to current crisis and associated feelings of helplessness and frustration.	Parents will verbalize accurate understanding of pt's condition and treatments as well as realistic expectations.	– Be available during physician explanations of pt's condition to later clarify and reinforce the information. – Encourage family members to ask questions prn. – Provide them with opportunity to ventilate feelings and concerns daily. – Demonstrate support for family's desire to participate in care by performing teaching, giving positive feedback. – Maintain open communication with social service.
5. Actual and potential impaired skin in-tegrity 2° surgical incisions, traumatic abrasions, immobility, and Decadron.	Pt's skin will regain integrity through routine care and cleansing, monitoring of wound healing, nutritional support, and Decadron taper in progress.	– Observe all wounds and incisions for cleanliness, drainage, signs of inflammation or infection, odor q shift. – Assess vital signs q 4°. – Assess WBC/differential as obtained. – Provide trach care in sterile manner, cleansing with ½ strength hydrogen peroxide, rinsing with saline, drying with 4 x 4 94° + prn as ordered. – Apply dry sterile dressing to gastrostomy incision and stoma qd and prn.
	Prevent further breakdown in skin integrity through appropriate preventive measures.	– Apply air mattress to bed. – Keep skin clean and well lubricated with lotion. – Reposition pt side to side 92°. – Inspect entire skin for signs of pressure points with each turn. – Provide with adequate nutrition.
6. Nutritional deficit 2° inability to take oral nourishment.	Pt will receive adequate nutrition and begin slow weight gain through use of feeding gastrostomy tube.	– Administer G-tube feedings of osmolyte HN with vegetable oil and propac at 80 cc/° via pump as ordered. – Observe pt for signs of intolerance to tube feed (ex: loose stools, high aspirates). – Obtain weight 3 times each week. – Assess cough, gag and swallow reflexes qd. – Use foods she likes when attempting oral intake ability--especially ice cream! – Consult occupational therapy for feeding evaluation when pt is ready.

NURSING DIAGNOSIS	EXPECTED OUTCOME	NURSING CARE PLAN WITH NURSING ORDERS
7. Self care deficit (total) 2° severe motor deficit and cognitive/perceptual impairment.	Pt will demonstrate beginning participation in ADL's through aggressive physical and occupational therapies with assist from devices or others as needed, beginning before discharge.	— Perform activities of daily living for pt while she is unable to participate. — Assess pt for readiness to begin to participate. — Follow through with therapists' interventions. — Reinforce teaching with family.

Patient Care Referral Form

FROM: Beth Israel Hospital	Patient's Hospital Record # _____

PATIENT NAME: Betsy H.

Unit/Clinic 7 North	ADDRESS: 12 River St.
ADDRESS Boston	Bayside, MA TEL. 333-2222

		FLOOR	APT. #	BIRTHDATE 11/6/62
ADM. DATE 5/13/85	DISCH. DATE 7/2/85	AGE 22	SEX M	MARITAL STATUS S M W D SEP.	RELIGION Hebrew

	RELATIVE OR GUARDIAN: Mother - Mrs. H.
TO: Rehabilitation Hospital	
ADDRESS: Boston	ADDRESS: 1331 Tadd Street
TEL.	Bridge, MA TEL. 414-4444

MEDICARE NO. & LETTER	PLAN A X	BLUE CROSS NO. 543210	SOC. SEC. NO. 222-55-8888	OTHER

CLINIC APPOINTMENTS	DATE	TIME	Agency Worker Office Address Telephone

DIAGNOSIS (S) Surgery Performed and Date, Allergies or Infections R temporal lobe herniation, mult. brain contusions, acute subdural hematoma, 1 basilar skull fracture, scalp lacerations, 1 epidural hematoma, R pneumothorax, tracheitis, 1 deep vein thrombosis. SURG - 5/13 - R temporal lobectomy (partial). 5/14 - epidural clot evac via craniectomy & chest tube. 5/23 - tracheostomy and gastrostomy. NKA

Is Patient Family aware of diagnosis?	Date of last physical 7/2/85
PHYSICIAN'S ORDERS: (Include specific orders for Diet, Lab Tests, Speech, and O.T.)	TRANSPORT BY: X Ambulance ☐ Car

MEDICATION	STRENGTH AND FREQUENCY	DATE & TIME OF LAST DOSE
Tegretol	400 mg per GT tid	7/2 8A
Carmadin	10 mg per GT qd	7/1 8P
Multivitamins	1 per GT qd	7/2 8A
Iron - K_2SO_4		
Mycostatin	5 cc to mouth qid	
tube feed - osmolyte HN & veg. oil & propac 80 cc/°		
daily physical, speech, occupational therapy		
PT/PTT qd/qod until Coumadin dose stabilizes		

TREATMENTS & FREQUENCY: Follow-up CT scan in 2 months

DIET: as above

PHYSICAL THERAPY: Restrict Activity X Yes ☐ No   Sensation Impaired X Yes ☐ No

Precautions   Weight Bearing Status - Non-Weight X   Partial-Weight ☐   Full-Weight ☐

SPECIFIC TREATMENT & FREQUENCY: _____

ANTICIPATED GOALS: Recover nearly full motor movement with residual L wkness. Independence in ADL's.

REHABILITATION POTENTIAL IS: Good

HOME HEALTH SERVICES:	☐ NURSING	☐ OCC. THERAPY	☐ SPEECH THERAPY	☐ SOCIAL WORK	☐ H.H. AIDE	☐ OTHER - SPECIFY

The above services require Level of Care: ☐ I ☐ II ☐ III ☐ IV

If Chronic Hospital, why? _____

CERTIFICATION: ✱(when applicable)
Services above needed to treat condition for which patient was hospitalized ☐ Yes ☐ No
I certify that the above named patient is: (check one)
☐ Under my care (or has been referred to another physician having professional knowledge of patient's condition); is home bound except when receiving out-patient services; requires skilled nursing care on an intermittent basis or physical or speech therapy as specified in the orders.
☐ Requires skilled nursing care on a continuing basis for any of the conditions for which he/she received care during this hospitalization.

_____ M.D.
Signature
John James
_____ M.D.
Print Name
Tel. 777-7777 Date 7/1/85 Will follow X Yes ☐ No - If no, who?
_____ M.D.
ADDRESS: _____ TEL. _____

9/85
282-956

APPROVED BY THE MASSACHUSETTS DEPARTMENT OF PUBLIC HEALTH

Page 2
Patient Care Referral Form

Name ___Betsy H.___

Record # _____

Transfer to: _____

NURSING: Self Care Status Check Functional Level	Inde-pendent	Needs Assist-ance	Unable
Ambulation Bed–Chair			
Walking			
Stairs			
Wheelchair			
Crutches			
Walker			
Cane			
Activities Bathe self			
Dress self			
Feed self			
Brushing teeth			
Shaving			
Toilet			
Commode			
Bedpan/Urinal			

Bowel & Bladder Program ☐ Yes ☐ No
Incontinence: Bladder ☐ Bowel ☐
Date of Last Enema
Catheter: Type
Date last changed:

Weight	Height	Date
Anointed Yes ☐ No ☐		Date

Check if Pertinent: (describe at right) ▷

DISABILITIES
☐ Amputation
☐ Paralysis
☐ Contractures
☐ Decubitus
☐ Other

IMPAIRMENTS
☐ Speech
☐ Hearing
☐ Vision
☐ Sensation
☐ Other

COMMUNICATION
☐ Can Write
☐ Talks
☐ Understands Speaking
☐ Understands English
☐ If no, Other Language?
☐ Reads
☐ Non-Verbal

BEHAVIOR
☐ Alert
☐ Forgetful
☐ Noisy
☐ Confused
☐ Withdrawn
☐ Wanders
☐ Other

REQUIRES
Mark "S" if sent; "N" if needed

☐ Colostomy Care   ☐ Dentures
☐ Cane   ☐ Eye Glasses
☐ Crutches   ☐ Hearing Aid
☐ Walker   ☐ Prosthesis
☐ Wheelchair   ☐ Side Rails
☐ Other

PATIENT CARE PLAN
(Explain details of care, medications, treatments, teaching, habits, preferences, and goals.)

Medications: Note time last dose given on day of discharge.

Betsy H. is a 22-year-old right-handed single female admitted to BIH 5/13/85 with head trauma after being struck by a van. Had emergency surgery for right partial temporal lobectomy, acute subdural hematoma evacuation, and revision of left occipital laceration p̄ CT scan showed right temporal herniation and contusions. Also had left basilar skull fracture, bilateral scalp lacerations, and multiple trunk and extremity abrasions. Developed left parietal epidural hematoma on 5/14 and had evacuation via craniectomy. (Had complication of right pneumothorax during surgery, since resolved.) Post-op, she was comatose with periods decerebrate and decorticate posturing unequal and sluggish pupils, vital sign changes (high blood pressure with low pulse), and agitation despite diuretics, hyperventilation, Decadron, Fentanyl, and Pavulon. Was put in Pentothal coma to help reduce intracranial pressure, with good results.

Pt has shown marked neurological improvement over the past month. She is now awake for increasing periods during day and is becoming more attentive. Has periods of agitation, worse when first wakes, that respond to stimulation and brief re-orientation. Follows one-step and, inconsistently, more complex commands. Moves right arm against resistance and right leg against gravity – both very ataxic. Left arm recently began to move laterally. Left leg withdraws to painful stimuli. Pupils unequal, left is larger, and both reactive to light. Of note is that she has not yet begun to vocalize. She has begun to communicate using hand signals (see speech therapy referral). No signs of seizure activity have been observed. Most recent CT scan showed improvement in mild hydrocephalus.

_____
Signature of Nurse
Telephone _____ Date _____

NUTRITION: (discuss food preferences, understanding of diet, teaching needs and goals)   Diet enclosed ☐ Yes ☐ No

Betsy is a 22-year-old female admitted to BIH 5/13/85 with head trauma. She was receiving the following blended tube feeding: 9 cans of osmolyte HN, 4 tbsp vegetable oil, and 6 tbsp Propac. This provides about 2923 kcal. Would encourage a minimum of 2000 cc per day for continued slow weight gain. Her usual weight is 125 lbs, present weight is 46-48 kg. Beginning oral intake, but amount not sufficient for nutritional needs at present.

821-640 9/85

APPROVED BY THE MASSACHUSETTS DEPARTMENT OF PUBLIC HEALTH

_____
Nutritionist Signature   Telephone   Date

White - Receiving Facility   Canary - Medical Records   Pink - C.C. Services

Page 2
Patient Care Referral Form

Name ___ Betsy H. ___

Record # _____

Transfer to: _____

NURSING: Self Care Status Check Functional Level		Inde- pendent	Needs Assist- ance	Unable
Ambulation	Bed-Chair			
	Walking			
	Stairs			
	Wheelchair			
	Crutches			
	Walker			
	Cane			
Activities	Bathe self			
	Dress self			
	Feed self			
	Brushing teeth			
	Shaving			
	Toilet			
	Commode			
	Bedpan/Urinal			

Bowel & Bladder Program	☐ Yes ☐ No
Incontinence: Bladder ☐ Bowel ☐	
Date of Last Enema	
Catheter: Type Date last changed:	

Weight	Height	Date
Anointed Yes ☐ No ☐	Date	

Check if Pertinent: (describe at right) ▷

DISABILITIES
- ☐ Amputation
- ☐ Paralysis
- ☐ Contractures
- ☐ Decubitus
- ☐ Other

IMPAIRMENTS
- ☐ Speech
- ☐ Hearing
- ☐ Vision
- ☐ Sensation
- ☐ Other

COMMUNICATION
- ☐ Can Write
- ☐ Talks
- ☐ Understands Speaking
- ☐ Understands English
- ☐ If no, Other Language?
- ☐ Reads
- ☐ Non-Verbal

BEHAVIOR
- ☐ Alert
- ☐ Forgetful
- ☐ Noisy
- ☐ Confused
- ☐ Withdrawn
- ☐ Wanders
- ☐ Other

REQUIRES
Mark "S" if sent; "N" if needed
- ☐ Colostomy Care
- ☐ Cane
- ☐ Crutches
- ☐ Walker
- ☐ Wheelchair
- ☐ Other
- ☐ Dentures
- ☐ Eye Glasses
- ☐ Hearing Aid
- ☐ Prosthesis
- ☐ Side Rails

PATIENT CARE PLAN
(Explain details of care, medications, treatments, teaching, habits, preferences, and goals.)

Medications: Note time last dose given on day of discharge.

Betsy had tracheostomy and feeding gastrostomy tubes inserted 5/23 without any problem. Was removed from ventilator 5/30. Had tracheostomy tube removed 7/1. Has had no respiratory distress. Had tracheobronchitis with fever treated with antibiotics, now resolved.

She developed left leg deep vein thrombosis 6/16, treated with bedrest and intravenous heparin drip. Is not on Coumadin. This has slowed progress with physical and occupational therapies.

Family has been participating in her care with ADL's and various therapies. Each member has visited daily and mother spends most of day here. Social service has been seeing parents almost daily (see social service referral).

Betsy is now stable enough for transfer to Rehabilitation Hospital.

Past medical and surgical history includes acne, low back pain after prolonged sitting, and tonsillectomy as child.

Discharge needs include Tegretol 400 mg po tid, Coumadin 10 mg po qhs (last dose received 7/2 8 pm), Multivits 1 po qd, $FeSO_4$ 300 mg po tid, and Mycostatin 5 cc swish and swallow. Last doses given 7/3 at 8 am except as indicated.

No known food or drug allergies.

_____
Signature of Nurse

Telephone _____ Date _____

NUTRITION: (discuss food preferences, understanding of diet, teaching needs and goals)　Diet enclosed ☐ Yes ☐ No

APPROVED BY THE MASSACHUSETTS DEPARTMENT OF PUBLIC HEALTH

821-640　9/85

_____
Nutritionist Signature　　Telephone　　Date

Page 3
Patient Care Referral Form

Name: <u>Betsy H.</u>

Record # _____

Transfer to: _____

SOCIAL SERVICE:

Prior to hospitalization, patient lived:
- [ ] Alone
- [ ] Nursing Home
- [ ] With Family
- [ ] With Friends
- [x] Other <u>roommate</u>

SOCIAL INFORMATION (including patient's personality, attitude toward illness and family constellation and inter-relationships)

Betsy H. is a 22-year-old single female who was struck by a van while crossing street; admitted to BIH 5/13/85. Extent of injuries well documented in nursing and medical summaries.

Betsy was living with a roommate, not far from family's home. Significant others include parents, brother, sister, and boyfriend. They've all been very involved in her care and supportive of each other as well. Each visits daily.

Identified Problems:

Plan (include short and long range plans)

Will referring unit social worker plan to follow patient: Yes [ ] No [ ]

Name	Signature & Title	Phone	Date

THERAPIES (P.T., O.T., Speech)   Instructions enclosed: Yes [ ] No [ ]

P.T.:

Betsy H. is a 22-year-old single female admitted to BIH 5/13/85 with head trauma. History well documented by other sources.

Pt has made significant progress since her accident. Presently alert and responsive to simple commands. Nonverbal with some ability to use hand signals to communicate. Progress has been limited by short attention span and agitation/ irritability and by left leg deep vein thrombosis and subsequent bedrest.

<u>Range of motion:</u> Possibly is normal in all extremities. Tight left shoulder girdle and slightly tight heel cords.

<u>Motor:</u> Minimal movement of left arm with increased tone in left shoulder girdle. Left leg flaccid without spontaneous movement. Right arm has good strength, moves purposefully but very ataxic. Right leg moves almost constantly, usually rotating, has normal tone and fair strength.

<u>Sensation:</u> All extremities react to painful stimuli.

<u>Mobility:</u> Dependent in all bed mobility and transfers. Head control has improved, still poor to fair, leans to right. Poor unsupported and supported sitting balance. Assists rolling to left with verbal cueing. Can push self to supine with right arm. Does not bear weight on arms or extend neck when prone. Have been working on purposeful activities and grabbing objects to increase cognition, and on head control, balance, rolling, trying to bear weight with arms. We've been limited because of deep vein thrombosis.

Signature of Therapist   Phone   Date

620-17M - 681-282   9/85

APPROVED BY THE MASSACHUSETTS DEPARTMENT OF PUBLIC HEALTH

RECEIVING FACILITY
DISTRIBUTION: **WHITE**-RECEIVING FACILITY; **CANARY**-MEDICAL RECORD; **PINK**-C.C. SERVICE

Page 3
Patient Care Referral Form

Name: _____ Betsy H. _____

SOCIAL SERVICE:

Record # _____

Prior to hospitalization, patient lived:

Transfer to: _____

☐ Alone ☐ Nursing Home
☐ With Family ☐ With Friends
☐ Other _____

_____

SOCIAL INFORMATION (including patient's personality, attitude toward illness and family constellation and inter-relationships)

They were initially fearful that she would die and they would lose her that way. They, especially parents, now speak of a different loss, that of losing her as they knew her because of her present physical and cognitive deficits. They are feeling helpless, frustrated, and sad, focusing on the slow progress. Members, especially mother, want and need to be involved in all aspects of Betsy's care and planning. They are also realistic and know that she needs to "struggle" on her own in order to keep making progress and achieve some level of independence. They are very verbal,

Identified Problems

easy to approach, and open to new information and ideas.

Plan (include short and long range plans)

Will referring unit social worker plan to follow patient: Yes ☐   No ☐

_____ _____ _____ _____

Name   Signature & Title   Phone   Date

_____

THERAPIES (P.T., O.T., Speech)   Instructions enclosed: Yes ☐ No ☐

O.T.:

Betsy H. is a 22-year-old single female admitted to BIH 5/13/85 with head trauma. History well documented in referral. Lived with roommate in second floor apartment and worked as pianist/composer.

Communication: Alert, presently non-verbal, can point to appropriate objects. Uses hand signals (see speech referral). Wears glasses for near-sightedness.

Perceptual-Motor/Cognition: Difficult to assess with short attention span, but able to follow one-step directions, knows body parts, right/left discrimination intact, can perform some imitation of movement, can point to and recognize family members.

Upper Extremity Status: Right dominant. Right range of motion normal, very ataxic, has difficulty holding hand signal positions. Left has splint, normal passive range of motion, and now demonstrates wrist extension, elbow flexion, and some finger flexion.

Lower Extremities: Has bilateral footdrop splints.

Activities of Daily Living Status: Fully independent before admission. Is able to swallow soft solids and does better after oral stimulation. Needs maximal assist in all other areas.

_____ _____ _____

Signature of Therapist   Phone   Date

APPROVED BY THE MASSACHUSETTS DEPARTMENT OF PUBLIC HEALTH

620-17M - 681-282   9/85

RECEIVING FACILITY
DISTRIBUTION: **WHITE**-RECEIVING FACILITY; **CANARY**-MEDICAL RECORD; **PINK**-C.C. SERVICE

Page 3
Patient Care Referral Form

Name: Betsy H.

Record #

Transfer to:

<u>SOCIAL SERVICE:</u>

Prior to hospitalization, patient lived:
- [ ] Alone
- [ ] With Family
- [ ] Other
- [ ] Nursing Home
- [ ] With Friends

SOCIAL INFORMATION (including patient's personality, attitude toward illness and family constellation and inter-relationships)

They see her transfer as a sign of progress yet feel a bit uneasy about the loss of established support here and about how well she will do in a rehabilitation setting.

Mother has taken leave of absence from work and stays with Betsy all day. She benefits from and appreciates regular social service contacts. I would encourage early intervention to help ease the transition.

Identified Problems:

Plan (include short and long range plans)

Will referring unit social worker plan to follow patient: Yes [ ] No [ ]

Name	Signature & Title	Phone	Date

THERAPIES (P.T., O.T., Speech)   Instructions enclosed: Yes [ ] No [ ]

O.T. CONTINUED

<u>Facial Status:</u> Can stick out tongue, has good lateral movement, full lip closure, good obicularis oris strength. Clamps teeth when objects put in mouth. Poor head control in flex/extension with fair lateral.

<u>Endurance:</u> Unable to assess because of bed rest.

<u>Assessment:</u> Has made good improvements in cognition, attention span, and right arm movement. This is expected to continue. Has very supportive family and friends who will follow through with all treatment ideas.

SPEECH:

Betsy H. is a 22-year-old single female, right handed, admitted to BIH 5/13/85 with head trauma. History well documented in other disciplines. No significant past history.

Pt was changed to fenestrated trach 6/24, and it was removed 7/1 without any respiratory compromise. She remains non-verbal. Was referred for evaluation of communicative status, which was limited by short attention span and agitation.

Auditory comprehension skills were functional for processing one-step commands, but had difficulty with multi-steps. Uses hand signals for yes/no. "Yes" is the o.k. sign. "No" is thumb under second finger.

Signature of Therapist   Phone   Date

RECEIVING FACILITY
DISTRIBUTION: **WHITE**-RECEIVING FACILITY; **CANARY**-MEDICAL RECORD; **PINK**-C.C. SERVICE

APPROVED BY THE MASSACHUSETTS DEPARTMENT OF PUBLIC HEALTH

620-17M - 681-282   9/85

Page 3
Patient Care Referral Form

Name: _____ Betsy H. _____

Record # _____

Transfer to: _____
_____

SOCIAL SERVICE:

Prior to hospitalization, patient lived:
- ☐ Alone
- ☐ With Family
- ☐ Other _____
- ☐ Nursing Home
- ☐ With Friends

SOCIAL INFORMATION (including patient's personality, attitude toward illness and family constellation and inter-relationships)

Identified Problems:

Plan (include short and long range plans)

Will referring unit social worker plan to follow patient: Yes☐   No☐

Name	Signature & Title	Phone	Date

THERAPIES (P.T., O.T., Speech)   Instructions enclosed: Yes☐ No☐

SPEECH CONTINUED:

Verbal expressive skills assessment showed non-verbal state with no response to stimulation. Buccofacial praxis mildly impaired. Uses hand signal to indicate need for toilet: thumb under first finger.

Reading comprehension skills were functional for processing one-step command, with difficulty and inconsistency on multi-steps. Unable to evaluate written formulation skills because of right arm ataxia.

Summary: Difficult to evaluate with short attention span and intolerance to structure. Her communication status is adequate for processing simple conversation and commands. Expressively non-vocal with some "sign" ability.

Given ability to do above, use of communication board should be considered as well as further development of a sign system.

Family has been counseled in methods to improve communication.

Recommend on-going evaluation and refinement of communication system and continued family counseling. Consider possibility of ear, nose, and throat service consults.

Signature of Therapist   Phone   Date

RECEIVING FACILITY
DISTRIBUTION: **WHITE**-RECEIVING FACILITY; **CANARY**-MEDICAL RECORD; **PINK**-C.C. SERVICE

620-17M - 681-282   9/85

APPROVED BY THE MASSACHUSETTS DEPARTMENT OF PUBLIC HEALTH

HIP FRACTURE

FHPAA

General Summary

Mr. S. is a 90-year-old, widowed man, who fell today and sustained a fracture of the neck of the right femur. He was found conscious on the floor of the bathroom at the Seaside Rehabilitation Center (SRC), where he lives. This is his second Beth Israel Hospital admission. He is scheduled to undergo surgery this evening for the insertion of a Moore's prosthesis in the right femur.

Mr. S. was admitted at 2 PM today from the emergency ward by stretcher, accompanied by a transporter. He was alert, but disoriented to place and time. His vital signs were recorded as follows: temp, 36.8°C; pulse rate, 88 beats per minute; respirations, 22/min; BP, 142/76. His weight was 163 lb. His height could not be determined, but an old record gives it as 5 ft 1 in. He had no known allergies. The patient had one pair of glasses (bifocals) and upper dentures—no lowers; his right ear had a hearing aid in place; he had no other valuables. The right lower extremity was externally rotated and shortened. He was incontinent of urine. An attempt was made to orient the patient to his new environment. He appeared anxious. Pattern areas had to be addressed through observation and the information received on referral; the patient was not a good historian at that time. Generally, however, the patient appeared to be a very healthy 90-year-old person.

Pattern Areas

Health Perception–Health Management

The patient's past medical history and medication includes the following:

- cataract, OS—timolol maleate (Timoptic) drops, BID
- chronic UTIs—Bactrim (not presently taking)
- constipation—docusate sodium (Colace), 100 mg, TID; bisacodyl (Dulcolax), PRN
- dementia
- deaf in left ear; hearing aid in the right ear

His past surgical history includes the insertion of a Richard's screw in his left hip in January 1981. The patient does not smoke or use alcohol. His admitting diagnosis was a fracture of the neck of the right femur. An ecchymotic area was observed on the right hip and the right elbow. No head trauma was apparent.

The patient's physician has been Dr. K.

Self-Perception–Self-Concept

The patient complains of pain at the right hip site. Because of his confusion at this time, no further assessment can be made.

Roles-Relationship

Mr. S. is a retired print-shop worker. He has been a widower for 27 years and has no children. He has been an active resident of SRC since his wife's death.

Coping-Stress

The patient appears to be anxious. He needs a lot of reassurance and contact because of his confused state and the change of environment.

Cognitive-Perceptual

Mr. S. speaks English. He can sense pain. The patient wears glasses (bifocals), is deaf in the left ear, and wears a hearing aid. He is alert, but is disoriented to place and time; there is a history of dementia. He is a high risk for slips and falls.

Activity-Exercise

The referral documents indicate the patient's "minimal use of a cane; independent with ambulation." The patient, however, is unable to address this area.

Nutritional-Metabolic

Mr. S. keeps a Kosher diet. He is obese. Because he uses only upper dentures, he limits his diet to ground meat. His skin integrity is good. There are no pressure sores or lesions, but there are ecchymotic areas on the right hip and the right arm.

Elimination

The patient has a history of constipation. His last BM was two days before admission. Bisacodyl (Dulcolax) was given q3d at SRC if the patient had no BM. Mr. S. was incontinent of urine when he arrived. His urine was cloudy and foul smelling. A Texas condom catheter was applied. Urinalysis was sent for culture and sensitivity evaluation.

Sleep-Rest

Further data are needed.

Values-Beliefs

The patient is a Jew. He observes kosher practices.

Sexuality-Reproductive

No pertinent information is available.

Anticipated Discharge Status

The patient will be able to ambulate by using a walker and with the assistance of one person. He can return to SRC.

Assessment and Plan

The patient's general appearance is that of a well-groomed, well-cared-for 90-year-old gentleman. He appears to be physiologically intact. He is obese. His ability to care for himself is questionable because of stiffening of the joints. He appears frightened and angry, and is gruff in speech.

His disoriented mental status is reflected in his assertion that he is "at home." He has very good long-term memory but no recall of his fall.

His vitals signs are as follows: temp, 36.8° C; pulse rate, 88 beats per minute, regular; BP, 162/76. The patient's oral cavity is dry; he has no permanent teeth. There are no lesions.

Although Mr. S. is unable to fully extend his upper extremities, he is able to reach food on the tray and bring it to his mouth.

The patient's thorax is symmetric and has no visible scars. His breath sounds are clear (respirations, 18/min). The rate and rhythm of the heart sounds are regular. His abdomen is hard—tympanic. Bowel sounds are present.

Assessment of the two lower extremities can be summarized as follows:

1. baseline unaffected left extremity
   - circulation: pulses are moderate; color, pale
   - sensation: positive in all areas
   - movement: limited flexion, good extension, muscle strength weakened.
2. affected right extremity
   - circulation: pulses are weak; color, pale
   - sensation: decreased in all areas, but present
   - movement: minimal at command; otherwise, very weak

A continuing care plan for initial problems can be listed as follows:

- Discharge planning: Return the patient to the SRC and call for further data.
- Immobility (2°) due to fracture of the neck of the right femur: Schedule patient for the OR this evening, and begin pre-op teaching.
- At risk for slips and falls: Assess patient's mental status; provide safety measures, as needed (Posey and side rails); assist the patient to orient to person, place, and time.
- Pain management: Medicate the patient before moving and positioning him.
- Sensory deficit: Maintain the patient's use of glasses and a hearing aid.
- Elimination: Make changes in diet and medication PRN; prepare full FHPA.

FHPA

Because the patient is not a good historian, the following information has also been acquired through direct observation, referrals, and a telephone call to the SRC.

On July 8, Mr. S. underwent the insertion of a Moore's prosthesis in the right femur. This assessment reflects further data since his admission and any change in his status.

Pattern Areas

Health Perception–Health Management

The patient states, "I feel pretty good; my leg is sore, though." However, he is unable to recall his prior admission and states only that his eyes are bad. The nurse from SRC, Ms. C., states that he had been seen regularly (for 8 mo) by the house physician, Dr. K. The patient has had no known allergies. He participated in physical, educational, and vocational activities, but over the past year, his interest and energy had been decreasing.

Mr. S. states, "My family was never very well. I have one living relative—my nephew. My wife had cancer. I don't remember about the rest."

Nutritional-Metabolic

Mr. S. is obese (5 ft 1 in, 163 lb). His present weight represents a 10-lb increase over the past year. Otherwise, he appears to be healthy. Has upper dentures and the minimal flexion and extension of the upper extremities are leading him to tolerate only easily chewable or handled food (eg, with a spoon or straw). He asks to be fed and does eat independently at SRC.

The patient has a history of constipation because he cannot chew food with natural roughage. Therefore, bran is added to his diet; the amounts of cheese and bananas are decreased, and fluids are increased. He also takes multivitamins every day. He says that he is always cold.

Observation of the patient's skin integrity reveals an intact suture line on the right hip, but no redness or swelling. His coccyx is beginning to redden and dry areas have appeared on his heels.

Elimination

For his constipation, Mr. S. takes docusate sodium (Colace) and bisacodyl (Dulcolax) supositories, PRN. The nurse states that they usually give the suppository q2d; then, if there is no result, they give Fleet enemas to disimpact the bowel.

The patient has suffered from urinary incontinence for many years. Chronic UTIs have been treated with Bactrim. He has had a GU workup, but with no result. A Texas catheter has been maintained in an attempt to assure skin integrity and patient comfort.

Activity-Exercise

Mr. S. was an active member of the SRC, although his activity had decreased over the past year. He attended an exercise class three times each week, participated in group activities, and walked to the cafeteria for meals; but he had a "sedentary" job in occupational therapy. He did not make a habit of climbing stairs (he uses the elevator). These past levels of activity are the baseline.

Presently, Mr. S. is on bedrest for the next 24 hours, with legs abducted or externally rotated. Physical therapy will follow. ROM exercises are being done by nursing.

Sleep-Rest

In the past year, Mr. S. has needed much encouragement to "get going"—especially in the morning. He naps in the afternoon and sleeps nine hours at night. Presently, Mr. S. is having some difficulty differentiating the time of day, which may be attributable to his dementia, the surgery, and the change of environment.

Cognitive-Perceptual

This pattern assessment can be summarized as follows:

- Mental Status: The patient is alert to persons, not to place or time.
- Memory: He has excellent long-term memory, but short-term memory loss.
- Balance: The baseline is questionable; present status cannot be assessed.
- Speech: The patient's speech is clear, but he speaks in short, incomplete sentences.
- Vision: He requires glasses for reading and for distance. He has cataracts, OS.
- Hearing: The patient is deaf in his left ear. He wears a hearing aid in the right ear but can only hear a loud or low speaking voice on the right side.
- Pain: The patient complains of discomfort when he is moved; otherwise he appears comfortable.
- Circulation-Sensation-Motion: On the basis of the initial assessment, all three are decreased in the right leg. The patient has good color, a good pulse is

present, sensation is intact, and there is limited motion (also noted on the unaffected side).

Self-Perception–Self-Concept

This pattern cannot be assessed at present.

Roles-Relationship

Mr. S. is a 27-year resident of the SRC. Because he was without other supportive family members, he was encouraged by his nephew to take residence there after his wife's death. They had no children. The charge nurse from SRC has been calling every day about his status.

Sexuality-Reproductive

Assessment of this pattern is not appropriate for this admission.

Coping-Stress

SRC reported that he was easy going, involved with the staff and other patients. More time is needed, however, to assess his ability to cope with this hospitalization.

Values-Beliefs

Mr. S. is an Orthodox Jew. He follows the prayer rituals and a kosher diet. He is active in religious activities at SRC.

Life Patterns and Life-styles

Mr. S. awakens at 7 AM. He washes up independently and uses his walker to walk to breakfast. He sits with the same group of friends each day. Then he participates in an occupational therapy program until 11 AM. Group exercise follows; then, lunch. The next three hours offer socialization activities, then relaxation until dinner at 5 PM. After dinner, the patient usually watches television. He goes to sleep by 10 PM. Mr. S. is in a semiprivate room. His roommate is 10 years younger, and slightly more independent.

Additional Problems

The following additional problems must be dealt with in continuing care discharge planning:

- Altered nutritional-metabolic pattern, 2°, due to decreased activity, and the inability to chew
- Altered elimination pattern, 2°, due to decreased bowel activity and urinary incontinence (history of UTIs)
- Altered mobility, 2°, due to insertion of a Moore's prosthesis

- Altered sleep pattern, 2°, due to a change in environment, routine, and medications
- Altered sensory perception and sensory deprivation, 2°, due to deafness, visual deficiencies, memory loss, pain, and surgery

- At risk for slips and falls, 2°, due to history of dementia
- Altered skin integrity, 2°, due to surgery and bedrest
- Potential clot formation, 2°, due to decreased activity

NURSING CARE PLAN

FORMULATED BY Susan Kinell, R.N.   DATE 7/9/85

NURSING HISTORY

Mr. S. is a 90-year-old widowed male who fell on 7/8/85, sustaining a right femoral neck fx. He was found conscious on the floor of the bathroom where he lives at the Seaside Rehabilitation Center. On 7/9/85 a Moores prosthesis was inserted. Med Hx includes cataract OS, chronic UTI, constipation, and dementia; surgical Hx left Richard's screw to left hip 1/81. Wife died 27 years PTA. Has been a resident of the center since. No known allergies. Medications include Timoptic, Bactrim, Colace, Dulcolox, MOM, codeine, Coumadin. Alert to person — not to place and time.

NURSING DIAGNOSIS	EXPECTED OUTCOME	NURSING CARE PLAN WITH NURSING ORDERS
1. Discharge planning.	Will return to SRC when medically stable.	Continue to keep in contact with nursing at SRC. References will be needed.
2. Altered nutritional metabolic pattern 2° to decreased activity, inability to chew.	Short term goal: Pt's PTA status will be maintained post-op. Long-term goal: Weight reduction, food with higher nutritional value will be introduced.	Enc. fluids at least 2,000 cc/day. Maintain kosher diet. Explore foods high in fiber/bulk, yet easy to chew. ? Lower teeth (only has uppers) Dental consult.
3. Altered elimination pattern 2°: a. bowels – decreased activity, dietary limitations b. bladder – Hx UTI	Bowels: will have regular BM's Bladder: UTI will be eliminated	Bowels: enc. diet as above, increase activity as tolerated. Meds: Colace with Dulcolox q 2 days, followed by Fleets if no results. Bladder: enc. fluids Texas catheter check C+S results Cont. bactrim
4. Altered mobility 2° to insertion of a Moores prosthesis right hip.	Short term goal: Activity will increase. Long term goal: Will return to PTA activity level.	Bedrest at present. ROM to all extremities DT consult OOB to chair 7/11/85 Maintain external rotation, abduction Turn to affected side only

NURSING DIAGNOSIS	EXPECTED OUTCOME	NURSING CARE PLAN WITH NURSING ORDERS
5. Altered sleep pattern 2° to change in environment/routine, medications.	Sleep/wake cycle will be maintained.	Offer stimulating environment during the day to keep awake. – TV, radio – Contact with staff – Lights Offer quiet environment NEC
6. Altered sensory perception with sensory deprivation a. Sensory loss – Hearing – Vision – Memory b. Hx dementia c. Pain management d. Circulation, sensation, motion of right hip	Care will be planned around sensory deficiencies. Pain will be controlled. CSM of right hip will return to PTA status.	Hearing aid in right ear – speak loud and in a low voice. Glasses on while awake. Orient to person/place/thing. Maintain PTA schedules AMAP. Position/offer codeine prn Check circulation/sensation/motion 94° (right hip), record any change.
7. At risk for slips & falls Hx falls Sensory deficits	Pt will not fall.	Alert other health team members of this risk; maintain safe environment. – Posey vest at NOC – Frequent checks – Side rails up; bed in low position
8. Altered skin integrity – right Moores – pressure areas	Suture line will heal without infection. Skin will not break down.	Keep suture line clean and dry. Check for any change qs. Dry heels – Lanolin/booties/keep heels off pressure Coccyx reddened – turn 92° unbleached linen sheepskin keep dry (incontinent) air mattress
9. Potential clot formation – at risk for bleed Coumadin precautions	Will not bleed.	Coumadin 9 D as ordered, monitor labs Guial stool Herne urine Check wound (right hip) for bleeding

Patient Care Referral Form

Patient's Hospital Record # _____

FROM: Beth Israel Hospital	PATIENT NAME ___ Mr. S. ___
Unit/Clinic ___ 12th floor ___	ADDRESS: Seaside Rehabilitation Center
ADDRESS ___ Boston, MA ___	TEL. 333-6000

	TEL.	FLOOR	APT. #	BIRTHDATE
ADM. DATE 7/8/85	DISCH. DATE 7/23/85	AGE 90	SEX M F	MARITAL STATUS S M W D SEP.	RELIGION Hebrew

TO: Seaside Rehabilitation Center

RELATIVE OR GUARDIAN: Mr. S.

ADDRESS: 2 Parway, Centersite, MA

ADDRESS: 5-B Site Ave. Bilford, MA

TEL. 342-6000

TEL. 123-0987

MEDICARE NO. & LETTER 012-34-5678A	PLAN A B	BLUE CROSS NO.	SOC. SEC. NO. 111-11-1111	OTHER
CLINIC APPOINTMENTS	DATE	TIME	Agency Worker Office Address Telephone	

DIAGNOSIS (S) Surgery Performed and Date, Allergies or Infections

7/9 S/P R Moores prosthesis for a R femoral neck Fx. No known allergies. Hx chronic UTI tx c̄ Bactrim. No other infections.

Is Patient ___ Family ___ aware of diagnosis?

Date of last physical _____

PHYSICIAN'S ORDERS: (Include specific orders for Diet, Lab Tests, Speech, and O.T.)

TRANSPORT BY: ☐ Ambulance ☐ Car

MEDICATION	STRENGTH AND FREQUENCY	DATE & TIME OF LAST DOSE
Timoptic 1%	ii gtts bid ou	7/23 8A
Bactrim	i TAB po qid	7/23 8A
Coltek	100 mg po qid	7/23 8P
Ducolox suppos.	÷ pr prn	7/21 11A
Coumadin D/c'd 7/22		
codeine	30 mg po prn	7/22 8P
MOM	30 cc po prn	

TREATMENTS & FREQUENCY: ___ Hip x-ray done q wk ___

DIET: Kosher

PHYSICAL THERAPY: Restrict Activity ☐ Yes ☒ No   Sensation Impaired ☒ Yes ☐ No

Precautions   Weight Bearing Status - Non-Weight ☐   Partial-Weight ☐   Full-Weight ☒

SPECIFIC TREATMENT & FREQUENCY: ___ Cont. amb c̄ walker and assist of 1. strength

ANTICIPATED GOALS: ___ walk c̄ walker

REHABILITATION POTENTIAL IS: ___ good

HOME HEALTH SERVICES: ☐ NURSING ☐ OCC. THERAPY ☐ SPEECH THERAPY ☐ SOCIAL WORK ☐ H.H. AIDE ☐ OTHER - SPECIFY

The above services require Level of Care: ☐ I ☐ II ☐ III ☐ IV

If Chronic Hospital, why? _____

CERTIFICATION: ✱(when applicable)
Services above needed to treat condition for which patient was hospitalized ☐ Yes ☐ No
I certify that the above named patient is: (check one)
☐ Under my care (or has been referred to another physician having professional knowledge of patient's condition); is home bound except when receiving out-patient services; requires skilled nursing care on an intermittent basis or physical or speech therapy as specified in the orders.
☐ Requires skilled nursing care on a continuing basis for any of the conditions for which he/she received care during this hospitalization.

_____ M.D.
Signature

Dr. A.

_____ M.D.
Print Name

Tel. 871-3000 Date 7/23/85 Will follow ☐ Yes ☒ No - If no, who?

Dr. B. _____ M.D.

ADDRESS: HRCA   TEL. 321-0000

282-956 9/85

DISTRIBUTION — WHITE — RECEIVING   PINK — MEDICAL RECORDS   YELLOW — C.C. SERVICE

Page 2
Patient Care Referral Form

Name __Mr. S.__

Record # _____

Transfer to: _____ SRC _____

NURSING: Self Care Status Check Functional Level		Inde- pendent	Needs Assist- ance	Unable
Ambulation	Bed-Chair		X	
	Walking		X	
	Stairs			X
	Wheelchair		X	
	Crutches			X
	Walker		X	
	Cane			X
Activities	Bathe self		X	
	Dress self			X
	Feed self		X	
	Brushing teeth	X		
	Shaving	X		
	Toilet		X	
	Commode		X	
	Bedpan/Urinal		X	

Bowel & Bladder Program	X Yes	No
Incontinence: Bladder X		Bowel X
Date of Last Enema		

Catheter: Type __Texas__
Date last changed: __7/22/85__

Weight __158__	Height __5'1__	Date __7/22/85__
Anointed Yes☐	No☐	Date

Check if Pertinent: (describe at right) ▷

DISABILITIES
- ☐ Amputation
- ☐ Paralysis
- ☒ Contractures /stiffness of
- ☐ Decubitus   extremities
- ☐ Other

IMPAIRMENTS
- ☐ Speech
- ☒ Hearing
- ☒ Vision
- ☐ Sensation
- ☐ Other

COMMUNICATION
- ☒ Can Write
- ☒ Talks
- ☒ Understands Speaking
- ☒ Understands English
- ☐ If no, Other Language?
- ☐ Reads
- ☐ Non-Verbal

BEHAVIOR
- ☒ Alert
- ☒ Forgetful
- ☐ Noisy
- ☐ Confused
- ☐ Withdrawn
- ☐ Wanders
- ☐ Other

REQUIRES
Mark "S" if sent; "N" if needed

☐ Colostomy Care	☒	Dentures
☐ Cane	☒	Eye Glasses
☐ Crutches	☒	Hearing Aid
☐ Walker		Prosthesis
☐ Wheelchair		Side Rails
☐ Other		

PATIENT CARE PLAN
(Explain details of care, medications, treatments, teaching, habits, preferences, and goals.)

Medications: Note time last dose given on day of discharge.

Mr. S. is a 90-year-old male familiar to you. On 7/9 he underwent a right Moores prosthesis for a right femoral neck Fx.

1. Elimination: Cont. to be incont. – 2 more days of Bactrim planned for UTI. Bowel routine with Colace, Dulcolox supp. & morn followed by Fleets if no results. Last BM 7/22.

2. Mobility: Walker, assist of 2, PWB.

3. Sleep pattern: Cont. with many naps during day, sometimes awake at no1.

4. Sensory: Seen by dental clinic – full set of dentures obtained. Pain minimal – occasional cod 30 po prn. CSM checks to both extremities equal, but somewhat weak (baseline).

5. Slips and falls risk: Safety measures maintained – Posey, freq. checks, side rails.

6. Skin integrity: wound clean and dry – no redness. No pressure areas.

7. Coumadin precautions: Coumadin decreased on 7/22. Keep on precautions till 7/24. A very pleasant man- no complications in evidence from surgery. Will do well returning to familiar environment. Has been disoriented to time and place.

_____
Signature of Nurse
Telephone _____ Date _____

NUTRITION: (discuss food preferences, understanding of diet, teaching needs and goals)   Diet enclosed ☐Yes ☐No

Kosher - eliminated constipating foods (cheese, bananas) and added increased fluids (2000 cc/day), fiber/roughage to diet. With upper and lower dentures, has been able to increase the consistency of his diet (fruits and vegetables).

_____
Nutritionist Signature   **Telephone**   **Date**

9/85

821-640

APPROVED BY THE MASSACHUSETTS DEPARTMENT OF PUBLIC HEALTH

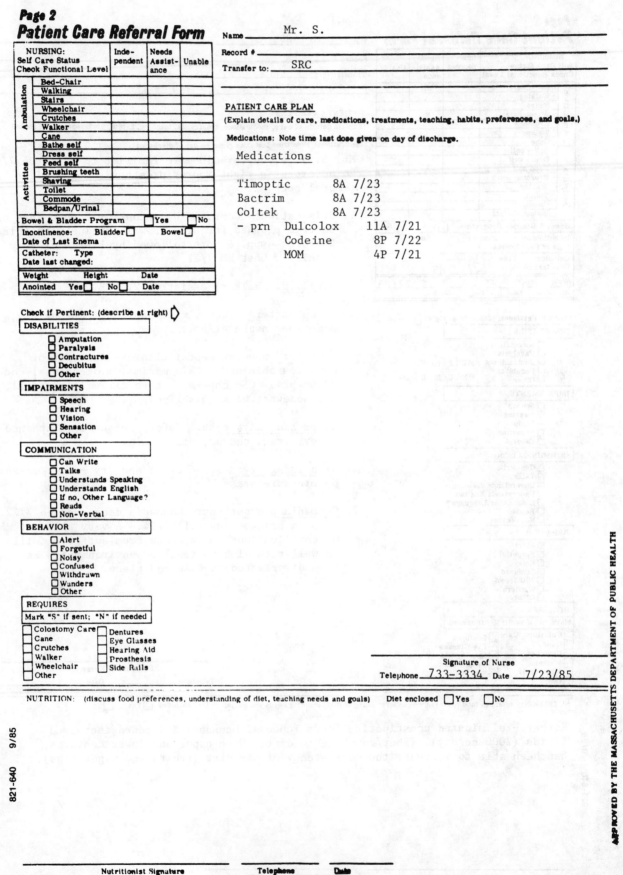

Page 2
Patient Care Referral Form

Name _____ Mr. S. _____

Record # _____

Transfer to: _____ SRC _____

NURSING: Self Care Status Check Functional Level		Independent	Needs Assistance	Unable
Ambulation	Bed-Chair			
	Walking			
	Stairs			
	Wheelchair			
	Crutches			
	Walker			
	Cane			
Activities	Bathe self			
	Dress self			
	Feed self			
	Brushing teeth			
	Shaving			
	Toilet			
	Commode			
	Bedpan/Urinal			

Bowel & Bladder Program ☐ Yes ☐ No

Incontinence: Bladder ☐ Bowel ☐
Date of Last Enema

Catheter: Type
Date last changed:

Weight	Height	Date
Anointed Yes ☐ No ☐	Date	

Check if Pertinent: (describe at right) ▷

DISABILITIES
☐ Amputation
☐ Paralysis
☐ Contractures
☐ Decubitus
☐ Other

IMPAIRMENTS
☐ Speech
☐ Hearing
☐ Vision
☐ Sensation
☐ Other

COMMUNICATION
☐ Can Write
☐ Talks
☐ Understands Speaking
☐ Understands English
☐ If no, Other Language?
☐ Reads
☐ Non-Verbal

BEHAVIOR
☐ Alert
☐ Forgetful
☐ Noisy
☐ Confused
☐ Withdrawn
☐ Wanders
☐ Other

REQUIRES
Mark "S" if sent; "N" if needed
☐ Colostomy Care
☐ Cane
☐ Crutches
☐ Walker
☐ Wheelchair
☐ Other
☐ Dentures
☐ Eye Glasses
☐ Hearing Aid
☐ Prosthesis
☐ Side Rails

PATIENT CARE PLAN
(Explain details of care, medications, treatments, teaching, habits, preferences, and goals.)

Medications: Note time last dose given on day of discharge.

Medications

Timoptic	8A	7/23
Bactrim	8A	7/23
Coltek	8A	7/23
- prn Dulcolox	11A	7/21
Codeine	8P	7/22
MOM	4P	7/21

Signature of Nurse _____
Telephone _733-3334_ Date _7/23/85_

NUTRITION: (discuss food preferences, understanding of diet, teaching needs and goals)   Diet enclosed ☐ Yes ☐ No

821-640   9/85

APPROVED BY THE MASSACHUSETTS DEPARTMENT OF PUBLIC HEALTH

Nutritionist Signature _____   Telephone _____   Date _____

White - Receiving Facility   Canary - Medical Records   Pink - C.C. Services

Page 3
Patient Care Referral Form

Name: _____ Mr. S. _____

Record # _____

Transfer to: _____ SRC _____

_____

SOCIAL SERVICE:

Prior to hospitalization, patient lived:
- ☐ Alone
- ☐ Nursing Home
- ☐ With Family
- ☐ With Friends
- ☐ Other ___ HRCA ___

SOCIAL INFORMATION (including patient's personality, attitude toward illness and family constellation and inter-relationships)

Mr. S. has interacted well with staff. His mental status has improved as he moved past his surgical date. He is anxious to return to you.

Identified Problems:

Plan (include short and long range plans)

To return to SRC and return to his usual ADL.

Will referring unit social worker plan to follow patient: Yes ☐ No ☒

Alice Smith		735-5555	7/23/85
Name	Signature & Title	Phone	Date

THERAPIES (P.T., O.T., Speech)   Instructions enclosed: Yes ☐ No ☐

Mr. S. underwent a Moores prosthesis on 7/9/85.

1st day OOB was 7/11. Since that time he has progressed from max. asst. of 2 c̄ walker, to his present level of min. assist of 1 with walker.

Goals: increase strength
        increase endurance
        continue to assess pt stability in relation to safety
        ROM to all extremities
        progress to a cane when stable

        Call with any questions.

	722-2222	7/23/85
Signature of Therapist	Phone	Date

620-17M - 681-282   9/85

APPROVED BY THE MASSACHUSETTS DEPARTMENT OF PUBLIC HEALTH

RECEIVING FACILITY
DISTRIBUTION: **WHITE**-RECEIVING FACILITY; **CANARY**-MEDICAL RECORD; **PINK**-C.C. SERVICE

HYPERTENSION

FPHAA

General Summary

The patient is an 82-year-old feisty, pleasant, A+O×3 black woman with a past medical history of hypertension since 1980; polymyalgia rheumatica since 1982 (with bilateral leg, hip, thigh, shoulder, and back pain); adult onset of diabetes mellitus; degenerative joint disease (DJD); glaucoma; and recent, new congestive heart failure (January 1985). She was admitted June 19, 1985. Her chief complaint was of frequent falls, light-headedness, and difficult ambulation for one month before admission. Her medications included methyldopa (Aldomet), since 1980; furosemide (Lasix), and Atenolol, since January 1985, secondary to 2+ pedal edema and mild congestive heart failure; prednisone (an attempt to decrease this dosage in 1983 caused an exacerbation of her signs and symptoms); ibuprofen (Motrin); tolbutamide (Orinase); Timolol; CaCO₃; and Vitamin D. The patient lives with her husband (a WWII paraplegic) in a third floor walk-up apartment in Boston.

The patient, accompanied by a friend, was admitted to the emergency ward from her home by ambulance on June 28, 1985, at 2 PM for evaluation of recent, frequent falls; light-headedness; increased pedal edema; and evaluation of left lower extremity pain and difficulty ambulating.

The patient's vital signs were recorded as follows: temp, 36.5° C, p.o.; pulse rate, 64 beats per minute; respirations, 22/min; BP, 148/92. Her height was 5 ft 2 in; her weight, 160.5 lb. She denied having chest pain, palpitations, and shortness of breath. Auscultation of her lungs disclosed rales at normal baseline bilaterally with 2+ pedal edema. An ECG showed normal sinus rhythm (62). A chest roentgenogram showed mild congestive heart failure. Patient complained of dizziness on standing initially; however, it resolved in a few seconds. Her eyes were without nystagmus; the fundi were obscured by cataracts. Her pupils were equal, round, and reacted to light. Her neck was supple and without nodes. The abdomen was obese and nontender. A rectal examination was not done; but the patient's BM was large, soft, and brown. Urinalysis showed a trace of ketones, yellow with a moderate amount of white blood cells. Laboratory studies disclosed the following values: hematocrit, 33.7%; hemoglobin, 11.4g/dL; potassium, 4.1 mEq/L; sodium, 134 mEq/L; blood glucose, 134 mg/dL; BUN, 34 mg/dL; creatinine 1.1 mg/dL; lactic dehydrogenase, 235 units; creatine phosphokinase, 152 units/L. The patient had the following valuables: bifocal glasses and a cane.

Pattern Areas

Health Perception–Health Management

M.C. or Mamie, as she likes to be addressed, believes that good health keeps her independent. She considers herself a strong "able-bodied" person who has "always managed." She states that she "always does her best and puts her trust in God, and whatever happens, they'll deal with it." She feels her illness is a test from God. She is concerned about her declining health and has agreed to this hospitalization in order to get well and go home quickly. She does not smoke and does not use alcohol.

The patient's past medical history includes hypertension, recent new congestive heart failure, adult onset of diabetes mellitus, polymyalgia rheumatica, and glaucoma. She has no known allergies. Her blood group is A-positive.

The patient's medicines include the following:

- methyldopa (Aldomet), 250 mg, TID
- furosemide (Lasix), 20 mg, QD
- Atenolol, 50 mg, QD
- prednisone, 5 mg, QD
- ibuprofen (Motrin), 400 mg, QID
- tolbutamide (Orinase), 250 mg, BID
- Timolol, one gtt, o.u. TID
- CaCO₃, 750 mg, QD
- Vitamin D, 2 times each week

Roles-Relationship

Mamie lives with her husband, a WWII paraplegic, in a rented apartment in Boston. It is on the 3rd floor and is without an elevator. She retired as a housekeeper in the 1960s. They have no children but many supports. As Mamie put it, "I have so many adopted children and grandchildren, I don't have time to have my own." She has a young friend—and a major support—whom Mamie calls her "adopted granddaughter"; she lives nearby and makes sure that Mamie gets to the doctor and the market, and that her prescriptions get filled. The patient's husband does the cooking, and she does the household business. They live on their social security benefits, and, Mamie states, they have some money "tucked away."

Coping-Stress

Mamie states that her usual way of dealing with stress is to worry a little, then pray to God. "I do my best to remedy the problem, and if it ain't good enough to change it, I learn to live with it—cause it's God's will."

Cognitive-Perceptual

Mamie is articulate, A+O×3, with good hearing (the date of her last examination is not known). She wears bifocals and has some difficulty reading newsprint. She is unsteady on her feet, so, with the cane in one hand, she reaches out with the other to hold on to things. Mamie describes her tolerance to pain as high but states that lately the pain has "slowed her down." She describes her memory as occasionally lacking. If she cannot remember whether she has taken all of her pills for the day, she may take more the next day to make up for it—" if she sees fit." Mamie had very little schooling, but she learned to read and write.

Activity-Exercise

Lately, minimal activity produces fatigue, weakness, and pain. She denies having chest pains, shortness of breath, and palpitations. She states, however, that six months ago she could walk independently with the use of her cane and managed the stairs without much fatigue.

Nutritional-Metabolic

A decreased appetite, which persisted for six months and was secondary to increased pain, caused a 10-lb weight loss. The patient denies having indigestion. She states that she tries to avoid salt and sugar. They eat a lot of canned and boxed prepared foods. Mamie has her own teeth. Her skin is dry. She has a vitiliginous chin and no eyebrows secondary to scalding burns she received as a child.

Elimination

The patient complains of increased urination and some stress incontinence secondary to the use of furosemide (Lasix). She states that at times she "skips" the furosemide (Lasix), if it's convenient, and takes two the next day. She reports a large, soft BM every other day with the help of milk of magnesia.

Sleep-Rest

Mamie takes no sedatives to promote sleep. She is in bed at any time from 6 to 8 PM but "nods off" before that time. She gets up at 2 AM and has coffee; then she goes back to bed and remains there until 6 AM, when she gets up for the day. (She also naps during the day.) Lately, increased need to urinate has awakened her "in a start."

Values and Beliefs

Religion and God are important to the patient. She used to take the bus to church every week, and misses doing that. She believes strongly that her health is her independence. The goal, then, of this hospitalization is to go home. She agrees, however, that she will need help.

Anticipated Discharge Status

Mamie's anticipated discharge status is independent function, with maximum home supports—including VNA, home health aid, and a homemaker.

Her hypertension is poorly controlled because of her poor dietary habits and the medication regimen that resulted in her heart failure (right side), the associated pedal edema, and the mild congestive heart failure. With the addition of beta-blockers and a diuretic as an antihypertensive therapy, her habit of "doubling up" her diuretics—and possibly her other pills—could possibly be the cause of her reported lightheadedness, secondary to the acute hypotensive reactions. The diagnosis of polymyalgia rheumatica as the cause of the pain and weakness only increases her risk of falling and having a potential fracture.

Assessment and Plan

The patient's continuing care assessment can be summarized by the following factors:

- The potential for injury due to lightheadedness, fatigue, and weakness, secondary to acute hypotensive reactions
- The potential for ineffective gas exchange due to the patient's recent new congestive heart failure
- The alteration in comfort due to diffuse pains and weakness, secondary to the polymyalgia rheumatica
- The alteration of glucose metabolism due to increased blood sugar, which is secondary to steroid therapy and the adult onset of diabetes mellitus
- The patient's knowledge deficit about diet, medications, and the disease process
- The alteration in the patient's sleep-rest pattern due to increased urination and stress incontinence, which are secondary to the use of diuretics
- The potential for ineffective coping secondary to anxiety about getting home quickly
- Discharge planning and its potential for ineffective home health maintenance

The following continuing care plan focuses on eight areas of concern:

1. Determine whether the patient's orthostatics are symptomatic. Check her vital signs q4h and provide antihypertensive therapy—methyldopa (Aldomet) 250 mg, TID; furosemide (Lasix), 20 mg, QD; Atenolol, 50 mg, QD as ordered. Assess the patient's ambulation while she is using a cane and her ability to carry out ADL. Document the progress. Have the patient ambulate at least QID, and assess for symptoms and vital sign changes.
2. Check the patient's weight QD and assess her lungs every shift. Assess the respiratory rate and for

evidence of shortness of breath, dyspnea on exertion, or orthopnea. Assess also for pedal edema. Document the changes and progress.

3. Administer steroid and antiinflammatory therapies as ordered. Give antacids or meals with the medicines as ordered. Provide a heating pad PRN. Provide range-of-motion exercises or ambulation at least QID. Provide a back brace and instruction for putting it on by occupational therapy. Provide physical therapy QD for ambulation and the use of the TENS unit as ordered. Offer oxycodone HCl with acetaminophen (Percocet), one to two tablets, q6h, PRN, as ordered. Assess the level of pain post epidermal steroid injection. (Planned for 7/1.)

4. Check fasting blood sugar every AM as ordered. Arrange for a diet consultation to provide an 1800-calorie ADA diet, as ordered, for home instruction. Administer tolbutamide (Orinase), 250 mg, BID, as ordered. Check for sugar and acetone QS. Assess the patient's appetite and signs or symptoms of hyper- or hypoglycemia.

5. Give written and verbal information to the patient about hypertension—what it is, the signs and symptoms to watch for and report, and how often to see the physician. Make a medication card for the patient. Tape pills to the card, and give the times, the doses, the action, and the side effects. Give the card to the patient while she is in the hospital, and teach her with each administration of the medication. Also provide a diet consultation and secure a no-added-sodium (NAS), low-cholesterol, 1800-calorie ADA diet. Instruct the patient to do the following:

   • Weigh yourself daily and notify your physician of a 2-lb weight loss or gain.
   • Lie down immediately if you feel faint, light-headed, or nauseous; put your feet higher than your head.
   • Avoid hot baths.
   • Rise slowly and dangle your feet before standing from a lying position.
   • Avoid standing motionless for a long time.
   • Use the elastic stockings prescribed by your physician, and keep your feet up when sitting.

6. Provide a bedside commode and maxi- or minipads for stress incontinence, PRN. Reinforce, for the patient, the importance of taking the Lasix when she gets up in the AM in order to avoid the urgency to urinate at night; reinforce also the importance of following the prescribed dosage for all medications: do not skip one day and then double the dose on the next.

7. Explain all procedures and plans. Encourage questions and conversation. Involve social services. Give emotional support.

8. Discharge the patient to home with maximum supports, including VNA, HHA, homemaker, meals-on-wheels (if she is eligible) and the ride-for-the-elderly program.

FHPA

Pattern Areas

Health Perception–Health Management

Mamie is an 82-year-old, independent black woman who had never seen a physician until 1980. Because she feels that her "health is her independence," she is concerned about her declining health. She has agreed to this hospitalization in order to get well so that she can return home quickly. She is followed by Dr. H. (internal medicine) and a consulting rheumatologist. She has Medicare and Medicaid. Her last complete examination was in 1983. She feels that "it's too expensive to be having all those unnecessary tests." Her "granddaughter" picks up her medicines from the pharmacy.

Nutritional-Metabolic

With the increase in her pain, Mamie reports a decrease in her appetite over the past six months and a 10-lb weight loss. She states that she has had swelling in her ankles since January. She is an obese woman, 5 ft 2 in and 160 lb. According to Mamie, the diet restrictions have been loosely followed. They try to avoid salt and concentrated sugar. She states they eat a lot of prepared foods, both boxed and canned (these foods are usually very high in sodium and sugar). They eat "things that can keep . . . because I only shop once a week for essentials." The foods they eat often are soups, pork and beans, and breads. The do not buy fresh meat, other than cold cuts. She denies having indigestion with any particular foods. They used to like salads and vegetables, but now she feels that it is too much work to prepare them. Mamie states that she does not think much about food or meals because of the pain; she just snacks when she is hungry. She prefers juice or coffee to water or milk. She says that she took a Vitamin D supplement at home whenever she thought of it. Mamie has her own teeth—no dentures or plates.

Her skin is dry; she has a vitiliginous chin, multiple scars, and no eyebrows, secondary to scalding burns as a child. She denies having a problem with healing but is aware that she should watch her feet for cuts and massage them with a lotion. She denies having an intolerance for heat or cold.

Elimination

The patient has a large BM every other day. If she is feeling constipated, she takes milk of magnesia. She complains of increased urination because of the furosemide

(Lasix), which she feels is very inconvenient. She has noticed some stress incontinence; when she feels the urge to go, it comes on quicker than she can move. She states that sometimes she gets so frustrated that she does not take the furosemide—"But not that often. . . . I just take two the next day."

Activity-Exercise

Activity is minimal because of her pain and light-headedness. With her cane, however, she gets along fine. Ambulating 50 feet with supervision produces extreme fatigue; yet, Mamie plans on returning home and walking up and down three flights of stairs to go about her business.

Sleep-Rest

Mamie states that she has no particular hobbies. She either listens to the radio or sleeps when she is not busy. She describes an unusual routine. She denies taking any sleeping aids. She goes to bed between 6 and 8 PM and is up at 2 AM, when she has coffee. Then she goes back to bed till 6 AM, when she gets up for the day. Her husband has a similar routine—8 PM to 6 AM. She describes herself as being tired a lot. She really doesn't sleep while she is in bed; she awakens and dozes throughout the night and then naps during the day. She attributes her sleeplessness to the pain. She denies experiencing orthopnea.

Cognitive-Perceptual

Mamie is an articulate, $A+O \times 3$, delightful black woman who has a contagious laugh and enjoys conversation. She has retained her southern drawl and charm. Mamie describes her hearing as "too good." Her eyes are not as good; she wears bifocals and reads newsprint only with some difficulty. She has a history of glaucoma, for which she uses Timolol drops. She describes her vision as getting worse for reading, but not bad enough to prevent her from getting around. Mamie walks with a cane very slowly. Her balance is off, and she tends to reach out to hold on to other objects. She attributes this problem to her occasional light-headedness and to the pains in her body. She further describes the pain as the reason she has slowed down. She says that being still for too long makes her stiff. She has good range of motion in her extremities. She describes her tolerance to pain as high.

Mamie describes her memory (with slight disdain) as occasionally lacking: "I'm not as sharp as I used to be a few years ago." She states that she never had much formal schooling but that she was taught how to read and write by the family for whom she worked.

Self-Perception–Self-Concept

The patient considers herself to be a strong "able-bodied" person who has "always managed." She feels that she always does her best and puts her trust in God; whatever happens, happens for a reason, and she will deal with it. She perceives her illness as a test from God. Her husband, a WWII paraplegic, gets around the apartment with braces on both legs. They take care of each other.

Roles-Relationships

The person to be notified in case of an emergency is M.J., her "adopted granddaughter" who lives nearby. "I ain't got no family," Mamie explains.

I was brought to Boston from Alabama by a white family in 1930 or so, and I was their housekeeper for 30 years. I met my husband while he was in the Merchant Marine, and we married. We never had no children; then he was hurt in the war. I retired in 1960 as a housekeeper, but I did ironing and laundry for families in Newton on my own time. We got an apartment in Boston. I've got me plenty of adopted children and grandchildren. The closest one is M.J. who oversees us and makes sure we get along.

Mamie and her husband make decisions mutually in the household. Her husband does the cooking and Mamie does "the picking up." She realizes that she may not be able to take care of the banking and the shopping in the future. They live off their social security benefits and, most likely, receive a government check as well. Mamie states that they have some money "tucked away." The incapacitation resulting from her illness has frightened Mamie, but she refuses to discuss any other options besides going home.

Sexual-Reproductive

Mamie never had children. She believes that she ceased menstruating in the 1950s. She denies examining her breasts. Intercourse was not discussed.

Coping-Stress

The major stresses for Mamie have been her gradually developing illness, which has slowly prevented her from getting around. Her usual way of dealing with stress had been to "worry a little, pray to God, and work it out. I can only do my best, and if it ain't good enough to change the situation, I learn to live with it, because it's God's will. I've learned to live with a lot of things." She used to go to church weekly by bus, but lately she has been doing her praying at home.

Values-Beliefs

Religion and God are important to Mamie. She states that she was a Baptist, but since she did not know any "black folk" in the 1930s, she went to services with the family for whom she worked. They were Methodists. Mamie misses not getting to church weekly. The three things she values most in her life are (1) her independence, (2) her love of God, and (3) her loved ones—her husband and her granddaughter.

NURSING CARE PLAN

FORMULATED BY Kathleen Smith   DATE 6/29/85

NURSING HISTORY

This is an 82-year-old fiesty, pleasant, A+Ox3 BF with PMH or HTN since 1980, PMR (polymyalgia rheumatica - a collagen inflammatory disease) since 1982 with c/o bilateral leg, hip, thigh, shoulder, and back pain, AODM, DJD, glaucoma, and recent new CHF (1/85). Admitted 6/19/85 with cc of frequent falls, lightheadedness, LLE pain, and difficulty walking one month PTA. Her medications include Aldomet 250 mg tid, Lasix 20 mg qd, and Atenolol 50 mg qd since Jan. 85 secondary to 2+ pedal edema and mild CHF; Prednisone 5 mg qd (in 1983 an attempt to decrease this dose caused an exacerbation of her S/S), Motrin 400 mg qid, Orinase 250 mg bid, Timolol one gtt ou tid, CaCO$_3$ 750 mg qd, and Vit D+2x/week. She lives with her husband (WWII paraplegic) in a 3rd floor walk-up apt. in Boston.

NURSING DIAGNOSIS	EXPECTED OUTCOME	NURSING CARE PLAN WITH NURSING ORDERS
1. Potential for injury d/t lightheadedness, fatigue, weakness 2° acute hypotensive reactions.	BP WNL Apostural Safe independent ambulation with cane	Orthostatics if symptomatic, Q4 VS with antihypertensive meds as ordered (Aldomet, Lasix, & Atenolol). Assess amb. with cane and ability to carry out ADL. Document progress and assess for S/S + VS.
2. Potential ineffective gas exchange d/t h/o recent new CHF.	No SOB No CHF	QD Wt., assess lungs qs. CXR per HO. Monitor I/O. Lasix qam as ordered. Assess RR, evidence of SOB, DOE, or orthopnea. Assess for pedal edema. Document changes and progress.
3. Alteration comfort d/t diffuse pain: legs, hips, back, & shoulders 2° PMR.	Pain control to allow for maximum ADL at home	Administer steroid and anti-inflammatory meds as ordered. Give antacids or meals with meds as ordered. Heating pad prn. ROM or amb. at least qid. Back brace and instruction for putting it on by OT. Pt qd for amb. and use of TENS unit (pain control) offer Percocet 1-2 tabs q6 prn as ordered. Assess level of pain post-epidural steroid injection (7/1).
4. Alteration glucose metabolism d/t increased BS 2° steroid therapy + AODM.	BS WNL	Check FBS qam as ordered. Diet consult as ordered for 1800 ADA diet for home instruction. Orinase 250 bid as ordered. Check s/a qs. Assess appetite and S/S of hyper/hypoglycemia.

NURSING DIAGNOSIS	EXPECTED OUTCOME	NURSING CARE PLAN WITH NURSING ORDERS
5. Knowledge deficit re diet, medications, and disease process.	Describe HTN, list S/S to notify M.D. about. List 4 types of foods high in Na and sugar. Avoid hypotension; list meds, dose, time, and action	- Give written and verbal info. about HTN, what it is, S/S to report, and how often to see M.D. - Make med card with pills taped to card with times, doses, action, and side effects. Give med. card to pt while in hospital and teach with each administration. - Diet consult for NAS low chol. 1800 ADA diet. - Instruct patient to: 1. Weigh self daily and notify M.D. of a 2 lb wt. gain or loss. 2. Lie down immediately if feeling faint, lightheaded, or weak and put feet higher than head. 3. Avoid hot baths. 4. Rise slowly and dangle feet before standing from a lying position. 5. Avoid standing motionless for long periods of time. Use elastic stockings prescribed by M.D. and keep feet up when sitting.
6. Alteration sleep-rest pattern d/t increased urination and stress incontinence 2° diuretics.	Maintain dryness, integrity, and safety	Bedside commode. Maxi/mini pads for stress incontinence prn. Reinforce to patient the importance in taking Lasix in am to avoid urgency at night and reinforce not to skip one day and double the dose on the next.
7. Potential ineffective coping 2° to anxiety re getting home quickly.	Trust and compliance	Explain all procedures and plans. Emotional support. Encourage questions and conversation. Involve social service.
8. Discharge planning + PTL. Ineffective home management.	Home with maximum supports	VNA + HHA 3x/wk, homemaker 1x/wk, Meals-on-Wheels service, The Ride (elderly transport service) F/U with PMD. Write and call in VNA referral.

Patient Care Referral Form

Patient's Hospital Record # _____

FROM: Beth Israel Hospital

Unit/Clinic 11R

ADDRESS 330 Brookline Ave.

Boston, MA   TEL. 777-7777

ADM. DATE 6/28/85   DISCH. DATE 7/3/85

TO: _____

ADDRESS: _____

PATIENT NAME M.C.

ADDRESS: 22 South Road
Southmore, MA   TEL. 333-9999

FLOOR 2nd   APT.# 2   BIRTHDATE 12/28/02

AGE 82   SEX M ☒   MARITAL STATUS S ☒ W D SEP.   RELIGION Protestant

RELATIVE OR GUARDIAN: Husband

ADDRESS: Same   TEL.

MEDICARE NO. & LETTER 212-11-1111D	PLAN A B	BLUE CROSS NO.	SOC. SEC. NO. 222-11-1111	OTHER

CLINIC APPOINTMENTS   DATE   TIME   Agency Worker Office Address Telephone

DIAGNOSIS(S) Surgery Performed and Date, Allergies or Infections

CHF and AODM

Is Patient Family aware of diagnosis? YES

Date of last physical 1/85

PHYSICIAN'S ORDERS: (Include specific orders for Diet, Lab Tests, Speech, and O.T.)

TRANSPORT BY: ☐ Ambulance ☒ Car

MEDICATION	STRENGTH AND FREQUENCY	DATE & TIME OF LAST DOSE	
Aldomet	250 mqm TID	8-2-8	8 am
Atenolol	50 mqm qd	8 am	8 am
Lasix	20 mqm qd	8 am	8 am
Prednisone	5 mqm qd	8 am	8 am
Motrin	600 mqm qid	8-23-4-8	8 am
Orinase	250 mqm bid	8 am-8 pm	8 am
Timolol	one qH ou tid	8-2-8	8 am
C_aCO_3	750 mqm qd	8 am	8 am

TREATMENTS & FREQUENCY: Monitor medication compliance. Teach diet, meds., wts., and disease process.
Monitor VS 3x/week. Assess lungs, pedal edema, wt. pattern for signs of CHF.

DIET: 1800 ADA, NAS, low cholesterol

PHYSICAL THERAPY: Restrict Activity ☐ Yes ☒ No   Sensation Impaired ☐ Yes ☒ No

Precautions   Weight Bearing Status - Non-Weight ☐   Partial-Weight ☐   Full-Weight ☐

SPECIFIC TREATMENT & FREQUENCY: _____

ANTICIPATED GOALS: _____

REHABILITATION POTENTIAL IS: _____

HOME HEALTH SERVICES: ☒ NURSING   ☐ OCC. THERAPY   ☐ SPEECH THERAPY   ☐ SOCIAL WORK   ☒ H.H. AIDE   ☒ OTHER - SPECIFY homemaker

The above services require Level of Care: ☐ I   ☐ II   ☐ III   ☐ IV

If Chronic Hospital, why? _____

CERTIFICATION: ✱(when applicable)
Services above needed to treat condition for which patient was hospitalized ☒ Yes ☐ No
I certify that the above named patient is: (check one)
☒ Under my care (or has been referred to another physician having professional knowledge of patient's condition); is home bound except when receiving out-patient services; requires skilled nursing care on an intermittent basis or physical or speech therapy as specified in the orders.
☐ Requires skilled nursing care on a continuing basis for any of the conditions for which he/she received care during this hospitalization.

_____ M.D.
Signature
Dr. Smith _____ M.D.
Print Name
Tel. 777-7777 Date 7/3/85   Will follow ☒ Yes ☐ No - If no, who?
_____ M.D.
ADDRESS: _____ TEL. _____

282-956   9/85

APPROVED BY THE MASSACHUSETTS DEPARTMENT OF PUBLIC HEALTH

DISTRIBUTION — WHITE — RECEIVING   PINK — MEDICAL RECORDS   YELLOW — C.C. SERVICE

Page 2
Patient Care Referral Form

Name _____ M.C. _____

Record # _____

Transfer to: _____

NURSING: Self Care Status Check Functional Level		Inde-pendent	Needs Assist-ance	Unable
Ambulation	Bed–Chair	X		
	Walking	X		
	Stairs			X
	Wheelchair			
	Crutches			
	Walker			
	Cane	X		
Activities	Bathe self	X		
	Dress self	X		
	Feed self	X		
	Brushing teeth	X		
	Shaving			
	Toilet		X	
	Commode	X		
	Bedpan/Urinal			

Bowel & Bladder Program	☐ Yes	☐ No
Incontinence: Bladder ☐ Bowel ☐		
Date of Last Enema		

Catheter: Type	
Date last changed:	

Weight	Height	Date
Anointed Yes ☐ No ☐	Date	

Check if Pertinent: (describe at right) ▷

DISABILITIES
- ☐ Amputation
- ☐ Paralysis
- ☐ Contractures
- ☐ Decubitus
- XX Other

L wrist contracture d/t scarring 2° burn.

IMPAIRMENTS
- ☐ Speech
- ☐ Hearing
- XX Vision   bifocals
- ☐ Sensation
- ☐ Other

COMMUNICATION
- ☐ Can Write
- ☐ Talks
- ☐ Understands Speaking
- ☐ Understands English
- ☐ If no, Other Language?
- ☐ Reads
- ☐ Non-Verbal

BEHAVIOR
- ☐ Alert
- ☐ Forgetful
- ☐ Noisy
- ☐ Confused
- ☐ Withdrawn
- ☐ Wanders
- ☐ Other

REQUIRES	Sent: cane, glasses.
Mark "S" if sent; "N" if needed	

Needs: commode, rail in bathroom.

- ☐ Colostomy Care
- ☐ Cane
- ☐ Crutches
- ☐ Walker
- ☐ Wheelchair
- ☐ Other
- ☐ Dentures
- ☐ Eye Glasses
- ☐ Hearing Aid
- ☐ Prosthesis
- ☐ Side Rails

PATIENT CARE PLAN
(Explain details of care, medications, treatments, teaching, habits, preferences, and goals.)

Medications: Note time last dose given on day of discharge.

82-year-old fiesty, pleasant A+Ox3 BF with a PMH of HTN since 1980, PMR since 1982 with c/o bilateral leg, hip, thigh, shoulder, and back pain, AODM, DJD, glaucoma, and recent new CHF (1/85). Admitted with cc of frequent falls, lightheadedness, LLE pain, and difficulty walking one month PTA. She lives with her husband (WWII paraplegic) in 3rd floor walk-up apt. in Boston.

CVS W/u was neg. for DVT, fracture, or MI. Mild failure on admit was treated with 20 mg IVP Lasix and then 20 mg po qd. Denied SOB, CP, or palps. 60-66 NSR, 130-160/70-90. RR 18-22. Initial lightheadedness resolved by day #2. Apostural edema resolved by day #2. Pain 6/20-7/1 c/o with movement but able to perform ADL. Could only tolerate minimal ambulation with help of back brace and TENS unit (pt taught by OT and PT respectively). TENS unit d/c'd 7/1 post-steroid epidural injection which after 24 hours produced maximal relief enabling patient to ambulate 50 feet with fatigue but much less pain. Before epidural she required Percocet 2 tabs at least tid for pain control in addition to Motrin 600 qid and Prednisone 5 mg po qd. GI Percocet caused constipation and required Colace tid and qhs MOM. With cessation of Percocet she will probably only require MOM qod. Appetite much improved with decrease in pain. Wt. stable. GU stress incontinence and urgency at night somewhat relieved with taking am Lasix, but bedside commode and minipads helped increase self-esteem. AODM Stable FMS in 130's on Orinase. S/A Neg. On 1800 ADA, NAS, low chol. diet. Education Medications were taught in detail (Med-card was sent home with pt). Diet, daily weights, hypotension prevention tactics and S/S to notify M.D. were taught. Sleep Refused sleeping

_____
Signature of Nurse

Telephone _____ Date _____

NUTRITION: (discuss food preferences, understanding of diet, teaching needs and goals)   Diet enclosed ☐ Yes   ☐ No

821-640   9/85

_____
Nutritionist Signature   Telephone   Date

White - Receiving Facility   Canary - Medical Records   Pink - C.C. Services

Page 2
Patient Care Referral Form

Name _____ M.C. _____

Record # _____

Transfer to: _____

NURSING: Self Care Status Check Functional Level		Inde-pendent	Needs Assist-ance	Unable
Ambulation	Bed-Chair			
	Walking			
	Stairs			
	Wheelchair			
	Crutches			
	Walker			
	Cane			
Activities	Bathe self			
	Dress self			
	Feed self			
	Brushing teeth			
	Shaving			
	Toilet			
	Commode			
	Bedpan/Urinal			

Bowel & Bladder Program	☐ Yes		☐ No
Incontinence: Bladder ☐	Bowel ☐		
Date of Last Enema			
Catheter: Type			
Date last changed:			

Weight	Height	Date
Anointed Yes ☐ No ☐	Date	

Check if Pertinent: (describe at right) ▷

DISABILITIES
- ☐ Amputation
- ☐ Paralysis
- ☐ Contractures
- ☐ Decubitus
- ☐ Other

IMPAIRMENTS
- ☐ Speech
- ☐ Hearing
- ☐ Vision
- ☐ Sensation
- ☐ Other

COMMUNICATION
- ☐ Can Write
- ☐ Talks
- ☐ Understands Speaking
- ☐ Understands English
- ☐ If no, Other Language?
- ☐ Reads
- ☐ Non-Verbal

BEHAVIOR
- ☐ Alert
- ☐ Forgetful
- ☐ Noisy
- ☐ Confused
- ☐ Withdrawn
- ☐ Wanders
- ☐ Other

REQUIRES
Mark "S" if sent; "N" if needed
- ☐ Colostomy Care
- ☐ Cane
- ☐ Crutches
- ☐ Walker
- ☐ Wheelchair
- ☐ Other
- ☐ Dentures
- ☐ Eye Glasses
- ☐ Hearing Aid
- ☐ Prosthesis
- ☐ Side Rails

PATIENT CARE PLAN
(Explain details of care, medications, treatments, teaching, habits, preferences, and goals.)

Medications: Note time last dose given on day of discharge.

pills. She was usually awake from 2 a.m. – 6 a.m. and would sleep off and on during the day. She states her schedule is similar to this at home (asleep at 6 p.m. till 2 a.m. then up till 3 or 4 a.m. then back to bed till 6 a.m.).

Assessment

M.C. is used to being very independent and it needs to be reinforced that help at home will keep her home and not in the hospital.
1. Potential for injury d/t lightheadedness, fatigue, and weakness secondary to acute hypotensive reactions PTA.
2. Potential ineffective gas exchange d/t h/o recent new CHF.
3. Alteration in comfort d/t diffuse pain: legs, hips, shoulders, and back secondary to polymyalgia rheumatica (improved post-steroid epidural).
4. Alteration glucose metabolism d/t increased BS secondary to steroid therapy and AODM.
5. Potential noncompliance with medications (especially diuretics) d/t poor memory and increased urination.
6. Potential ineffective Home Health Management d/t age, memory, pain, weakness, and fatigue.

Plan Suggestions

Homemaker one day a week for shopping and laundry.
Home health aide 3 days a week.
RN for general evaluation of home situation and health.
- Monitor medication taking and knowledge retained re diet, meds, and disease process.

_____
Signature of Nurse

Telephone _____ Date _____

NUTRITION: (discuss food preferences, understanding of diet, teaching needs and goals) Diet enclosed ☐ Yes ☐ No

9/85

821-640

_____
Nutritionist Signature

Telephone   Date

White - Receiving Facility   Canary - Medical Records   Pink - C.C. Services

Page 2
Patient Care Referral Form

Name ___M.C.___

Record # _____

Transfer to: _____

NURSING: Self Care Status Check Functional Level	Inde-pendent	Needs Assist-ance	Unable
Ambulation Bed-Chair			
Walking			
Stairs			
Wheelchair			
Crutches			
Walker			
Cane			
Activities Bathe self			
Dress self			
Feed self			
Brushing teeth			
Shaving			
Toilet			
Commode			
Bedpan/Urinal			

Bowel & Bladder Program ☐Yes ☐No

Incontinence: Bladder☐ Bowel☐

Date of Last Enema

Catheter: Type
Date last changed:

Weight	Height	Date

Anointed Yes☐ No☐ Date

Check if Pertinent: (describe at right) ▷

DISABILITIES
☐ Amputation
☐ Paralysis
☐ Contractures
☐ Decubitus
☐ Other

IMPAIRMENTS
☐ Speech
☐ Hearing
☐ Vision
☐ Sensation
☐ Other

COMMUNICATION
☐ Can Write
☐ Talks
☐ Understands Speaking
☐ Understands English
☐ If no, Other Language?
☐ Reads
☐ Non-Verbal

BEHAVIOR
☐ Alert
☐ Forgetful
☐ Noisy
☐ Confused
☐ Withdrawn
☐ Wanders
☐ Other

REQUIRES
Mark "S" if sent; "N" if needed
☐ Colostomy Care
☐ Cane
☐ Crutches
☐ Walker
☐ Wheelchair
☐ Other
☐ Dentures
☐ Eye Glasses
☐ Hearing Aid
☐ Prosthesis
☐ Side Rails

PATIENT CARE PLAN
(Explain details of care, medications, treatments, teaching, habits, preferences, and goals.)

Medications: Note time last dose given on day of discharge.

- Monitor VS 3x/week, assess lungs, pedal edema, weight pattern for signs of CHF.
- Evaluate pain control at home and ability to ambulate and carry out ADL.
- Check s/a, assess appetite and available food products (check pantry for high sugar, high salt products).
- Hook up with Meals-on-Wheels and The Ride services.
- Plan to visit early a.m. when awake.
- Obtain bedside commode.
- Assess if F/U appts. are made and kept.

Meds: Aldomet 250 mg tid, Atenolol 50 mg qd, Lasix 20 mg qd, Prednisone 5 mg qd, Motrin 600 mg qid, Orinase 250 mg bid, Timolol one gtt ou tid, $CaCO_3$ 750 mg qd, and Vit D 2x/week.

Telephone 777-7777 Signature of Nurse Date 7/3/85

NUTRITION: (discuss food preferences, understanding of diet, teaching needs and goals) Diet enclosed ☐Yes ☐No

Nutritionist Signature Telephone Date

White - Receiving Facility   Canary - Medical Records   Pink - C.C. Services

821-640   9/85

APPROVED BY THE MASSACHUSETTS DEPARTMENT OF PUBLIC HEALTH

STROKE

FHPAA

General Summary

The patient is an 87-year-old white woman who was admitted at 10 PM to the emergency unit after a fall at home. She was accompanied by her sister, who was near her. On examination, the patient was found to be alert, but not oriented to place or time, and was unable to obey commands. Her left side was flaccid; her speech was slurred; and the pupils of her eyes were sluggishly reactive, with marked deviation to the right. (Normal strength remained in her right side.) Gag reflex was present, though decreased. Because of the weakened gag reflex and the poor p.o. intake, a pediatric feeding tube was placed. She was found to be restless, showed intermittent lethargy, and has been incontinent two times since admission. These episodes were followed by urinary retention. A Foley catheter was then placed. The patient has no known allergies. Her vital signs were recorded as follows: BP, 160/92; pulse rate, 68 beats per minute; respirations, 16/min; and temp, 37.2°C. Her medications were thyroid tablets and hydralazine. The patient had both upper and lower dentures. Her valuables were sent home with her sister. The history was obtained from the patient's sister and two daughters.

Pattern Areas

Health Perception–Health Management

The patient has been followed regularly by a physician and has been in good health, except for hypertension that has been managed by medications. She has no known allergies. Her medications include thyroid tablets, 1.5 grain, p.o. QD and hydralazine HCl, 25 mg, p.o. QD.

Self-Perception–Self-Concept

The family states that the patient has always felt good about herself. She is strong-willed. A stylish dresser, the patient enjoys socializing with friends, vacationing, and visiting two daughters in Oregon. For transportation outside of walking distance she uses a taxi.

Roles-Relationship

The patient has many friends and a supportive family. Two sisters live nearby, and two daughters are living in Oregon.

Coping-Stress

The patient has experienced many loses in her life, and her strong will and positive attitude have assisted her through these periods. Her friends also are a source of strength to her.

Cognitive-Perceptual

Presently, the patient is alert, oriented only to self and recognizing family members. No discomfort is apparent at present.

Activity-Exercise

Until the onset of the stroke, the patient was independent, took frequent vacations, and spent social time with friends.

Nutritional-Metabolic

The patient has both upper and lower dentures. Before admission, she had a healthy appetite. Nevertheless, her weight was within normal limits; no gain or loss of weight has been reported.

Elimination

Her sisters report that the patient has history of incontinence and that she has been on a bowel regimen.

Sleep-Rest

The family does not know of any problems in this area of concern.

Values-Beliefs

The patient practices the Jewish faith. Her religion is very important to her.

Sexuality-Reproductive

Assessment has been deferred.

Anticipated Discharge Status

It is anticipated that, under the present circumstances, the patient will need to be transferred to a chronic care hospital. Her daughters are requesting a transfer to the state of Oregon. They are distressed at the sudden change in her health status. She requires assistance with all ADLs, has total flaccidity of the left side, and has been cognitively impaired. It is planned that the patient will be transported to a chronic care facility in Oregon that is near her daughters. The daughters will need much support in their preparation for this transfer. Social service, which has been asked to give assistance, has begun to provide support and is making initial plans for the eventual transfer.

Assessment and Plan

The alteration in cognitive thought process, due to the CVA on the right side, will require reorientation of the patient to self every shift and the anticipation of the patient's needs for comfort and protection.

The impaired physical mobility (2°), due to the paralysis of the left side, will require the following plan:

- positioning of patient
- bed-to-chair several hours each day
- ROM exercise, two times each day
- physical therapy and occupational therapy consultations
- water mattress for patient's bed
- skin care every shift

The self-care deficit will be approached by assisting the patient with bathing, feeding, and dressing, and by encouraging her to be as independent as possible.

The swallowing impairment, due to decreased gag reflex, will be dealt with by the following plan:

- Provide nutritional support by a nasogastric tube.
- Keep head of bed elevated at all times.
- Assess placement of feeding tube each shift.
- Change diet when it is properly assessed.

The impaired elimination will require Foley catheter care every day.

The body image disturbance (2°), due to the paralysis of the left side, will be dealt with through a plan that involves the family, involves social service, and anticipates chronic care placement.

FHPA

Pattern Areas

Health Perception–Health Management

The patient is an 87-year-old white woman who was living alone in her apartment and was fully independent in caring for herself. She had been followed by her physician biannually and was last seen by him approximately four months ago. Her health had been considered good, except for some hypertension, which is being treated currently with hydralazine HCl, 25 mg, p.o., QD.

The patient lives in a small apartment in a neighborhood primarily made up of an elderly Jewish population. It is a neighborhood in which there is much community feeling and support. The patient socialized frequently, sharing luncheons with friends and attending the weekly symphony orchestra performances. She also spent much time vacationing and visiting her two daughters in Oregon. She has no known allergies. In addition to the treatment with

hydralazine, the patient is being treated with thyroid tablets, 1.5 grain, p.o., QD.

Nutritional-Metabolic

The patient has both upper and lower dentures. Before admission, she had a healthy appetite. Her weight was within normal limits, and there was no reported gain or loss of weight. The patient has a gag reflex; however, it has decreased. Aspiration precautions are in effect. The head of the bed is elevated to 30° at all times. The patient can eat pureed foods, but p.o. intake has been very poor. A pediatric NG tube was placed and the patient was started on 1/4-strength Isocal at 50 mL/h.

Elimination

The patient does not have a history of incontinence. Nevertheless, she did have several episodes of urinary incontinence after admission; these were followed by urinary retention. A Foley catheter was placed. The patient has been placed on a bowel regimen of stool softeners, and bisacodyl (Dulcolax) suppositories, when necessary.

Activity-Exercise

Until the onset of the stroke, the patient had been fully independent; she took frequent vacations and spent much social time with her friends. Three days S/P CVA of the right side, the patient has retained normal strength in her side. Her left side has no movement. She requires assistance with all feeding, bathing, and dressing. Bed-to-chair transfers require the assistance of two to three persons. She has decreased functional mobility, decreased endurance, and decreased ability to stand at this time. The patient is being followed by occupational therapy and physical therapy, but she has been uncooperative and lethargic thus far.

Sleep-Rest

Before admission, the patient had no known difficulty obtaining the sleep she needed. Since admission, however, the patient has been known to be intermittently restless and agitated at night.

Cognitive-Perceptual

The patient is alert, but oriented only to self. She is able to state her name and address and recognizes family members; however, she is not aware that she is in the hospital—despite frequent reorienting. The patient is now able to follow simple commands; occasionally, she answers questions appropriately. The pupils of her eyes remain sluggishly reactive; speech continues to be slurred, and there is intermittent rambling. There is a notable decreased awareness of her left side.

According to the family, the patient does wear glasses. She does not require a hearing aid. There are no notable difficulties with memory, taste, or concentration and no complaints of pain.

Self-Perception–Self-Concept

The patient is alert, but oriented only to self. According to the patient's family, she has always felt good about herself and has been considered dapper. She has always dressed stylishly. Considered to be a strong-willed person, she generally did as she wished. When the patient was told that she had a stroke, she strongly denied it and refused to listen.

Roles-Relationship

The patient's supportive family members consist of her sister, who lives near her, and her two daughters, who live in Oregon. She had been living in a small apartment by herself and has been financially comfortable. Her main occupation during her lifetime has been that of a home-maker. Although the patient has been widowed for 15 years, she has developed many close friends who live nearby. She has also spent extensive periods visiting her daughters and has greatly enjoyed her two grandchildren during these visits.

Sexuality-Reproductive

The patient has been widowed for 15 years. She delivered and raised two children, both daughters.

Coping-Stress

The family states that the patient initially suffered tremendous grief upon the death of her husband, 15 years ago. However, her "strong will" pulled her through a most difficult time. In addition, she was very distressed over the sudden loss of her son-in-law, two years ago.

The patient's daughters are greatly distressed over their mother's sudden change in physical status. They are going to require much support, particularly about the placement of their mother in a chronic care facility. Social service is involved.

Values-Beliefs

The patient's religious denomination is Jewish. Her faith is important to her; she has always observed the Sabbath.

NURSING CARE PLAN

NURSING HISTORY

FORMULATED BY Evelyn Stelmack, R.N.   DATE 3/12/85

Pt is an 87-year-old woman, healthy except for history of HTN. Brought to the emergency unit on 3/11 following a fall at home. Upon exam, pt was alert but not oriented and unable to obey commands. Left side is flaccid, speech is slurred, and pupils very sluggish with marked deviation to the right. Pt diagnosed with a large right hemisperic CVA.

NURSING DIAGNOSIS	EXPECTED OUTCOME	NURSING CARE PLAN WITH NURSING ORDERS
1. Alteration in cognitive thought process 2° to right CVA.	Pt will be oriented to person. Pt's needs that she cannot communicate will be anticipated.	Nsg will reorient patient periodically during each shift. Nsg will anticipate pt's needs for comfort and protection.
2. Impaired physical mobility 2° to left side paralysis.	Pt will have enough body movement to prevent risks of contractures, decubiti, pneumonia, and osteoporosis.	- Pt will spend several hours per day up in chair as tolerated. - Pt will be turned and repositioned q 2°. - ROM exercises to be performed with pt 2x/day. - Pt to be followed by OT and PT. - Pt will wear splints alternatively on/off q2°. - Water mattress to be placed on bed. - Skin care - q shift.
3. Short term memory deficit 2° to right CVA.	Pt will have information repeated for her as needed.	Repeat information for pt as needed.
4. Self care deficit.	Pt's physical and nutritional needs will be met.	- Nsg will assist pt with bathing, feeding, and dressing. - Pt will be followed by occuaptional therapy to encourage her to be as independent as possible.

NURSING DIAGNOSIS	EXPECTED OUTCOME	NURSING CARE PLAN WITH NURSING ORDERS
5. Potential impairment of skin integrity.	Pt will not experience skin breakdown.	- Pt will be turned and repositioned at least every 2°. - Pt will spend several hours per day up in chair as tolerated. - Water mattress to be obtained. - Nutritional intake will be monitored to maintain adequate protein intake and prevent cachexia.
6. Swallowing impairment due to decreased gag reflex.	- Nutritional needs will be met either via feeding or po as tolerated. - Pt will not aspirate po intake.	- Pt to receive nutritional support via feeding tube until swallowing ability improves. - Assess pt's swallowing ability on a continuing basis. - Keep HOB elevated at least 30° at all times. - Assess for correct placement of feeding tube at least q shift. - If possible, change diet from tube feeding to pureed diet. - If pt is fed, she is to be positioned fully upright.
7. Impairment of elimination due to urinary incontinence/retention; potential for constipation.	Urinary incontinence will be prevented with use of foley catheter. Pt's skill will be kept dry and comfortable. Pt will have regular enemas.	- Foley care q day. - Monitor for potential UTI with indwelling foley catheter.
8. Body image disturbance 2° to left side paralysis.	Pt will feel more comfortable tolerating her physical compromise.	- Provide encouragement and positive reinforcement for the tasks that pt can do. - Provide emotional support. - Allow verbalization of frustrations.
9. Discharge plans.	Pt will be transferred to appropriate facility.	- Social Service involvement. - Expect placement to chronic care facility. - Provide emotional support to family.

Patient Care Referral Form

FROM: Beth Israel Hospital

Unit/Clinic 5F

ADDRESS 330 Brookline Ave.

Boston, MA   **TEL.** 777-0000

ADM. DATE 3/11/85   **DISCH. DATE** 3/30/85

TO: East Manor

ADDRESS: 3 Village Ave., Eastop, MA

TEL.

Patient's Hospital Record # _____

PATIENT NAME Mrs. M.

ADDRESS: 222 Road Street

Eastop, MA   **TEL.** 221-2121

FLOOR   **APT. #**   **BIRTHDATE** 2/2/98

AGE 87   **SEX** M X   **MARITAL STATUS** S M W D SEP.   **RELIGION**

RELATIVE OR GUARDIAN: Ms. Friend

ADDRESS: 220 Road St.

TEL. 221-2122

MEDICARE NO. & LETTER 222-22-222A

PLAN A B

BLUE CROSS NO.

SOC. SEC. NO. 222-22-2222

OTHER

CLINIC APPOINTMENTS   **DATE**   **TIME**   **Agency Worker Office Address Telephone**

DIAGNOSIS (S) Surgery Performed and Date, Allergies or Infections

1. Right hemispheric cerebrovascular accident.
2. Urinary tract infection.
3. Hypothyroidism; on thyroid supplementation.

Is Patient   Family   aware of diagnosis?

Date of last physical 12/83

PHYSICIAN'S ORDERS: (Include specific orders for Diet, Lab Tests, Speech, and O.T.)

TRANSPORT BY: [X] Ambulance   [ ] Car

MEDICATION	STRENGTH AND FREQUENCY	DATE & TIME OF LAST DOSE
Colace 100 mg po tid		
Miniheparin 5,000 m sc. bid		
Thyroid tablets 1.5 grains po qd		
Bactrim D.S. 1 po bid times 10 days		
Mylanta II 30 cc po qid		
Tylenol prn		

TREATMENTS & FREQUENCY: _____

DIET: pureed foods with assistance

PHYSICAL THERAPY: Restrict Activity [ ] Yes [X] No   Sensation Impaired [X] Yes [ ] No

Precautions   Weight Bearing Status - Non-Weight [X]   Partial-Weight [X]   Full-Weight [ ]

SPECIFIC TREATMENT & FREQUENCY: slow rehabilitation

ANTICIPATED GOALS: Maintain present status

REHABILITATION POTENTIAL IS: poor

HOME HEALTH SERVICES: [ ] NURSING   [ ] OCC. THERAPY   [ ] SPEECH THERAPY   [ ] SOCIAL WORK   [ ] H.H. AIDE   [ ] OTHER - SPECIFY

The above services require Level of Care: [ ] I   [ ] II   [ ] III   [ ] IV

If Chronic Hospital, why? _____

CERTIFICATION: *(when applicable)
Services above needed to treat condition for which patient was hospitalized [X] Yes [ ] No
I certify that the above named patient is: (check one)
[ ] Under my care (or has been referred to another physician having professional knowledge of patient's condition); is home bound except when receiving out-patient services; requires skilled nursing care on an intermittent basis or physical or speech therapy as specified in the orders.
[ ] Requires skilled nursing care on a continuing basis for any of the conditions for which he/she received care during this hospitalization.

Signature _____ M.D.

Dr. Jones _____ M.D.

Print Name

Tel. 770-0000   Date 3/29/85   Will follow [X] Yes [ ] No - If no, who? _____ M.D.

ADDRESS: _____ TEL. _____

282-956   9/85

APPROVED BY THE MASSACHUSETTS DEPARTMENT OF PUBLIC HEALTH

DISTRIBUTION — WHITE — RECEIVING   **PINK — MEDICAL RECORDS**   **YELLOW — C.C. SERVICE**

Page 2
Patient Care Referral Form

NURSING: Self Care Status Check Functional Level		Inde- pendent	Needs Assist- ance	Unable
Ambulation	Bed--Chair		X	
	Walking			X
	Stairs			X
	Wheelchair			X
	Crutches			X
	Walker			X
	Cane			X
Activities	Bathe self		X	
	Dress self		X	
	Feed self		X	
	Brushing teeth		X	
	Shaving			
	Toilet		X	
	Commode			
	Bedpan/Urinal			

Bowel & Bladder Program	☐ Yes	☐ No

Incontinence: Bladder ☒   Bowel ☒
Date of Last Enema

Catheter: Type Foley cath 3/29
Date last changed:

Weight	Height	Date
Anointed Yes ☐	No ☐	Date

Check if Pertinent: (describe at right) ▷

DISABILITIES
- ☐ Amputation
- ☐ Paralysis
- ☐ Contractures
- ☐ Decubitus
- ☐ Other

IMPAIRMENTS
- ☒ Speech
- ☐ Hearing
- ☐ Vision
- ☐ Sensation
- ☐ Other

COMMUNICATION
- ☐ Can Write
- ☐ Talks
- ☐ Understands Speaking
- ☐ Understands English
- ☐ If no, Other Language?
- ☐ Reads
- ☐ Non-Verbal

BEHAVIOR
- ☒ Alert
- ☐ Forgetful
- ☐ Noisy
- ☐ Confused
- ☐ Withdrawn
- ☐ Wanders
- ☒ Other

REQUIRES
Mark "S" if sent; "N" if needed
- ☐ Colostomy Care
- ☐ Cane
- ☐ Crutches
- ☐ Walker
- ☐ Wheelchair
- ☐ Other
- ☐ Dentures
- ☐ Eye Glasses
- ☐ Hearing Aid
- ☐ Prosthesis
- ☒N Side Rails

Name _____ Mrs. M. _____

Record # _____

Transfer to: _____ East Manor _____

PATIENT CARE PLAN
(Explain details of care, medications, treatments, teaching, habits, preferences, and goals.)

Medications: Note time last dose given on day of discharge.

Nursing referral

Pt is an 87-year-old woman, healthy except for history of HTN. Admitted to hospital after fall at home with onset of new L hemiparesis. Pt was diagnosed with large R hemispheric CVA.

Alteration in neuro status

Pt has experienced some recovery in her cognitive and functional losses since admission. Her mental status waxes and wanes between being alert, talkative, and appropriate to that of increased lethargy on other days. Speech is garbled but understandable.
Left side is flaccid; right side has normal strength.

Alteration in mobility

Pt does not bear weight and is a heavy 2 person transfer. She has been followed by occupational therapy and physical therapy, however she has frequently been uncooperative; little progress has been made.
Pt is able to tolerate activity increase to chair for several hours/day in spaced intervals.
Pt wearing left extremity splints alternatively on and off q 2°.
Receiving ROM exercises bid.

Self care deficit

Pt is unable to feed or dress self. She does have use of her right hand but has been unable to use it to coordinate self-feeding. Pt does need to be bathed, though she does like to assist with the upper body.

_____
                        Signature of Nurse
Telephone _____ Date _____

NUTRITION: (discuss food preferences, understanding of diet, teaching needs and goals)   Diet enclosed ☐ Yes ☐ No

620-22M - 821-640   9/85

APPROVED BY THE MASSACHUSETTS DEPARTMENT OF PUBLIC HEALTH

_____
Nutritionist Signature   Telephone   Date

Page 2
Patient Care Referral Form

Name _____ Mrs. M. _____

Record # _____

Transfer to: _____ East Manor _____

NURSING: Self Care Status Check Functional Level		Inde- pendent	Needs Assist- ance	Unable
Ambulation	Bed-Chair			
	Walking			
	Stairs			
	Wheelchair			
	Crutches			
	Walker			
	Cane			
Activities	Bathe self			
	Dress self			
	Feed self			
	Brushing teeth			
	Shaving			
	Toilet			
	Commode			
	Bedpan/Urinal			

Bowel & Bladder Program	☐Yes	☐No

Incontinence: Bladder☐ Bowel☐
Date of Last Enema

Catheter: Type
Date last changed:

Weight	Height	Date
Anointed Yes☐	No☐	Date

Check if Pertinent: (describe at right) ⇨

DISABILITIES
- ☐ Amputation
- ☐ Paralysis
- ☐ Contractures
- ☐ Decubitus
- ☐ Other

IMPAIRMENTS
- ☐ Speech
- ☐ Hearing
- ☐ Vision
- ☐ Sensation
- ☐ Other

COMMUNICATION
- ☐ Can Write
- ☐ Talks
- ☐ Understands Speaking
- ☐ Understands English
- ☐ If no, Other Language?
- ☐ Reads
- ☐ Non-Verbal

BEHAVIOR
- ☐ Alert
- ☐ Forgetful
- ☐ Noisy
- ☐ Confused
- ☐ Withdrawn
- ☐ Wanders
- ☐ Other

REQUIRES
Mark "S" if sent; "N" if needed
- ☐ Colostomy Care
- ☐ Cane
- ☐ Crutches
- ☐ Walker
- ☐ Wheelchair
- ☐ Other
- ☐ Dentures
- ☐ Eye Glasses
- ☐ Hearing Aid
- ☐ Prosthesis
- ☐ Side Rails

PATIENT CARE PLAN
(Explain details of care, medications, treatments, teaching, habits, preferences, and goals.)

Medications: Note time last dose given on day of discharge.

Impairment of elimination
Urinary: Pt was incontinent followed by retention. Pt now has indwelling foley catheter (gauge 14 Fr) and is currently on Bactrim for UTI.
Bowel: Pt has been fecally incontinent. She requires use of Colace and occasional Dulcolax suppository.

Potential impairment of skin integrity
(Please see under Mobility)
Pt requires turning and repositioning q2°.
Water mattress has been helpful.
Pt has been maintaining adequate po protein intake in her progression from tube feeding to pureed foods.

Swallowing impairment due to decreased gag reflex.
Pt has progressed from nutritional support via tube feeding to a diet of pureed foods. Pt's swallowing ability has been assessed on a continual basis. HOB is kept elevated at least 30° at all times, and pt is fed only in full upright position.

Alteration in individual and family coping
Although pt has been informed about her stroke, it upsets her and she denies it. At times, she is frustrated and restless. Her 2 devoted daughters have been quite stressed by the effects of the CVA upon their mother. In addition, making the arrangements for their mother's transfer from Oregon to Nevada has been an additional stress for them.

Alteration in CV status
H/O persistent HTN - currently not being treated.
$\frac{150-190}{70-90}$ HR 64-87.

Signature of Nurse
Telephone _____ 777-7777 _____ Date _____ 3/30/85 _____

NUTRITION: (discuss food preferences, understanding of diet, teaching needs and goals)   Diet enclosed ☐Yes ☐No

APPROVED BY THE MASSACHUSETTS DEPARTMENT OF PUBLIC HEALTH

821-640   9/85

_____ Nutritionist Signature _____   Telephone   Date

Page 3
Patient Care Referral Form

Name: Mrs. M.

Record # _____

Transfer to: East Manor

SOCIAL SERVICE:

Prior to hospitalization, patient lived:
- ☐ Alone
- ☐ With Family
- ☐ Other _____
- ☐ Nursing Home
- ☐ With Friends

SOCIAL INFORMATION (including patient's personality, attitude toward illness and family constellation and inter-relationships)

87-year-old woman who lives alone on first floor of a duplex. Enjoys friends; is close to her sisters and visits daughter in Oregon. Active woman, presently unable to communicate needs.

Identified Problems:

Alteration in coping of immediate family members regarding illness and long term needs.

Plan (include short and long range plans)

1. Support to pt and family.
2. Weekly meetings with sisters.
3. Communicate with daughters.
4. Set up transfer plans to Oregon.

Will referring unit social worker plan to follow patient: Yes ☐   No ☒

Barbara Smith		777-7777	3/29/85
Name	Signature & Title	Phone	Date

THERAPIES (P.T., O.T., Speech)   Instructions enclosed: Yes ☐   No ☐

_____   _____   _____
Signature of Therapist   Phone   Date

Appendix B.   Community Resources

This appendix is intended to assist those persons responsible for planning continuing care services for their patients and clients. The resource list, which is not intended to be exhaustive, is organized under a health problem classification. It is designed to provide sources of information about local organizations that can assist in supporting community resources for the patient.

Adult Day Care

Directory of Adult Day Care Centers
Health Standards and Quality Bureau
Dogwood East Building
1849 Gwynn Oak Avenue
Baltimore, MD 21207

State Associations

- Alabama Association of Adult Day Care
  East Alabama Mental Health
  P.O. Drawer 2425
  Opelika, AL 36801
- Alaska Adult Daycare Association
  Chugiak Senior Center
  P.O. Box 414
  Chugiak, AK 99567
- Arizona Association of Adult Day Care
  Foundation for Senior Adult Living
  1017 North 3rd Street, Suite 20
  Phoenix, AZ 85004

- California Association for Adult Day Health Services
  Marin Senior Day Services
  P.O. Box 692
  Mill Valley, CA 94942
- Connecticut Association of Adult Day Care Centers
  Jewish Home for the Elderly of Fairfield County
  175 Jefferson Street
  Fairfield, CT 06432
- Florida Association of Adult Day Care
  Department of Aging Services
  305 North Morgan Street
  Tampa, FL 33602
- Illinois Association of Adult Day Care Providers
  Suburban Adult Day Center
  149 West Harrison
  Oak Park, IL 60304
- Indiana Adult Daycare Association
  6404 Castleway Court
  Indianapolis, IN 46250
- Iowa Association of Adult Day Care Programs
  Willis Adult Day Care
  Sixth and University Avenue
  Des Moines, IA 50314
- Kansas Adult Day Care Association
  6164 Charlotte
  Kansas City, MO 64110

- Louisiana Adult Day Care Association
  New Directions
  1523 North Dorgenois
  New Orleans, LA 70130
- Maryland Association of Adult Day Care
    Programs
  Winter Growth Adult Day Center
  P.O. Box 186
  Sandy Spring, MD 20860
- Massachusetts Association for Adult Day
    Health Services, Inc.
  Jewish Home for the Aged Adult Day Center
  629 Salisbury Street
  Worcester, MA 01609
- Michigan Association of Senior Adult Day
    Centers
  Center for Independent Living, Inc.
  1509 East Court Street
  Flint, MI 48503
- Senior Daytime Center
  1201 West Oakland, Suite 101
  Lansing, MI 48915
- Minnesota Adult Day Care Association
  Wilder Adult Day Care Center
  516 Humboldt
  St. Paul, MN 55107
- Missouri Adult Day Care Association
  Research Downtown Adult Day Center
  Admiral Boulevard at Oak
  Kansas City, MO 64106
- Nebraska Adult Day Care Association
  McAuley Bergan Center
  3552 Farnam Street
  Omaha, NE 68131
- New Jersey Adult Day Care Association
  Paterson Adult Day Center
  163 Graham Avenue
  Paterson, NJ 07501
- New Mexico Association of Adult Day Care
  Cornucopia, Inc.
  1734 Isleta Boulevard, SW
  Albuquerque, NM 87105
- New York State Adult Day Services Association
  Lockport Senior Citizens Center
  57 Richmond Avenue
  Lockport, NY 14094
- North Carolina Adult Day Care Association
  Life Enrichment Center
  610 Charles Road
  Shelby, NC 28150
- Ohio Association of Adult Day Care
  Today Center for Adults
  711 Dayton–Xenia Road
  Xenia, OH 45385

- Pennsylvania Adult Day Care Association
  Adult Day Care Center
  St. Joseph Villa
  Wissohickon and Stenton Avenue
  Flourtown, PA 19031
- Rhode Island Directors Association for Senior
    Citizens Programs
  Fruit Hill Adult Day Care
  399 Fruit Hill Avenue
  North Providence, RI 02911
- Adult Day Care Association of Texas
  North Texas Adult Day Health Care, Inc.
  5012 Justin Avenue
  Irving, TX 15060
- Vermont Association of Adult Day Centers
  Project Independence
  40 South Main Street
  Barre, VT 05641
- Virginia Institute of Adult DayCare
  Stuart Circle Center
  1605 Monument Avenue
  Richmond, VA 23220
- Washington State Association of Adult Day
    Centers
  Norwest Day Center for Adults
  9250—14th Street, NW
  Seattle, WA 98117
- Wisconsin Adult Daycare Association
  Independent Living
  1245 East Washington
  Madison, WI 53703
- Adult Day Center
  812 Wisconsin Avenue
  Madison, WI 53703

Addictions

National Nurses Society on Addictions
2506 Gross Point Road
Evanston, IL 60201

Alcoholism

Alcoholics Anonymous
468 Park Avenue, South
New York, NY 10016

Alzheimer's Disease and Related Disorders

ADRDA
360 North Michigan Avenue
Suite 601
Chicago, IL 60601

Anorexia

American Anorexia Nervosa Association
133 Cedar Lane
Teaneck, NJ 07666

Arthritis

Arthritis Foundation
1314 Spring Street, NW
Atlanta, GA 30309

Asthma

Asthma and Allergy Foundation of America
1302 18th Street, NW
Washington, DC 20036

Blindness

- American Foundation for the Blind
  15 West 16th Street
  New York, NY 10011
- American Optometric Association
  243 North Lindbergh Boulevard
  St. Louis, MO 63141
- National Association of Visually Handicapped
  305 East 24th Street, 17C
  New York, NY 10016
- National Society to Prevent Blindness
  79 Madison Avenue
  New York, NY 10016

Burns

Phoenix Society
11 Rust Hill Road
Levittown, PA 19056

Cancer

- American Cancer Society
  777 Third Avenue
  New York, NY 10017
- Candlelighter's Foundation
  2025 I Street, NW, Suite 1011
  Washington, DC 20006
- Compassionate Friends
  P.O. Box 1347
  Oak Brook, IL 60521
- National Hospice Organization
  1311A Dolly Madison Boulevard
  McLean, VA 22101
- Make Today Count
  514 Tama Building
  Box 303
  Burlington, Iowa 52601

- United Ostomy Association, Inc.
  2001 West Beverly Boulevard
  Los Angeles, CA 90057

Cardiovascular

- American Heart Association
  7320 Greenville Avenue
  Dallas, TX 75231
- Mended Hearts
  7320 Greenville Avenue
  Dallas, TX 75231

Cystic Fibrosis

Cystic Fibrosis Foundation
6000 Executive Boulevard
Rockville, MD 20852

Deafness

- A.G. Bell Association for the Deaf
  3417 Volta Place, NW
  Washington, DC 20007
- American Speech-Language-Hearing Association
  10801 Rockville Pike
  Rockville, MD 20852
- National Association of the Deaf
  814 Thayer Avenue
  Silver Spring, MD 20910

Diabetes

American Diabetes Association
2 Park Avenue
New York, NY 10016

Drug Abuse

Therapeutic Communities of America, Inc.
c/o Marathon House
179 Wayland Avenue
Providence, RI 02906

Epilepsy

Epilepsy Foundation of America
4351 Garden City Drive
Landover, MD 20785

Handicapped/Disabilities

- National Rehabilitation Association
  1522 K Street, NW
  Washington, DC 20005

- National Wheelchair Athletic Association
  40-24 62nd Street
  Woodside, NY 11377
- North American Riding for the Handicapped
  Association
  P.O. Box 100
  Ashburn, VA 22011
- Office for Handicapped Individuals
  Department of Health and Human Services
  388-D Hubert W. Humphrey Building
  Washington, DC 20201
- National Association of the Physically
  Handicapped
  70 Elm Street
  London, OH 43140
- National Easter Seals Society for Crippled
  Children and Adults
  2023 Ogden Avenue
  Chicago, IL 60612
- National Handicapped Sports and Recreation
  Assoc.
  4105 East Florida Avenue
  Denver, CO 80222

Hemophilia

National Hemophelia Foundation
25 West 39th Street
New York, NY 10018

Kidney

- National Kidney Foundation
  2 Park Avenue
  New York, NY 10016
- American Kidney Fund
  7315 Wisconsin Boulevard
  Bethesda, MD 20014
- National Association of Patients on Hemodialysis
  and Transplantation
  505 Northern Boulevard
  St. Louis, MO 63141

Neurological-Muscular

- American Parkinson Disease Association
  116 John Street
  New York, NY 10038
- Muscular Dystrophy Association
  810 Seventh Avenue
  New York, NY 10019
- Myasthenia Gravis Foundation
  15 East 26th Street
  New York, NY 10010

- National Head Injury Foundation
  184 Veron Street
  Framingham, MA 01701
- Spina Bifida Association of America
  343 South Dearborn, Room 319
  Chicago, IL 60604
- National Spinal Cord Injury Association
  369 Elliot Street
  Newton Upper Falls, MA 02164
- United Cerebral Palsy Associations, Inc.
  66 East 34th Street
  New York, NY 10016

Organizations for Physically or Developmentally Disabled

- Association for Retarded Citizens
  National Headquarters
  2501 Avenue J., P.O. Box 6109
  Arlington, TX 76011
- Goodwill Industries of America
  9200 Wisconsin Avenue
  Bethesda, MD 20814

Respiratory

American Lung Association
1740 Broadway
New York, NY 10019

Services: Children

- Association for the Care of Children's Health
  3615 Wisconsin Avenue, NW
  Washington, DC 20016
- Child Welfare League of America, Inc.
  67 Irving Place
  New York, NY 10003
- Shriners Hospital for Crippled Children
  323 North Michigan Avenue
  Chicago, IL 60601

Services: Aged

- Administration on Aging
  Department of Health and Human Services
  200 Independence Avenue, SW
  Washington, DC 20201
- American Association of Homes for the Aging
  1050 17th Street, NW
  Washington, DC 20036
- American Association of Retired Persons
  1909 K Street, NW
  Washington, DC 20006

- National Center on Black Aged
  1730 M Street, NW, Suite 811
  Washington, DC 20020

- National Indian Council on Aging
  P.O. Box 2088
  Albuquerque, NM 87103

- National Institute on Aging
  9000 Rockville Pike
  Bethesda, MD 20205

Sickle Cell Disease

National Association for Sickle Cell Disease
945 South Western Avenue, Suite 206
Los Angeles, CA 90006

Appendix C.   Abbreviations

ABG	arterial blood gases
AC	before meals
ADL	activities of daily living
AHA	American Hospital Association
AIDS	Acquired Immune Deficiency Syndrome
ANA	American Nurses' Association
AODM	adult onset diabetes mellitus
A-V	atrioventricular
BID	two times each day
BM	bowel movement
BP	blood pressure
BRCCN	Boston Regional Continuing Care Nurses
BUN	blood urea nitrogen
CC	chief complaint
C&S	culture and sensitivities
C/O	complains of
CHF	congestive heart failure
COPD	chronic obstructive pulmonary disease
CPK	creatine phosphokinase
CPT	chest physical therapy
CT	computerized tomography
CVA	cerebrovascular accident
d	day
DM	diabetes mellitus
DME	durable medical equipment
DOE	dyspnea on exertion
DRG	diagnostic related group
Dx	diagnosis
ETOH	alcohol
FBS	fasting blood sugar
FHPA	functional health pattern assessment
FHPAA	functional health pattern admission assessment
GI	gastrointestinal
gtt	drops
GU	genitourinary
HCT	hematocrit
HEENT	head, eyes, ears, nose, throat
HGB	hemoglobin
HHA	home health aide
HMO	health maintenance organization
H/O	history of
HS	hour of sleep
HTN	hypertension
ICP	intracranial pressure
ICU	intensive care unit
I/E	inspiration/expiration
I/O	intake/output
IV	intravenous
IVP	intravenous pyelogram

JCAH	Joint Commission on Accreditation of Hospitals
JVD	jugular vein distention
LLE	left lower extremity
LOC	level of consciousness
LOS	length of stay
MOM	milk of magnesia
NPH	neutral protamine Hagedorn (insulin)
NPO	nothing by mouth
NS	normal saline
N/V	nausea and vomiting
OOB	out of bed
OS	left eye
OT	occupational therapy
P	pulse
PC	after meals
PEEP	positive end-expiratory pressure
PERRL	pupils: equal, round and react to light
PMH	past medical history
p.o.	orally
PRN	whenever necessary
PRO	peer review organization
PSH	past surgical history
pt.	patient
PT	physical therapy
PTA	prior to admission
q	every
QA	quality assurance

QD	everyday
QHS	every evening at hour of sleep
QID	four times each day
QS	quantity sufficient
R	respirations
RAHN	room air heated nebulizer
ROM	range of motion (movement)
R/O	rule out
R/T	related to
Rx	treatment
SL	sublingual
SO	significant other
SOB	shortness of breath
S/P	status past
SQ	subcutaneous
S/S	signs and symptoms
Sx	symptoms
T, temp	temperature
TID	three times each day
Tx	therapy
U	unit
UA	urinalysis
UR	utilization review
UTI	urinary tract infection
VNA	Visiting Nurse Association
V/S	vital signs
W/U	workup
Y/O	year old

Bibliography

Accreditation Manual for Hospitals. Chicago, IL: Joint Commission on Accreditation of Hospitals, 1983.

Alfano, G.J. "The Nurse's Impact on Effective Discharge Planning." *Discharge Planning Update* (Summer 1982): 4–6.

American Hospital Association. *Introduction to Discharge Planning for Hospitals.* Chicago, IL: Association, 1983.

American Nurses' Association. *Continuity of Care and Discharge Planning Programs.* Kansas City, MO: ANA Publications (Code NP-49 3000), 1975.

———.*Guidelines for Review of Nursing Care at the Local Level.* Kansas City, MO: ANA Publications, 1976.

———.*Resolution on Admission and Discharge Planning* (Summary of Proceedings of ANA House of Delegates, 49th Convention). Kansas City, MO: ANA Publications (Code G-117-1500), 1975.

Anderson, Cynthia A. "Home or Nursing Home? Let the Elderly Patient Decide." *American Journal of Nursing* 7 (August 1979): 1449–1450.

Baulch, Evelyn M. *Home Care: A Practical Alternative to Extended Hospitalization.* Milbrae, CA: Celestial Arts, 1980.

Bayles, M. "The Value of Life—By What Standard?" *American Journal of Nursing* 8 (December 1980): 2226–2230.

Bertalanffy, L. von. *General Systems Theory.* New York: George Braziller, Inc., 1968.

Byrne, Majorie L., and Lida F. Thompson. *Key Concepts for the Study and Practice of Nursing.* St. Louis: C.V. Mosby Co., 1972.

Cahill, T.F. "Prospective Reimbursement: Its Effect on Discharge Planning Services." *Discharge Planning Update* (Fall 1982): 14–16.

Cohen, Elias. "Legal Consequences of Continuity of Care Decisions." *Coordinator* 3 (May 1984): 10–11.

Cohen, Kenneth P. *Hospice: Prescription for Terminal Care.* Rockville, MD: Aspen Publishers, Inc., 1979.

Conger, Shirley A., and L.F. Snider. "The Priority Component of Discharge Planning." *Coordinator* 2 (December 1983): 16–20.

Coser, R.L. *The Family: Its Structure and Function.* New York: St. Martin's Press, 1964.

Curtain, Leah. "Human Values in Nursing." *Supervisor Nurse* 3 (March 1978): 1–3.

Discharge Planning Guideline. Chicago, IL: American Hospital Association (catalog no. 004170. 15 M-6/84-4 0899), 11–12 April 1984.

Discharge Planning Standards. Boston, MA: Boston Regional Continuing Care Nurses, 1982.

Doenges, Marilyn E., Mary F. Jeffries, Mary Francis Moorhouse. *Nursing Care Plans: Nursing Diagnoses in Planning Patient Care.* Philadelphia, PA: F.A. Davis Co., 1984.

Drucker, P.F. *Management: Tasks, Responsibilities, Practices.* New York: Harper and Row, 1974.

Fanslow, Cathleen, and E. Massett. "Between Institutions." *American Journal of Nursing* 79 (August 1979): 1443–1445.

Gordon, Marjory. *Manual of Nursing Diagnosis.* New York: McGraw-Hill, Inc. 1982.

———, *Nursing Diagnosis: Process and Application.* New York: McGraw-Hill, Inc., 1982.

Gordon, M., M.A. Sweeney, K.M. McKeehan. "Nursing Diagnosis: Looking at Its Use in the Clinical Area." *American Journal of Nursing* 80 (April 1980): 672–674.

Habeeb, M.C. "Information Management in Discharge Planning: Future Directions." *Discharge Planning Update* (Spring 1982): 5–7.

———, Frank E. McLaughlin. "Including the Hospital Staff Nurse." *American Journal of Nursing* 79 (August 1979): 1443–1445.

Kantor, D., and W. Lehr. *Inside the Family.* San Francisco: Jossey-Bass Publishers, 1975.

Kim, M.J., and D.A., Moritz. eds. *Classification of Nursing Diagnoses: Proceedings of the Third and Fourth National Conferences* (April 1978 and 1980, St. Louis, MO). New York: McGraw-Hill, 1982.

Knight, Marilyn. "A Nursing Home: Sometimes the Only Answer." *HomeLife* (January 1984): 43–45.

Lurie, E., B. Robinson, J. Barbaccia. "Helping Hospitalized Elderly: Discharge Planning and Informal Support." *Home Health Care Services Quarterly* (Summer 1984): 25–43.

Maslow, A.H. *Motivation and Personality.* New York: Harper and Row, 1954.

McCann, B.A. "Hospice Care: A Challenge and an Opportunity for Discharge Planners." *Discharge Planning Update* (Fall 1983): 6–10.

McCarthy, E. "Comprehensive Home Care for Earlier Hospital Discharge." *Nursing Outlook* 24 (1976): 625–630.

McCarthy, S.A. "Discharge Planning in a Primary Nursing System." *Discharge Planning Update* (Fall 1983): 6–10.

McKeehan, K.M. *Continuing Care: A Multidisciplinary Approach to Discharge Planning.* St. Louis, MO: C.V. Mosby Co., 1981.

Moore, M.F. "Head Nurses Become Effective Managers in the Discharge Planning Process." *Discharge Planning Update* (Fall 1983): 15–17.

Peabody, S.R. "Assessment and Planning for Continuity of Care From Hospital to Home." *Nursing Clinics of North America* 4 (1969): 303–310.

Rasmusen, Linda. "A Screening Tool Promotes Early Discharge Planning." *Nursing Management* 5 (May 1984): 38–43.

Riehl, Joan P., and Sister Callista Roy. *Conceptual Models for Nursing Practice.* New York: Appleton-Century-Crofts, 1974.

Rosen, Rosalind P. "Alzheimers Disease, A Guide for the Discharge Planner." *Coordinator* 3 (January 1984): 11–19.

Rossen, Sallie. "Adapting Discharge Planning to Prospective Pricing." *Hospitals* 58 (1 March 1984): 71–79.

Rowland, H.S., and B.S. Rowland. "Patient Education and Patient Discharge." *Nursing Administration Handbook.* Rockville, MD: Aspen Publishers, Inc., 1980.

Roy, S.C. "Adaption: A Conceptual Framework for Nursing." *Nursing Outlook* 17 (March 1970): 42–45.

Schuman, J.E., and H.N. Willard. "Role of the Acute Hospital Team in Planning Discharge of the Chronically Ill." *Geriatrics* 31 (1976): 63–67.

Shahoda, Teri. "Preadmission Review Cuts Hospital Use." *Hospitals.* 58 (1 August 1984): 54–55.

Simmons, John C. "A Day in the Life of a Discharge Planning Director." *Coordinator* 4 (August 1985): 22–23.

Smith, Jennifer A., J. Buckalew, S. Rosales. "Coordinating a Workable System." *American Journal of Nursing* 79 (August 1979): 1439–1440.

Steffl, Bernita M., and Imogene Eide. *Discharge Planning Handbook.* Thorofare, NJ: Charles B. Slack, Inc., 1978.

Stone, Martha. "Discharge Planning Guide." *American Journal of Nursing* 79 (August 1979): 1446–1447.

Stone, S., M.S. Bergen, D. Elhart, *et al.,* eds. *Management for Nurses: A Multidisciplinary Approach.* St. Louis, MO: C.V. Mosby Co., 1976.

Tolkoff-Rubin, N., S. Fisher, J. O'Brien, R. Rubin. "Coordinated Home Care: The Massachusetts General Hospital Experience." *Medical Care* 16 (1978): 453.

Travelbee, J. *Interpersonal Aspects of Nursing.* 2d ed. Philadelphia: F.A. Davis Co., 1971.

Urosevich, Patti. "How Nurses are Learning to Live with DRGs." *Nursing Life* 2 (March-April 1984): 64–65.

Vlack, Jessie B., and Mary Grace Connelly. "When a Nursing Home is the Best Choice." *American Journal of Nursing* 79 (August 1979): 1450–1451.

Willihnganz, Greg. "The Next Step: Preadmission Planning for Discharge Needs." *Coordinator* 3 (April 1984): 20–21.

Winch, R.F. *The Modern Family.* New York: Henry Holt and Co., 1952.

Yura, Helen, and Mary B. Walsh. *The Nursing Process: Assessing, Planning, Implementing, Evaluating.* 2d ed. New York: Appleton-Century-Crofts, 1973.

Zarle, Nancy C. *Continuing Care: A Resource Booklet for the Primary Nurse.* Boston, MA: Beth Israel Hospital, 1982.

Zilligen, Katherine S. "Quality Assurance for Basic Discharge Planning." *Coordinator* 4 (August 1985): 24–26.

Index